Critical Theory

CRITICAL THEORY
Current State and Future Prospects

Edited by

Peter Uwe Hohendahl & Jaimey Fisher

Berghahn Books
New York • Oxford

First published in 2001 by

Berghahn Books

© 2001 Peter Uwe Hohendahl and Jaimey Fisher

Library of Congress Cataloging-in-Publication Data

Critical theory : current state and future prospects / edited by Peter Uwe Hohendahl,
Jaimey Fisher.
    p. cm.
  Includes bibliographical references and index.
  ISBN 1-57181-235-0 (alk. paper)
    1. Critical theory--Congresses. I. Hohendahl, Peter Uwe. II. Fisher, Jaimey.

B809.3 .C75 2000
142--dc21   00-058538

British Library Cataloguing in Publication Data

A catalogue record for this book is available from the British Library.

Printed in the United States on acid-free paper.

CONTENTS

Section III: In the Wake of Jürgen Habermas: Communicative Reason, Morality, and History

Section IV: A Contemporary Challenge to Critical Theory: Systems Theory

Section V: Epilogue

PREFACE

Peter Uwe Hohendahl and Jaimey Fisher

The essays appearing in this volume were delivered at a conference, "The Future of Critical Theory ... A Reassessment" held at Cornell University in April 1998. The conference was prompted by two important events marking the history of Critical Theory: first, the fiftieth anniversary of the publication of *Dialectic of Enlightenment* and, second, the recent retirement of Jürgen Habermas from his chair at the University of Frankfurt. While the year 1947 marked the most important philosophical intervention of the first generation of Critical Theory, the second event signals the transition from the generation of Habermas to a group of younger theorists, among them Axel Honneth and Christoph Menke. Habermas's project, that is, the systematic exploration of communicative rationality, has reached the point where both its achievements and limitations have become evident. Therefore a thoroughgoing assessment of both the current state and future prospects of Critical Theory seems timely.

The essays in this volume address the problems connected with this history and these transitions, partly by returning to the insights of the first generation (especially of Adorno and Benjamin), partly by focusing on problems in and posed by Habermas's work. In the volume's first essay, "From the Eclipse of Reason to Communicative Rationality and Beyond," Peter Uwe Hohendahl attends to one key element of the transition between the first, second, and now third generations of Critical Theory, namely, its relation to rationality. Against the presumed one-way trajectory from Adorno's and Horkheimer's vigorous critique of instrumental reason to Habermas's embrace of communicative rationality, Hohendahl demonstrates a plurality of positions on rationality from the first generation right through to the present.

After Hohendahl's opening discussion of broader trends in the history of Critical Theory, essays in the volume's first section attempt to reinvigorate some of the older generation's insights. Martin Jay's essay "Is Experience Still in Crisis? Reflections on a Frankfurt School Lament" investigates Adorno's inheritance of Benjamin's concept of experience by asking when, historically speaking, experience came into crisis and what consequences this crisis has for experience. In her essay, "Mega Melancholia: Adorno's *Minima Moralia*," Eva Geulen considers the notion of shame, including Adorno's "shameful" methodology, in *Minima Moralia*. For Geulen, the position of shame in *Minima Moralia*'s small ethics not only illuminates the generally neglected thematic around shame, but also speaks to various critics of Adorno. Like Geulen, Andrew Hewitt, in his essay "Stumbling Into Modernity: Body and Soma in Adorno," suggests that Adorno's conceptualization of language can lead out of the arrested impasse into which his relentlessly negative approach can lead. Hewitt takes up the question of the body and soma in Adorno's critique of the jitterbug and jazz, and reads Adorno against the occasional valorization of the somatic and its potential emancipation. Rounding out the essays solely concerned with the first generation of Critical Theory, Lutz Koepnick's "Aesthetic Politics Today: Walter Benjamin and Post-Fordist Culture" considers the contemporary relevance of Benjamin's famous concepts of auratic and postauratic art as well as his thesis on the aestheticization of politics. Koepnick rereads the "Work of Art in the Age of Mechanical Production" essay to demonstrate that Benjamin's own sensitivity to the historical contingency of concepts can yield a productive rethinking of his work.

Essays in the volume's next section take Jürgen Habermas's work as the point of departure for the current state of Critical Theory, but then also investigate its limits. In his essay, "Critique and Self-Reflection: The Problematization of Morality," Christoph Menke considers the status of moral philosophy in Critical Theory and sketches a process of the "self-reflection of morality" located between the first and second generations. Brian Jacobs's essay "Dialogical Rationality and the Critique of Absolute Autonomy" takes up the tenaciously persisting concept of subject autonomy in contemporary philosophy, especially in late Critical Theory, by returning to its Kantian roots. In her "Civil Society in the Information

Age: Beyond the Public Sphere," Jodi Dean contrasts three public spheres—Habermas's, Benhabib's, and that now emeging in "cyberia"—in order to highlight the limits of the traditional conceptualizations of the public sphere. In "Between Rights and Hospitality: Cosmopolitan Democracy, Nation and Cultural Identity," Max Pensky analyzes the limits of Habermas's notions of cosmopolitanism and cultural identity at its core, and suggests a different grounding for cultural identity, one that recognizes the obsolescence of, and then reconfigures, "authentic" cultural identity. Peter Dews traces a tension running through Habermas's entire work by contrasting his reconstructive methodology to the "strict reflexion" of his friend and colleague Karl-Otto Apel. Both theorists sense a need to balance the grounding of norms with empirically valid claims, though the methodology that they see meeting this challenge diverges greatly.

The volume's last section offers two essays lodging vigorous critiques of Critical Theory. Both critiques are informed by systems theory, which has posed the major challenge to Critical Theory in Germany in the last twenty years. In his essay, "Critical Theory and Systems Theory," Wolfram Malte Fues considers what he calls the modern "mediating subject" in modern philosophy: for Fues, Luhmann's critique of this subject has posed intractable problems for any philosophy relying on it, but he also sees the potential for some of Critical Theory's more dialectical moments to circumnavigate the trouble to which the great Hegelian subject can lead. In his "Observations on Observations: Some Remarks on Adorno's Aesthetic Theory," Haro Müller's considers the "observer position" from which Adorno theorizes; to understand Adorno's conceptual strategy, Müller examines Adorno's own self-observations in his autobiographical writings from *Ohne Leitbild. Parva Aesthetica.* The volume ends with a concluding essay by Jaimey Fisher in which he offers both a reading and a response to the pieces above. Tracing a theme running through almost all the essays, Fisher discusses the divergent understandings of normativity—the grounding and then deducing of norms—between the first and second generations of the Critical Theory. Fisher shows that, as Critical Theory moves into its third generation, there is no consensus on the status of normativity, but there is, for the project of Critical Theory, a persistingly connected vision.

Section I

INTRODUCTION

Chapter 1

FROM THE ECLIPSE OF REASON TO COMMUNICATIVE RATIONALITY AND BEYOND

Peter Uwe Hohendahl

By invoking Max Horkheimer's 1947 study *Eclipse of Reason* and Jürgen Habermas's 1981 *The Theory of Communicative Action*, my title suggests a significant transformation within the Frankfurt School between the late 1940s and the 1980s, a change that touches on the core concepts of reason and/or rationality. Moreover, the title reflects a specific understanding of the way in which this transformation occurred, namely, that the first generation's critique of instrumental reason was replaced by the second generation's more positive and clearly more differentiated approach to the concept of reason, most notably in the writings of Habermas. In this account, which is shared by most of the members of the second generation, the history of the Frankfurt School has to be read as a process of overcoming and also of theoretical improvement.[1] The most common narrative sketches a transition from the pessimism of Horkheimer and Adorno to the more pragmatic and realistic attitude of Habermas and his disciples. Another way of looking at the development would be (in Habermasian terms) to define it as a passage from metaphysical to postmetaphysical thought. What these two narratives have in common is their linear and teleological direction: they assert that Critical Theory has moved through a

Notes for this chapter begin on page 26.

number of phases until its final arrival at a theory of communicative rationality, a theory that not only redraws the boundaries of reason but also offers a very different outlook on contemporary social and political problems.

It is not my intention to reject this narrative out of hand—it is a convenient and, at least up to a certain point, persuasive account of the theoretical development within the Frankfurt School after World War II. Moreover, it represents the perspective of important insiders, among them Habermas and Axel Honneth, who have repeatedly emphasized a significant paradigm shift in the 1970s between the older and the younger generation. According to this model, the early work of Habermas, for example *The Structural Transformation of the Public Sphere* (1962) and *Knowledge and Human Interest* (1968), would still belong to the older paradigm, while *Legitimation Crisis* (1973) and *The Theory of Communicative Action* (1981) would be part of the postmetaphysical paradigm that then becomes the standard for the third generation of Critical Theorists.

There are, however, external observers like Fredric Jameson—much more sympathetic to Adorno and Benjamin than to Habermas's later work—who have acknowledged and commented on the paradigm shift, if only to reject it as a loss of the original impetus of Critical Theory. In his reading of Adorno's work in *Late Marxism* (1989), Jameson pleads for Critical Theory's original project as it was defined by Horkheimer and Adorno in the 1940s and later worked out in the mature writings of Adorno. Similarly, the recent work of Peter Bürger, who had more or less adopted a Habermasian perspective in *Theory of the Avant-Garde* (1974), reassimilates themes and forms of Adorno's thought, combining it with a stronger acknowledgement of French poststructuralist theory. These voices suggest the possibility of a different understanding of the theoretical development of the Frankfurt School, a more complex configuration in which the older theoretical model is not simply replaced but reintegrated, potentially even deployed as a challenge to the conception of communicative rationality. In such a configuration the work of Albrecht Wellmer certainly also comes to mind: Wellmer never absolutely abandoned the theoretical foundations of the first generation and has continued to emphasize the importance of Adorno's aesthetic theory for the debate on postmodernism.

Two additional elements do not fit neatly into the presumed picture of a linear development from a critique of reason to communicative rationality. First, there is the complicated case of Herbert Marcuse. The work of Marcuse, which spanned three decades, did not foreground an eclipse of reason or a loss of belief in the possibility of revolutionary change. During the 1960s he became one of the most outspoken revolutionary social critics in the United States, arguing that the structures of advanced capitalist societies were not immutable.[2] Marcuse also undeniably influenced the German Left, including the young Habermas. In fact, it was partly through Marcuse's writings that the young Habermas could reformulate the project of Critical Theory in Germany, especially in overt opposition to the position that Max Horkheimer considered most appropriate for West Germany. Second, there is the case of Walter Benjamin, or more precisely, the case of his impact in the 1970s and 1980s. Benjamin's reception in Germany (as well as in the United States, for that matter) does not easily fit the evolutionary narrative I have outlined above. During the 1960s and 1970s he became the hero for the radical Left as they became increasingly disenchanted with the political position of the Frankfurt School (including that of Habermas).[3] Later he was sometimes seen as an altogether isolated figure whose writings anticipated the philosophical and cultural criticism of French poststructuralism. Habermas's response to the radical Marxist appropriation of Benjamin is telling: he argued that it is Adorno rather than Benjamin who carried on the Marxist tradition, thereby marginalizing Benjamin's importance for Critical Theory. [4] In any case, I would like to underscore that Benjamin's multifaceted reception is at odds with the official narrative of the school.

How, then, ought one to conceptualize the development of Critical Theory after World War II? First of all, I would like to suggest that if one wants to apply an evolutionary model, one has to distinguish at least three phases: the early years of the Institute for Social Research; the restructuring of the project after 1944; and finally, the paradigmatic shift in the 1970s under the leadership of Jürgen Habermas after the death of Adorno. Moreover, one will have to keep in mind that this model tends to eliminate or marginalize countertendencies or moments of repetition and recurrence.

Before focusing on the best-known works of the older generation such as *Eclipse of Reason* and *Dialectic of Enlightenment,* I would like first to sketch the project of the Institute for Social Research as it emerged during the 1930s. To this end, I shall offer a symptomatic reading of one of Herbert Marcuse's early essays,

"Philosophy and Critical Theory" (1937), that attempts to define the method and the goal of Critical Theory. In character and intent the Marcuse essay remains close to Horkheimer's more famous essay "Traditional and Critical Theory," which argues for a special and distinct status of Critical Theory vis-à-vis philosophy. Marcuse emphasizes those aspects of the German Idealist tradition that Critical Theory has appropriated. For Marcuse, modern European philosophy contains a critical element: "Reason was established as a critical tribunal."[5] In this vein, Marcuse quotes Hegel's lectures on the history of philosophy to underline the link between philosophy and freedom: "To speculative philosophy belongs the knowledge that freedom is that alone that is true of mind."[6] For Marcuse the philosophical concept of reason *(Vernunft)* therefore remains a limited, but clearly positive, asset of the project of freedom with which he identifies. The limitations of reasons have to do with two aspects of philosophy: first, philosophy's blindness to the material aspects of life, which only an economic theory can conceptualize; and second, the way in which reason, by way of philosophical reflection, merely reconstitutes the world. Marcuse criticizes philosophy's inability to offer a truly critical approach to the actual development of the world. He argues: "For at its conclusion [philosophy] arrives at nothing that did not already exist 'in itself' at the beginning. The absence of concrete development appeared to this philosophy as the greatest benefit."[7] The critical moment that philosophy cannot produce by itself emerges in connection with the struggle of oppressed groups for better living conditions. This means that "the realization of reason no longer needs to be restricted to pure thought and will"[8]; instead, only through the intertwinement of, on the one hand, the pressure of material conditions and, on the other, the conception of reason as a "critical tribunal," does a truly Critical Theory that is bent on social transformation materialize. Thus Critical Theory, unlike philosophy, derives its progressive tendencies from its involvement with the present social process.

The proximity of this definition of Critical Theory to Marxian theory is hard to overlook. Yet it is important to note that Marcuse does not want Critical Theory to be confused with economics, i.e., with certain orthodox forms of Marxism for which German Idealism is nothing but bourgeois ideology. While Marcuse agrees with Marxism's characterization of the goal—freedom of the masses—he insists on the potential contribution of philosophy in this struggle, therefore maintaining the concept of reason as it is defined and sustained by the philosophical tradition. The universality of rational concepts, although they are abstract, remains for Marcuse a necessary correlate to the processes of material changes and revolutionary transformations. In other words, Marcuse perceives reason's utopian moment as an aid, not as a hindrance, for emancipation: "Critical theory's interest in the liberation of mankind [sic] binds it to certain ancient truths. It is at one with philosophy in maintaining that man [sic] can be more than a manipulatable subject in the production process of class society."[9]

This argument implies not only that Critical Theory should take cognizance of Kant and Hegel, but also that it should recuperate a concept of reason brought forth by these philosophers. Nowhere does the essay suggest that the concept of reason is in itself problematic or unsuitable for the process of emancipation. For instance in *One-Dimensional Man* (1964), Marcuse differentiated more clearly between reason as "Vernunft" and instrumental reason, yet he continued to link reason and liberation—thereby also insisting on the revolutionary potential of reason. This is, I would like to suggest, the strand of Critical Theory that the young Habermas picked up in the 1960s in his initial opposition to the late work of his teachers in Frankfurt.

Habermas's first major project, *The Structural Transformation of the Public Sphere,* has a pivotal position in the postwar development of the Frankfurt School. It is a perplexing and ambivalent book since its epistemology is certainly indebted to Horkheimer and Adorno, while its politics are only partly compatible with the teachings of the older generation. It was not accidental, therefore, that they rejected the study and forced Habermas to seek his Habilitation at the University of Marburg.[10] When one scrutinizes the study more carefully, it becomes apparent that Habermas actually lodges an implicit critique of *Dialectic of Enlightenment.* Not only does he offer a much more positive evaluation of the European Enlightenment and its philosophical accomplishments than Adorno and Horkheimer, but he also develops a political perspective that his teachers were unwilling to share. While they might have agreed on the need for democracy in Germany, their assessment of the necessary strategies differed, although more implicitly than explicitly. In psychological and political terms, *Structural Transformation* was too radical and Marxist for Horkheimer's taste, while *Dialectic of*

Enlightenment remained too pessimistic for the early Habermas. In particular, they clashed over the question of modernity. While Horkheimer and Adorno, following Nietzsche, wrote a harsh, unrestrained indictment of modernity, Habermas offers a first version of what he would later come to call "the incomplete project of modernity." Although his critique of the decline of the public sphere in the late nineteenth century is clearly indebted to *Dialectic of Enlightenment*, especially to the famous chapter on the culture industry, Habermas ultimately wanted to explore the ground for a rehabilitation of the public sphere—in other words, he meant to investigate the political and social institutions on which a radical democracy could be built. In this context, as I shall try to demonstrate, the concept of reason as well as the classical German philosophical tradition from Kant to Marx take on a different meaning than in *Dialectic of Enlightenment*.

Habermas's implicit disagreement with his teachers has to do with their relentless critique of the very concept of reason that had sustained the essay of Herbert Marcuse as well as, more broadly speaking, the Institute's project of the 1930s. Both in historical and systematic terms *Dialectic of Enlightenment* attacks the concept of reason as the cardinal failure of Western civilization, which had "progressed," on the one hand, from its early stages couched in mythology to the nominalism of modern positivism, and, on the other, "progressed" from the human sacrifice of early civilizations to the mass murder of contemporary fascism. The failure of reason is the central argument of the book. The introduction speaks of the "self-destruction of the enlightenment"[11] and argues "We are wholly convinced—and therein lies our *petitio principii*—that social freedom is inseparable from enlightened thought. Nevertheless, we believe that we have just as clearly recognized that the notion of this very way of thinking , no less than the actual historic forms—the social institutions—with which it is interwoven, already contains the seed of the reversal universally apparent today."[12]

What is wrong with reason as it functions in modern discourse? Where do Horkheimer and Adorno perceive its shortcomings and problems? They offer a number of different criticisms, some of them relating to its context and functions in modernity, others linked more intimately to reason's genealogy. Because its application to scientific and social problems is exclusively determined by pragmatic concerns that are rooted in strategies for survival, reason, they note, has lost its transcendent quality and its relation to truth. This line of the argument is closely connected with the problem of commodification, that is, the problem that "thought becomes a commodity and language the means of promoting that commodity,"[13] obviously an echo from Lukács's analysis of reification in *History and Class Consciousness*. But whereas Lukács grounded his analysis in the modern phenomenon of commodity fetishism, Horkheimer and Adorno develop a much broader critique that reaches all the way back to the original split between subject and object in the era of mythology. For instance, in a move against the historical European Enlightenment, they argue that, in Kant, the formation of the subject is not the result of autonomy, but the consequence of adaptation to survive through the domination of nature. From this perspective, the self-interpretation of the historical Enlightenment—as well as its focus on humanism—comes across as an ideology that serves darker purposes under the aegis of modern capitalism and imperialism.

Horkheimer and Adorno were quite aware of the inner contradiction of their study. Despite their all-out attack on the Enlightenment, they insisted on the legitimacy of substantive reason as well, a performative contradiction that Adorno later tried to work out in *Negative Dialectics* (1966), in which the epistemological consequences of the earlier critique are finally brought into the foreground.

Although the Frankfurt School still presented a common front to the public, the differently invested project of the second generation was already emerging. In their critique of the radical students, for instance, Habermas and Adorno apparently worked out a mutual position.[14] But the appearance of a common front was deceptive, for when one looks more closely at the arguments that Adorno and Habermas developed in dealing with student unrest, it becomes obvious that Adorno's resistance to revolutionary action was one based on principle while Habermas's criticism was determined by strategic considerations. Adorno was convinced that the time for revolutionary mass movements had passed, that they would be counterproductive in the age of late capitalism. Habermas, on the other hand, believed that the time for revolution had not yet come, that the students were mistaken when they expected a major revolutionary transformation in the immediate future.[15]

This subtly complicated position on the student movement returns us back to the early work of Habermas. Both *Structural*

Transformation and his early essays collected in the volume *Theory and Practice* (1963) are grounded in a concept of history that is largely indebted to Marx, seen through the lenses of western Marxism and the older Critical Theory. I would suggest that the young Habermas partially recuperated the project of the 1930s, though with a much more critical eye for those moments of Marx's work that had to be revised. Along these lines, Habermas reconstructed the history of the public sphere by demonstrating its determination by material conditions. In sum, the bourgeois public sphere rose and fell with the class that had promoted it. In his reconstruction of the public sphere, Habermas simultaneously emphasizes the need for a normative grounding of it. By defining the ideal bourgeois public sphere *(Öffentlichkeit)* as a discursive field based on reason, he sets up a tension between historical reality and the ideal. Using the public sphere of the Enlightenment and, in particular, Kant's definition of it as the trope for this ideal, Habermas moved away from the historical-philosophical *(geschichtsphilosophisch)* model of the older Critical Theory, at least in some respects, although not consistently and systematically. When, some thirty years later, Habermas wrote a new introduction for the 1990 edition of *Structural Transformation* he clarified precisely this point[16]: because he had, during the 1970s, become dissatisfied with the theoretical underpinnings of his first book, in *The Theory of Communicative Action* he tried a very different kind of theoretical grounding. He replaced historical hermeneutics with linguistic theory and clearly preferred normative considerations over historical ones.

Before I sketch Habermas's path to communicative rationality, however, I want to mention, at least in passing, that Habermas's solution to the implicit tension between historical and normative aspects in *Structural Transformation* was not the only one within the Frankfurt School. In their 1972 *Public Sphere and Experience* Oskar Negt and Alexander Kluge propose a very different solution. In their critique of Habermas, they radicalize the historical approach by charging that he failed to understand the deeply ideological nature of the bourgeois public sphere. Their reconstruction not only broadens the scope of the investigation by including the proletarian public sphere, it also reinforces its Marxist tenets— therefore arguing that the liberal public sphere cannot be recuperated at all. By insisting on the radical historicity of the public sphere (or, rather, of the configuration of competing public spheres), Negt and Kluge mean to block—in epistemological as well as political terms—the normative bent of Habermas's theory.

By the end of the 1960s Habermas was left with two fundamental problems: on the one hand, he had to develop a theoretical perspective that would enable him to describe and address social and political problems; on the other hand, he had to formulate a theory that would allow him to articulate normative moral and ethical positions. For a short span of time, Habermas was convinced that the common denominator for these projects would be a combination of an advanced form of philosophical hermeneutics (a critical extension of the work that Hans-Georg Gadamer had begun) and critical reflection in the tradition of ideology critique.

In this approach theory and material interests are linked through the concept of *"erkenntnisleitende Interessen"* (knowledge-constitutive interests) that are inevitably at the bottom of human communication and social action. In this approach the concept of reason is differentiated along the lines of basic forms of human orientation. Building on the methodological differences among the natural sciences, the social sciences, and the humanities, Habermas argues that the traditional understanding of theory that has dominated philosophy from Plato to Husserl falsely treats theory and interests as a strict opposition, since it fails to analyze the hidden premises of knowledge. Instead of eradicating human interests as constitutive for knowledge, Habermas proposes a tripartite structure as the basis for the development of knowledge: "The specific viewpoints from which, with transcendental necessity, we apprehend reality ground three categories of possible knowledge: information that expands our power of technical control, interpretations that make possible the orientation of action within in common traditions, and analyses that free consciousness from its dependence on hypostatized powers. These viewpoints originate in the interest structures of a species that is linked in its roots to definitive means of social organization: work, language, and power."[17]

What Habermas gained from this approach was a rather different take on the problem of reason: the tripartite structure redirects the critique of reason in the work of Horkheimer and Adorno elaborated above. On the one hand, it acknowledges instrumental reason as a legitimate concern of the human species to gain control over its environment; on the other, it criticizes the unreflected application of scientific standards and methods to the humanities and the social sciences where humans ought to be concerned with different forms of truths. In this configuration the concept of reason, with respect to theory, loses its overpowering central position since it is conceived and applied in a variety of contexts and is shown to be grounded in the lifeworld. Thus Habermas concludes: "The insight that the truth of statements is linked in the last analysis to the intention of the good and true life can be preserved today only on the ruins of ontology."[18] Although Habermas's later work did not continue this line of argument, because he had increasing doubts about the mode of transcendental grounding applied in *Knowledge and Human Interest*, it gives a clear indication of the general direction of his theory, distinguishing a variety of forms of rationality and therefore emphasizing the need for a variety of critical approaches. Ideology critique is only one of several methods of analysis.

In the ongoing discussion of the paradigm shift in Habermas's work, scholars often emphasize the so-called linguistic turn that was already suggested in *Knowledge and Human Interest*. Of equal interest, however, is the problem of historical reconstruction because it resonates against his approach to social criticism. In his early work, Habermas, as I have indicated above, followed a Marxian trajectory in the treatment of the public sphere. During the 1970s, however, he critically revised his approach. In *Zur Rekonstruktion des historischen Materialismus* (1976), Habermas attempted to explore the continued feasibility of a Marxian concept of history while simultaneously exploring another strand of his theory, moving in the direction of a general theory of communication in which the traditional concept of reason had to be substantially redefined. Still, the question remains: how do these two strands hang together? How, more specifically, does Habermas reconcile a theory of social evolution indebted to the Marxist tradition with a general theory of communicative rationality based on linguistic theory? One can best understand this relationship as a three-tiered research project. To use a succinct formulation of Thomas McCarthy: "The ground level consists of a general theory of communication ... at the next level this theory serves as the foundation for a general theory of socialization in the form of a theory of the acquisition of communicative competence, finally, at the highest level, which builds on those below it, Habermas sketches a theory of social evolution which he views as a reconstruction of historical materialism."[19]

I would like to begin with what McCarthy calls the highest level, i.e., Habermas's theory of social evolution. While it claims to stand in the Marxist tradition, it does not retain many of the typical building blocks of Marxist theory. In this respect Habermas turns out to be a radical revisionist who reassembles and modifies traditional Marxism in order to recuperate its most important feature—its critical and practical intent. Part of this strategy is the inclusion of other theoretical traditions, among them phenomenology (Schütz), pragmatism, and functionalism (Parsons, Luhmann). Thus Habermas argues: "I do not see, why [my critical] intentions would oblige me to take over more or less dogmatically the assumptions of a theory which is rooted in the nineteenth century."[20] In his own approach, the problems of meaning *(Sinn)*, aspects of action (communicative versus strategic), and hierarchies of communications (symbolically-mediated interaction, propositionally-differentiated actions, discursive speech) play an important role. Specifically, Habermas underlines the relevance of learning for the social system and its evolution. This emphasis is directed, on the one hand, against traditional Marxism, and, on the other, against Luhmann's theory. By emphasizing the crucial importance of learning processes and steering mechanisms, Habermas distances himself from the Marxist assumption that the dialectic between the forces of production and the relations of production can sufficiently explain social evolution. Moreover, this accent implies a critique of systems theory's belief that evolution can be sufficiently explained in terms of differentiation.

In "Towards a Reconstruction of Historical Materialism" (1976), Habermas tries to demonstrate how a materialist theory can both make use of Marx and must at the same time go beyond him. I would like to indicate the ways in which Habermas deviates from the tenets of Marxian theory. First, he maintains that there is no need for a collective subject *(Gattungssubjekt)* that is treated as the substratum of the evolutionary process. Second, the logic of the evolutionary process does not demand the assumption of linearity or necessity and continuity. Instead, he wants to access evolution by way of a consistent distinction between events and structures. These structures are the basis for evolutionary changes, but the actual process of evolution remains contingent—hence, the central importance of learning processes. Third and finally, the observation and analysis of (increased) complexity does not suffice for a complete description of social evolution. More specifically, Habermas argues that the primary importance of the economic system for social evolution, as Marx defined it, was not meant as a universal law, but as a specific model of explanation for the transition from a feudal to a capitalist society. For a more plausible understanding of social evolution, Habermas insists on a categorical distinction between communicative action, on the one hand, and instrumental and strategic action, on the other. By separating out communicative action, he arrives at a different understanding of the dialectic between the forces of production and the relations of production. Moreover, he distances himself from the Marxian assumption that the forces of production ultimately take the lead in social evolution—for him, neither the emergence of the original civilization nor the origins of western capitalism can be explained in terms of the impact of new forces of production.[21]

How, then, does one explain the major shifts in the social structure? Habermas's answer reads: "the species learns not only in the dimension of technically useful knowledge decisive for the development of productive forces but also in the dimension of moral-practical consciousness decisive for structure of interaction. The rules of communicative action do develop in reaction to the changes in the domain of instrumental and strategic action; but in doing so they follow *their own logic*."[22] This means that the concept of the mode of production that underlies Marxian theory is, according to Habermas, not abstract enough to explain the more general character of social evolution.[23] Consequently, Habermas wants to move in the direction of increased conceptual abstraction to analyze organizational principles. This would include, for instance, a clear separation between the mode of production and the social formation that is linked to the dominant mode of production.[24] And more specifically he means to foreground the role of symbolic interactions, which Marxist theory has traditionally treated as secondary for the process of social evolution. This, then, is the place where a theory of communicative action begins to help in the conceptualization of social evolution—and also where he has turned entirely from Horkheimer and Adorno's critique of reason.

I would like to offer just one example to demonstrate how this approach would unfold in the description of social evolution. To pinpoint the transition from one stage to the next, Habermas gives a pattern of attitudes and responses that define a specific phase of social organization. In the case of social evolution some of them are changed but not necessarily all of them. Thus Neolithic societies and early civilizations share a conventionally structured system of action, as well as mythic world views, [25] but in developed civilizations this mythic world view is already separated from the system of action and therefore can have a legitimating function for the ruler.

In such examples, I would like to underscore the general perspective of Habermas's understanding of social evolution in terms relating back to the status of reason and rationality. Whereas Horkheimer and Adorno in *Dialectic of Enlightenment* treated the history of the modern world as essentially the failure of rationality, Habermas views social evolution, which of course includes increased rationality, as a more neutral process. Not that he tries to derive general laws of progress from it as nineteenth-century evolutionists did, but he sees in human history a potential for better social, political, and moral solutions based on learning processes. Yet there are, as he repeatedly argues, no transcendent guarantees (Lessing) nor metaphysical logic (Hegel). Habermas's understanding of social evolution is strictly postmetaphysical. In other words, Habermas's materialism has distanced itself from the belief in preordained laws of evolution. History can be theorized, but only through the intertwinement of empirical methods and a systematic theoretical framework. Strictly speaking, there is no place for the philosophy of history anymore that, as observed above, still guides Habermas's early work.

The primary difference between Habermas's early work and his mature writings arise in the fundamental changes in his theoretical grounding, changes that occurred at the level of the general theory of communication that Habermas began to explore in the 1970s and then articulated in the *Theory of Communicative Action*.[26] The first major step was taken in the groundbreaking essay "What is a Universal Pragmatics?" that tries to reconstruct the universal conditions of possible understanding (*Verständigung*) and identify them as basic to other forms of action such as conflicts, competition, and strategic action. Following Karl Otto Apel, Habermas focuses on speech acts and distinguishes four aspects of linguistic communication: the moment of utterance, the aspect of the content, the moment of articulation (the speaker), and finally, the aspect of reception by another person. Habermas claims: "The goal of coming to an understanding is to bring about an agreement (*Einver-*

ständnis) that terminates in the intersubjective mutuality of reciprocal understanding, shared knowledge, mutual trust, and accord
with one another."[27] To be sure, this structure does not represent
the average case of communication—far from it. In most cases communication remains partial, incomplete, possibly hindered, muti-
lated, and subverted. In most cases, therefore, interpretation is
necessary for speaker and recipient to achieve adequate, if not ideal
communication. For Habermas, however, the crucial question is not
the factuality of disrupted and partial communication, but a reconstruction of the general conditions of communication. To put it suc-
cinctly: what does one already presuppose when one speaks of
failure in communication? There are always validity claims, for
instance, that can be affirmed or negated. In addition, there are
grammatical structures. Hence Habermas distinguishes: (1) the
grammatical level; (2) the level of intersubjective recognition (claims
of truthfulness); (3) the aspect of justification of validity claims (for
instance through arguments, appeals to intuition etc.). Like Apel,
Habermas thus underlines the importance of the pragmatic properties of language, simultaneously distancing himself from positivism,
structuralism, or any type of linguistic theory that treats the pragmatic aspect of language as a mere empirical problem.

The goal Habermas pursues with his analysis relies on a notion
of a transcendental deduction. Yet the term "transcendental" no
longer carries the strong connotations it has in Kant's first *Critique*.
Following the discussion of modern logic, Habermas is inclined
towards a weaker conception of the transcendental that allows for
adaptations and modifications in the analysis.

It would be too time-consuming to develop the specific steps of
his argument here, one that is strongly indebted to Searl and Austin.
Instead, I would like to focus on the consequences of the steps and,
specifically, on the problem of the transition from linguistic to social
theory as well as on its consequences for reason and rationality in
his theory. Why does a social theorist feel the need to integrate linguistic theory? The concise, albeit abbreviated answer, would be:
Habermas is concerned with what he calls "*Geltungsansprüche*"
(validity claims) that are, he argues, basic for social interaction. To
underline this point I want to quote from the essay's final para-
graph where Habermas summarizes his findings: "In speech, speech
sets itself off from the regions of external nature, society, and internal nature, as a reality *sui generis*, as soon as the sign-substrate,

meaning, and denotation of a linguistic utterance can be distinguished."[28] With this statement Habermas foregrounds the linkage between language and the world in which humans live and act—in this scheme, however, the function of speech is differentiated from the world. Representation of facts correlate with the world of external nature; the social world needs speech for the establishment of legitimate interpersonal relations; and the world of internal nature (the subject) uses speech to disclose the speaker's subjectivity. In terms of validity claims, we therefore have to distinguish truth, rightness, and truthfulness.[29]

It would be a nearly impossible task—but the one to which my argument for better and for worse tends—to sketch how Habermas's linguistic turn has affected his social theory in *The Theory of Communicative Action*. This massive two-volume study (the English translation has almost 900 pages) proceeds simultaneously historically and systematically. It develops its argument by returning to older theories—for instance, to those of Weber, Durkheim, Mead, Lukács, and Adorno—in order to frame the theory of communicative action through a redemptive critique of the classics. Very much in the tradition of Critical Theory, yet even more consciously than the first generation, Habermas relies on a double strategy of critique and integration, which then leads to the articulation of the new theoretical position.

To bring this analysis back to the issues of reason and/or rationality, I would like to quote from Habermas: "If we assume that the human species maintains itself through the socially-coordinated activities of its members and that this coordination is established through communication—and, in certain spheres of life, through communication aimed at reaching agreement—then the reproduction of the species also requires satisfying the conditions of a rationality that is inherent in communicative action."[30] Rationality is clearly decoupled from the concept of instrumental reason, as one finds it in Horkheimer and Adorno, and even from a concept of reason developed out of subjective consciousness. Instead, Habermas shifts his attention more to social action through communicative interaction. The social, in other words, cannot be achieved without language and speech: social action depends on interpretive accomplishments. But, of course, the act of reaching an understanding does not exhaust communicative action. Rather, it prepares the coordination of social actions in which the particular aims of the agents come to the fore.[31]

As McCarthy points out: "Communicative competence is not just a matter of being able to produce grammatical sentences. In speaking we relate to the world about us, to other subjects, to our own intentions, feelings and desires."[32] To generalize this point, one can say that for Habermas the world is largely (though not exclusively) constructed through language. And it is through language that humans are able to foster a process of social organization that is at any given moment incomplete and therefore open to social development. In this process examined above, rationality plays an important role: "The rationality proper to the communicative practice of everyday life points to the practice of argumentation as a court of appeal that makes it possible to continue communicative action with other means when disagreement can no longer be repaired with everyday routines and yet are not to be settled by the direct or strategic use of force."[33] Apart from their conventional or functional use, language and communication contain, for Habermas, a critical dimension that is crucial for social interaction and especially for cultural and moral evolution. What I underscored above as a moment of idealization in the initial concept of the public sphere in 1962, now returns as the claim for a universal communicative rationality in 1981. In short, the concept of reason must not be rejected but redirected, differentiated, and delimited in its function.

In the last section of this chapter, I would like to turn to the emergence of a post-Habermasian version of Critical Theory. One can elaborate this post-Habermasian trajectory in two directions: on the one hand, one that would analyze the work of the third generation of Critical Theorists, among them Axel Honneth in Germany and Thomas McCarthy and Seyla Benhabib in the United States; on the other hand, one that would address internal tendencies of returning to older theoretical positions or seeking an alliance with different theoretical traditions—trajectories that one finds in the writings of Peter Bürger and Albrecht Wellmer. In some instances this return to Adorno or Benjamin is also characterized by a strong anti-Habermasian sentiment: their positions cast Habermas as the rationalist spoiler of Critical Theory. While the members of the third generation have, by and large, accepted the foundations of Habermasian thought and, therefore, developed their critiques on the basis of this theory, some "outsiders," who are not directly connected to the Frankfurt School as an institution, have been stronger in their resistance to the force of the theory of communicative action and all it stands for. This is, I feel, particularly true in the field of aesthetic theory, a field that has received only marginal attention in Habermas's writings. And again in the official transition from Habermas to Axel Honneth, who was recently appointed Habermas's successor at the University of Frankfurt, the aesthetic question, which was so prominent in the work of Adorno and Benjamin, has been moved to the background.

Before turning to the situation of the third generation, I would like first to focus briefly on Peter Bürger and Albrecht Wellmer, who are only a few years younger than Habermas himself. Important in both cases is a somewhat uneasy arrangement reached with Habermas's conception of communicative rationality, which, as I indicated above, cannot easily be applied to the tradition of aesthetic analysis from the early Lukács to the late Adorno. Bürger is quite conscious of this tension when he explains in the first chapter of his 1988 study *Prosa der Moderne* that his concept of reason or rationalism is more indebted to the older tradition of western Marxism than to Habermas. He talks about an *"eingeschränkter Begriff von Zweck-rationalität"* (delimited concept of instrumental reason) [34] to distinguish himself from Habermas's differentiated concept of rationality. Bürger's central thesis returns self-consciously to the conceptual framework of the first generation of Critical Theory, for instance in his definition of autonomous art: "Autonomous art comes into being as answer to the experience of alienation that a person has in a world that is his product but that confronts him everywhere nonetheless as alienated."[35] In this view the process of social differentiation, which in Habermas's work is seen as neutral, takes on a definitely negative character: alienation becomes the very experience that modern art has to oppose or subvert. Modern art, Bürger suggests, resists the process of differentiation as such, "because the concept of form that constitutes art stands at an angle to the concept of rationality."[36] It is quite consistent therefore that Bürger begins with a reconstruction of the category of the modern and modernism in the work of Hegel, Lukács, and Adorno. Still, this reiteration of Habermas's strategy has a different aim since Bürger holds on to a concept of substantive aesthetic truth as it can be found in Adorno's aesthetic theory, a theory that Habermas and his immediate disciples would certainly no longer defend. While in *The Theory of the Avant-Garde* of 1974 Bürger treated Adorno's theory as no longer satisfactory for the postwar situation, in *Prosa der Moderne* (1988) he reverts in his analysis of modernism to the aporetic dialectic of Adorno's aesthetic theory. This theory maintains, on the one hand, that art cannot give up its autonomous status as well as its truth claims, but has, on the other hand, to come to grips with the fact that the modern social system, i.e., advanced capitalism, has marginalized art and subverted its truth claims. Bürger defines the basic experience of modern art as aporetic insofar as it is at the same time necessary and impossible.[37] This definition, I would argue, stays closer to Adorno and Benjamin than to Habermas.

This repositioning and return to older Critical Theorists becomes even more apparent in Bürger's most recent work. In *Das Denken des Herrn* (1992) Bürger begins to distance himself from the notion of a systematic theory (that has guided Habermas's work from the very beginning) and seeks refuge in the essay form that the early Lukács and the mature Adorno had cultivated as the most appropriate form for critical thought. This formal decision should not merely be taken as a light change of genre. Now the nonsystematic—even antisystematic—format of the essay is consciously brought back to articulate those moments of critical and self-reflexive thought that the rigor of systematic theory represses or misses. Where Habermas prefers closure (even in his essays), Bürger now propagates the refusal of closure. He suggests: "The essay yields no exits, such exits would make it clearly the wrong path. It is a form of unending delay. Its inner temporal form is the future, even where it speaks of the past. If there is a process of the essayist, then it is the trust in the distancing (*Abliegende*). From such distancing the essayist hopes to find the impetus for a reversal of knowledge. To this degree the essayist shares with Benjamin the surrealist inclination to expectation ... "[38] "Verkehrung des Wissens" (reversal of knowledge) signals a situation where the construction of knowledge, theoretical as well as empirical, has become a disappointing experience—*Endzeitstimmung*. One cannot fail to notice the growing pessimism in Bürger's late work—possibly one reason why all of a sudden Adorno seems to be a more attractive guide than Habermas.[39]

Albrecht Wellmer takes up both a different strategy and a different position. Unlike Bürger, he actually engages Habermas's theory and makes a serious attempt to fuse the Adornian problematics with the framework of the theory of communicative action. In fact, the essay "Truth, Semblance, Reconciliation" (1985) takes Habermas's critique of Adorno as its point of departure. Looking back at Adorno's work from the perspective of communicative rationality, Wellmer suggests that Adorno's epistemology, especially its subject-object split, makes it virtually infeasible to grasp the "communicative moment of the spirit"[40]; it forces Adorno to develop a theory of mimesis that has to fill the gap left by a too-constrained concept of rationality. Wellmer follows Habermas in assuming that communicative rationality can overcome the conflict between subjectivization and alienation, which had to remain an unresolved dialectical tension in Adorno and Horkheimer's work.

Similarly, in the essay "Modernism and Postmodernism," Wellmer deploys the concept of communicative rationality to engage Lyotard's conception of postmodernism: Wellmer argues that the pluralism of language games and institutions that are expected to overcome the tyranny of enlightenment depend themselves on a different form of rationality. "But such a pluralism of institutions embodying the democratic self-organization of societies and groups would not be possible unless the fundamental mechanism by which action is coordinated were to take the form of communicative action in the sense that Habermas has defined it."[41] Particularity cannot be purchased without a moment of universality and vice versa. In this line of argument the problem of modern democracy is not simply a matter of supporting pluralism against authoritarian rationalism. What is at stake "is a shared basis of second-order social habits: the habits of rational self-determination, democratic decision-making, and the nonviolent resolution of conflicts."[42] It is interesting to note, however, that Wellmer defends this position not through ultimate principles and deductive reasoning. Instead, he suggests that "we cannot expect either ultimate justifications or final solutions to our problems."[43] Nonetheless, he underlines the need for a universalist perspective that guides the permeability of the various modes of discourse. In other words, Wellmer wants the unitary notion of reason to be replaced by "plurality of interacting rationalities."[44]

Though Wellmer's thought offers this strong Habermasian strand, ultimately more interesting is the question of where and to what extent he departs from the Habermasian position. While Wellmer stays convinced of the severe limitations of the epistemology developed in *Dialectic of Enlightenment* and views the weaknesses of Adorno's art criticism, at least in part, as their logical result, he takes the aesthetic theory of the first generation of Criti-

cal Theorists seriously and engages them both historically and systematically. In his search for an aesthetics of democracy, he carefully
distinguishes between moments of aesthetic traditionalism in the
work of Adorno and the unfolding of the internal logic of *Aesthetic
Theory,* which he sees as determined by the dialectic of subjectiva-
tion and alienation, specifically by the notion of an encroachment of
rationality into the work of art.

At this juncture Wellmer opts for the impulses that have come
from Benjamin's art criticism, in particular from Benjamin's reading
of modern mass culture, to distance himself from the Adornian cage
of aesthetic autonomy. Following Benjamin, Wellmer argues: "I
think that there is just as much positive potential for democratization and the unleashing of aesthetic imagination as there is potential
for cultural regression in rock music and the attitudes, skills and
modes of perception which have developed around it."[45] The structure of this argument, i.e., the rhetoric of "both/and," hovers at the
moment when Benjamin radically pushed the loss of aura as the
necessary secularization of the aesthetic. But, of course, this process
of democratic secularization is already completely taken for granted
by Wellmer and no longer deserves the defense that Adorno still put
up. One senses that Wellmer displays even a certain impatience with
Adorno when he holds onto the concept of the autonomous art
work in its classical or modernist version.

This criticism of Adorno, however, does not stand at the center
of Wellmer's essay. As he points out in his summary, his main interest lies in the possibility of a recuperative reading of Adorno in
which the concept of aesthetic truth is brought to the fore. Wellmer
wants to redeem, above all, the moment of communication in art,
a form of nonviolent communication that is inherent in the concept
of truth. This reading contains an interesting interpretative shift
since, for Adorno, the communicative aspect of the art work was of
secondary importance. Adorno was certainly not inclined to define
the truth-content of the art work in terms of communication. In
fact, his rabid criticism of reception studies makes this very clear. It
seems to me that Wellmer wants to create a bridge between the late
theory of Adorno and the mature work of Habermas by focusing
on the notion of the utopian: "The intention that has guided me in
these reflections," Wellmer states, "was to release the truth-content
of Adorno's aesthetics and develop it through critique and interpretation."[46] The idea of the utopian, one of the most essential and

powerful categories of Critical Theory, enables Wellmer to reintegrate Adorno's work into the mainstream of second-generation Critical Theory.

In many respects the third generation of Critical Theorists, most of them students of Jürgen Habermas, follow a similar path. Among them Axel Honneth stands out as perhaps most representative. His intellectual formation occurred during the 1970s and early 1980s in close proximity to Habermas, who taught for about a decade at the Max Planck Institute in Starnberg, returning to the University of Frankfurt in 1988. For Honneth the paradigm shift within the Frankfurt School had already happened when he joined Habermas's seminar and later became his assistant. Consequently, in Honneth's work the theory of communicative action, rather than *Negative Dialectics* or the late writings of Benjamin, became the point of departure. In this sense he represents the self-understanding of the School. Yet there is another side to his writings that is either absent or less developed in the thought of the second generation, namely, a strong interest in, and lasting familiarity with, French structuralism and poststructuralism. Unlike his teacher Habermas—who, for example, remained a suspicious reader of his French colleagues in the *Philosophical Discourse of Modernity*—Honneth tried to develop his own position through the appropriation of French theory, especially through Foucault. This comparative strategy defines the approach of his first major study, *The Critique of Power* (*Kritik der Macht*) (1985), but is also quite prominent in his essay collection, the fragmented world of the social (*Die Zerrissenheit des Sozialen*) (1990), that brought French social theory (Levi-Strauss, Merlau-Ponty, Castoriadis, and Bourdieu) to the attention of a broader German public. While *Critique of Power* still holds on to the perspective of the Frankfurt School, and ultimately favors the theory of communicative action over Foucault's analysis of power relations, the later essays demonstrate a greater appreciation of French thought as well as a broader and more generous framework of interpretation. What seems to attract Honneth to the French thinkers is the same moment that makes the older generation of Critical Theorists relevant again after Habermas's work superseded them—the preservation of motives and themes that did not find adequate expression in Habermasian theory, for example, the destructive character of the "rational" process of civilization. Thus Honneth characterizes Foucault in the following manner: "Foucault's heightened sensitivity for those forms of suffering, which arise from the culturally imposed repression of instinctual and imaginative impulses alone allows us to understand the difficult synthesis achieved by his works on the history of knowledge: the unusual combination of the knowledge of the scholar, the art of the narrator, the obsession of the monomaniac and the sensitivity of the injured—a synthesis mirrored in the physiognomy of Foucault's combination of analytical coldness and sympathetic sensibility."[47]

Nonetheless, as Honneth turns to the substance of Foucault's work, he notes the shortcomings as well, shortcomings seen from the perspective of a general theory of communication. In the essay "Foucault und Adorno" (1986) he underlines the failure of Foucault's early work in which Foucault unfolds the emergence and the passing of scientific discourses. Honneth interprets the shift to a theory of power in Foucault's later work as an indication that the structuralist approach to language and discourses had failed, and Honneth welcomes this shift as a significant step towards a social theory compatible with Adorno's late work. To make this point Honneth foregrounds the aspect of human suffering, especially the experience of bodily suffering, as a dimension common to both Adorno and Foucault: "The construction of the concept of rationality in Adorno and Foucault is guided by the compassionate awareness of the sufferings of the human body. This is the inner affinity in their critique of the modern age."[48] Common elements that Honneth emphasizes are the concept of rationalism, a notion of "bodily subjectivity,"[49] and the conception of modernity in which the process of enlightenment turns out to be a process of disciplinary and rationalist control in society (thus a totalizing critique of reason).

Ultimately, however, Honneth's essay stresses the differences between Foucault and Adorno. While Foucault means to demonstrate that human subjectivity is nothing but a field of manipulation, Adorno, following a Marxist analysis of advanced capitalism, tends to stress the deformation of the individual. In the final analysis, Honneth favors Adorno's critique of the subject over Foucault's dismantling of the concept of subjectivity, since the latter approach strikes him as a reductive interpretation of the social along the lines of Luhmann's systems theory. The proximity of this critique to that of Habermas is fairly apparent. In *Critique of Power* Honneth offers a more systematic analysis of this line of interpretation. The study develops two lines of argument to unfold the main thesis; on the one hand, Honneth traces the internal development of the Frankfurt School, in particular the phase from Adorno to Habermas; on the other, he uses Foucault's theory of power relations to provide a contrasting reading of the social problems that Critical Theory addressed at various stages with various methods. In this regard Foucault might have a function similar to that of Nietzsche for Adorno and Horkheimer—a force of resistance to the idea of the self-reflexive and autonomous subject, especially to the idea of a subject-agent engaged in communicative interaction.

Even a cursory look at the latest constellation of Critical Theory confirms that the history of the Frankfurt School cannot be adequately conceptualized as a linear evolution toward rationality. Honneth himself seems to be somewhat aware of this more complex configuration when he suggests in his essay on the genealogy of Critical Theory that one has to distinguish between an inner and an outer circle of Critical Theorists. He then credits the "outsiders" such as Benjamin, Kirchheimer, Neumann, and Fromm with the preservation of a greater variety of theoretical models that the inner circle failed to maintain because it was locked into more narrowly defined thought patterns. The ideas of the outsiders would be picked up by the Critical Theory's second generation, in particular by Jürgen Habermas (and by extension, Honneth himself). Thus, in a surprising move Honneth claims that Habermas actually had little in common with his teachers whom he defines as functionalist Marxists.[50] Instead, by developing the insights of the outsiders, Habermas arrived at a nonfunctionalist social theory that "may be accepted as the only serious new approach within this tradition today."[51] While I find the latter part of this argument unconvincing, I find the distinction between insider and outsider useful and worth applying to the post-Adornian *Gestalt* of the Frankfurt School. One would have to turn to the work of Alexander Kluge and Oskar Negt, or to the writings of Peter Bürger and Christoph Menke, perhaps even to the essays of Karl Heinz Bohrer, to find the unorthodox impulses that the School might need to break the gridlock of its present articulation.

Still, the distinction between insiders and outsiders, as suggestive as it is, fails to capture the entire history of Critical Theory. The phenomenon of returns to older, seemingly outdated forms of theoretical articulation, as well as the moments of reiterations at a different level, have been at least as important for the development of Critical Theory. For example, as I have suggested above, the early work of Habermas "returned" to the project developed by the Institute during the 1930s. During the 1970s Negt and Kluge resisted the paradigm shift prepared by Habermas and returned to the Marxism of the first generation. During the 1980s and 1990s Wellmer and Bürger again returned to Adorno's aesthetic theory to make up for the aesthetic deficits of advanced Critical Theory. Of course, this moment of a return is not to be taken literally as the expression of a dogmatic belief. Rather, this move signals an awareness of the constraints of the dominant version of Critical Theory, i.e., the theory of communicative action and its concomitant communicative rationality, as well as an awareness of, and the need for, a new and fresh appropriation of previous theoretical patterns. In other words, it is a learning process for the future undertaken in consultation with the past.

Notes

1. Regarding the history of the Frankfurt School see Martin Jay, *The Dialectical Imagination. A History of the Frankfurt School and the Institute of Social Research 1923-1950* (Boston: Beacon, 1973); Rolf Wiggershaus, *The Frankfurt School. History, Theories, and Political Significance* (Cambridge: MIT Press, 1986).
2. Herbert Marcuse, *One-Dimensional Man, Studies in the Ideology of Advanced Industrial Society* (Boston: Beacon, 1964); Herbert Marcuse, *Counterrevolution and Revolt* (Boston: Beacon, 1972).
3. The two issues on Benjamin of the periodical *argumente* are symptomatic of this development; see the issues October/December 1967 and April/June 1968.
4. See Jürgen Habermas, "Consciousness-Raising or Redemptive Criticism: The Contemporaneity of Walter Benjamin," *New German Critique* 17(1979): 30-59.
5. Herbert Marcuse, *Negations: Essays in Critical Theory* (Boston: Beacon, 1968), 136.
6. Marcuse, *Negations*, 136.
7. Marcuse, *Negations*, 136.
8. Marcuse, *Negations*, 141.
9. Marcuse, *Negations*, 153.
10. See Wiggershaus, 537-55.

11. Max Horkheimer and Theodor W. Adorno, *Dialectic of Enlightenment* (New York: Herder and Herder, 1972), xi.
12. Horkheimer and Adorno, xiii.
13. Horkheimer and Adorno, xii.
14. Wiggershaus, 609-35.
15. Jürgen Habermas, "Die Scheinrevolution und ihre Kinder," in *Die Linke antwortet Jürgen Habermas* (Frankfurt am Main: Suhrkamp Verlag, 1968), 5-16.
16. Jürgen Habermas, "Further Reflections on the Public Sphere," in *Habermas and the Public Sphere*, ed. Craig Calhoun, (Cambridge: MIT Press, 1992), 421-61.
17. Jürgen Habermas, *Knowledge and Human Interests* (Boston: Beacon, 1972), 313.
18. Habermas, *Knowledge and Human Interests*, 317.
19. Thomas McCarthy, "Introduction," in Jürgen Habermas, *The Theory of Communicative Action*, vol. 1 (Boston: Beacon, 1984), xvii.
20. Jürgen Habermas, *Zur Rekonstruktion des historischen Materialismus* (Frankfurt am Main: Suhrkamp Verlag, 1976), 130: "Ich sehe andererseits nicht, warum diese Intentionen mich verpflichten sollten, die Konstruktionsmittel und die speziellen Annahmen einer im 19. Jahrhundert wurzelnden Theorie mehr oder wenig dogmatisch zu übernehmen." My translation—P.U.H.
21. Habermas, "Towards a Reconstruction of Historical Materialism," in Jürgen Habermas, *Communication and the Evolution of Society* (Boston: Beacon Press, 1979), 147.
22. Habermas, "Towards a Reconstruction of Historical Materialism," 148.
23. Habermas, "Towards a Reconstruction of Historical Materialism," 152.
24. Habermas, "Towards a Reconstruction of Historical Materialism," 153.
25. Habermas, "Towards a Reconstruction of Historical Materialism," 144.
26. Regarding the development of Habermas's philosophy, see Thomas McCarthy, *The Critical Theory of Jürgen Habermas* (Cambridge: MIT Press, 1978); Raymond Geuss, *The Idea of a Critical Theory. Habermas and the Frankfurt School* (Cambridge: Cambridge University Press, 1981).
27. Habermas, "What is Universal Pragmatics?" in Habermas, *Communication and the Evolution of Society*, 68.
28. Habermas, *Communication and the Evolution of Society*, 68.
29. Habermas, *Communication and the Evolution of Society*, 68.
30. Habermas, *The Theory of Communicative Action*, vol. 1, 397.
31. Habermas, *The Theory of Communicative Action*, vol. 1, 101.
32. McCarthy, "Introduction," in *The Theory of Communicative Action*, vol. 1, x.
33. Habermas, *The Theory of Communicative Action*, vol. 1, 17-18.
34. Peter Bürger, *Prosa der Moderne* (Frankfurt am Main: Suhrkamp Verlag, 1988), 18.
35. Bürger, *Prose der Moderne*, 17: ."Autonome Kunst entsteht als Antwort auf die Entfremdungserfahrungen, die der Mensch in einer Welt macht, die sein Produkt ist und ihm doch überall als eine ihm fremde entgegentritt."
36. Bürger, *Prose der Moderne*, 18: ."weil der sie konstituierende Formbegriff quersteht zum Begriff der Rationalität."
37. Bürger, *Prose der Moderne*, 447.
38. Peter Bürger, *Das Denken des Herrn: Bataille zwischen Hegel und dem Surrealismus* (Frankfurt am Main: Suhrkamp Verlag, 1992), 13: "Der Essay weist keine Auswege, es sei denn, um sie sogleich als Holzwege erkennbar zu machen.

Er ist die Form des unendlichen Aufschubs. Seine innere Zeitform ist das Futur, auch wo er von Vergangenem spricht.. Wenn es ein Verfahren des Essayisten gibt, dann ist es das Vertrauen auf das Abliegende. Von ihm erhofft er sich den Anstoß zur Verkehrung seines Wissens. Insofern teilt der Essayist mit Benjamin die surrealistische Haltung des Erwartens ... "

39. See also Peter Uwe Hohendahl, *Prismatic Thought. Theodor W. Adorno* (Lincoln: University of Nebraska Press, 1995).

40. Albrecht Wellmer, *Persistence of Modernity* (Cambridge: MIT Press, 1991), 13.

41. Wellmer, *Persistence of Modernity*, 92.

42. Wellmer, *Persistence of Modernity*, 92.

43. Wellmer, *Persistence of Modernity*, 93.

44. Wellmer, *Persistence of Modernity*, 94.

45. Wellmer, *Persistence of Modernity*, 33.

46. Wellmer, *Persistence of Modernity*, 35.

47. Axel Honneth, *The Fragmented World of the Social. Essays in Social and Political Philosophy*, ed. Charles W. Wright (Albany: SUNY Press, 1995) 123-24.

48. Honneth, *The Fragmented World of the Social*, 126.

49. Honneth, *The Fragmented World of the Social*, 127.

50. Honneth, *The Fragmented World of the Social*, 86.

51. Honneth, *The Fragmented World of the Social*, 86.

ADORNO AND BENJAMIN

Reemerging Questions of Epistemology, History, and Aesthetics

Chapter 2

Is Experience Still in Crisis?

Reflections on a Frankfurt School Lament[1]

Martin Jay

The identity of experience in the form of a life that is articulated and possesses internal continuity—and that life was the only thing that made the narrator's stance possible—has disintegrated. One need only note how impossible it would be for someone who participated in the war to tell stories about it the way people used to tell stories about their adventures.[2]

The war is "as totally divorced from experience as is the functioning of a machine from the movement of the body, which only begins to resemble it in pathological states ... Life has changed into a timeless succession of shocks, interspersed with empty, paralyzed intervals ... The total obliteration of the war by information, propaganda commentaries, with cameramen in the first tanks and war reporters dying heroic deaths, the mishmash of enlightened manipulation of public opinion and oblivious activity: all this is another expression for the withering of experience, the vacuum between men and their fate, in which their real fate lies."[3]

For those conversant with the history of Critical Theory, the lament expressed in these two citations will immediately sound familiar. If asked to identify the source, they would likely point to Walter Benjamin's celebrated essay "The Storyteller" (1936), in which World War I is blamed for starting a process that has impoverished something called experience (*Erfahrung*, not, for reasons to be discussed shortly, *Erlebnis*). It is here, after all, that one finds the now familiar lines: "for never has experience been contracted more thoroughly than strategic experience by tactical warfare, economic experience by inflation, bodily experience by mechanical warfare, moral experience by those in power."[4] Such an attribution would be logical, but, in fact, wrong. The first citation is from an essay written in 1954 by Adorno, entitled "The Position of the Narrator in the Contemporary Novel," and reprinted in *Notes to Literature*; the second comes from the aphorism "Out of the Firing Line," written in 1944 and published in *Minima Moralia* in 1951. The war in question is thus not World War I, but the second—the argument, however, is exactly the same. What Adorno has done is simply recycle Benjamin's claim that narrative continuity, and, with it, a certain notion of experience, has been shattered by the traumatic shocks and general unintelligibility of modern warfare.

I draw attention to this recycling not to undermine any claim to Adorno's originality—an issue of no great significance—but rather to pose the question: when exactly did something called experience come into crisis? Was it an actual historical event or process caused by a trauma like global warfare, or is something more ontological at issue? Is there, moreover, a coherent and unified notion of experience assumed by the lament, or does the word function in different ways in different contexts? And if different acceptations are to be discerned, can we say that all of them have withered to the same degree or even withered at all at the present time?

The assumption that something historical has indeed undercut the possibility of experience would seem to inform many of the Frankfurt School's formulations of the problem. It is in the work of Adorno that they most frequently appear.[5] For example, in *Aesthetic Theory*, he would write "The marrow of experience has been sucked out; there is none, not even that apparently set at a remove from commerce, that has not been gnawed away."[6] Similarly in his 1960 essay "Presuppositions," he would claim that in the modernist writings of Joyce and Proust one can see "the dying out of experience, something that ultimately goes back to the atemporal technified process of the production of material goods."[7] And in his essay of the previous year, "Theory of Pseudo-Culture," he would complain that experience—which he defined in almost Burkean terms as "the continuity of consciousness in which everything not present survives, in which practice and association establish tradition in the individual"—has now been "replaced by the selective, disconnected, interchangeable and ephemeral state of being informed which, as one can already observe, will promptly be cancelled by other information."[8]

Attempts to revive a robust variety of experience in the present, Adorno would moreover argue, are doomed to failure, especially when they seek to recover an alleged Ur-experience that is somehow deeper than the mediations of culture and society. In *The Jargon of Authenticity*, he would mock efforts by latter-day adepts of *Lebensphilosophie* to re-enchant the world:

> The contrast between primal experiences and cultural experiences, which [Friedrich] Gundolf invented *ad hoc*, for [Stefan] George, was ideology in the midst of superstructure, devised for the purpose of obscuring the contrast between infrastructure and ideology ... [Ernst] Bloch rightfully made fun of Gundolf for his belief in today's primal experiences. These primal experiences were a warmed-over piece of expressionism. They were later made into a permanent institution by Heidegger ... In the universally mediated world everything experienced in primary terms is culturally preformed.[9]

Here experience is understood more in terms of *Erlebnis* than *Erfahrung*, as prereflective immediacy without narrative continuity over time, but the point is the same: it is no longer available to us. As Adorno wrote in an essay of 1967 on the poetry of Rudolf Borchardt, "the poetic subject that did not want to give itself over to something alien to it had become the victim of what was most alien of all, the conventions of the long exhausted *Erlebnislyrik* [poetry of experience] ... The ideology of primal experience that Gundolf promulgated on George's behalf is refuted by Borchardt's poetic practice."[10]

In sum, there is an implied sense of loss of something that once existed and that has been seriously damaged, if not entirely destroyed, in the present. Variously attributed to the traumas of world war, modern technologies of information, and the "atemporal, technified process of the production of material goods," which seems another way to say capitalist industrialization, the decay of something called experience is for Adorno an index of the general crisis of modern life. How far back the roots of the crisis may go will be clearer if one turns briefly to the even more frequent bemoaning of the decay of experience in Benjamin, who provided, as shown above, an inspiration for many of Adorno's own ruminations on this theme. There is an enormous literature on the question of experience in Benjamin, which has culminated, at least for the moment, in Howard Caygill's just published *Walter Benjamin: The Colour of Experience*.[11]

Drawing on the hitherto ignored fragments of Benjamin's earliest writings on perception, visuality, and color, Caygill has con-

structed a carefully nuanced account of his lifelong preoccupation
with the possibility of reviving a lost experience. Prior to the articulation of that project in linguistic terms, in such essays as "On Language as Such and the Language of Man" (1916) and "On the
Program of the Coming Philosophy" (1918), Caygill shows that Benjamin experimented with expressing the loss of experience in visual
terms.[12] Reaching back beyond Kant's restriction of experience to
merely that which is filtered through the synthetic a priori function of
the understanding, the young Benjamin sought a frankly metaphysical alternative in the more immediate perception of prereflective intuition. According to Caygill, "Benjamin's speculative recasting of
Kant's transcendental account of experience involves the introduction of the absolute or infinite into the structure or forms of intuition—space and time—and the linguistic categories (*logoi*) of the
understanding. Benjamin sought to avoid both Kant's scission of
experience and the absolute, and what he regarded as Hegel's 'mys-
ticism of brute force' which for him reduced the absolute by expressing it in terms of the categories of finite experience."[13]

Color as opposed to form was particularly important in this
quest because of its infinite divisibility, a quality that eludes the cate-
gorizing reifications of a merely epistemological relation to the world,
based as it is on the rigid distinction of subject and object. In a fragment written in 1914-15, entitled "A Child's View of Color," Benjamin contended that "color is something spiritual, something whose
clarity is spiritual, so that when colors are mixed they produced
nuances of color, not a blur. The rainbow is a pure childlike image."[14]
Benjamin's subsequent valorization of Romantic aesthetic criticism,
in particular the work of Schlegel and Novalis, is foreshadowed here
in his celebration of childlike vision and the spiritual presence of
infinity in color. When in his later work, he turned toward modern,
urban experience, largely characterized in negative terms as a fallen
realm of shocklike, discontinuous *Erlebnisse*, he still sought traces or
prefigurations of the redeemed *Erfahrung* that he had glimpsed in his
earliest ruminations on visual intuition. Never abandoning his quest
for what Caygill rightly calls "a non-Hegelian account of speculative
experience,"[15] Benjamin believed that the absolute could somehow be
revealed through an immanent critique of even the most mundane of
phenomena. Thus, with this optimism he was able to avoid the paral-
ysis of nostalgia based on a simple inversion of the model of unidi-
rectional progress he so tellingly criticized.

Whether or not Benjamin's quest actually was successful is, of course, a matter of some dispute, as many of Benjamin's redemptive readings, like his political commitments, seem more like wishful thinking than anything else. Similarly, the precise chronology of the fall from grace, with which he tacitly worked, is not entirely coherent. At times, it seems as if Benjamin were making a typical Romantic argument about the loss of childhood innocence that would have done Wordsworth proud, an argument that is inherently ahistorical. At other times, he seemed to be saying that the fall came when the world of mimetic similarities, in which nature was a legible text, was supplanted by a dead world of deanimated objects, to be scrutinized by the scientific gaze and to be given philosophical justification by Kant's desiccated epistemology. Here his celebrated argument about the Baroque, as a period of mourning for the lost wholeness represented in Greek tragedy, a period of allegorical rather than symbolic representation, suggests that the absolute had already been driven out of experience and the infinite abjected from the finite by the seventeenth century. The technological transformations of more recent years—leading to the loss of the ritual, cultic aura around earlier art—thus merely continued and intensified a change that had begun much earlier. The unevenness of the process is shown, however, by his claim in a 1936 essay "The Storyteller" that Nikolai Leskov, a writer of the nineteenth century, was still able to convey genuine *Erfahrungen* in his tales in a fashion no longer available in the modern novel. Perhaps Russia was still the site of a ritualized, communal life allowing the narrative transmission from one generation to the next that was one expression of genuine *Erfahrung*. If so, Benjamin would not have been alone in finding an exception to the rule in Russian literature, another obvious example being the Dostoyevsky extolled by Lukács in his *Theory of the Novel*.

Be that as it may, Benjamin bequeathed to Adorno a strong belief in the importance of experience, once freed from its empiricist and Kantian limitations, as a locus of possible redemption, a place in which something called "the absolute" might make an appearance. His exaltation of color even found an occasional echo, as in the remark in *Negative Dialectics* that "the resistance to the fungible world of barter is the resistance of the eye that does not want the colors of the world to fade."[16] Benjamin also gave Adorno, as shown above, an unexamined assumption that at some indeterminate time in the past, actual lived experience came closer to this condition than it does today. Since that time a kind of fall from grace had occurred, causing experience in this metaphysical sense, to "decay" or "wither." Such a fall needed to be read dialectically, in the hope that something of what was lost might still be lurking in the debris—or even brought into the world anew with the fresh vision of every child.

Where Adorno, however, moved away from Benjamin was in his greater sympathy for Hegel's conceptualization of experience, which demonstrated his links with the other philosophers at the Frankfurt Institute. Perhaps the difference is best shown in his defense of Hegel against the attack launched by Martin Heidegger in the latter's *Holzwege* of 1950.[17] I do not want to conflate Benjamin and Heidegger—who were in many respects very different—but on the issue of experience they did share certain similar inclinations.[18] Both were, for example, hostile to the privileging of immediate "lived experience" or *Erlebnis* in *Lebensphilosophie*; both were against the reduction of experience to an epistemological category in the Kantian or empiricist sense; and both were anxious to transcend psychologistic subjectivism and restore a notion of experience prior to the split between subject and object. Heidegger, like Benjamin, was determined to return to more fundamental levels of truth—whether they be called the metaphysical absolute or the ontological real—than the tradition of disenchanted, secular humanism had allowed.

In *Holzwege*, Heidegger juxtaposes passages from Hegel's *Phenomenology of Spirit* with extended commentaries on their significance. He highlights the fact that Hegel had first called the work "Science of the Experience of Consciousness" and argues that his version of phenomenology is still deeply indebted to that project. Heidegger foregrounds Hegel's noncommonsensical definition of experience, which reads as follows: "this *dialectical* movement, which consciousness exercises on itself—on its knowledge as well as its object—is, *in so far as the new, true object emerges to consciousness* as the result of it, precisely that which is called *experience*."[19] Glossing this passage, Heidegger claims that Hegel means by "experience" the "Being of beings … Experience now is the word of Being, since Being is apprehended by way of beings *qua* beings."[20] Here he seems to be assimilating Hegel's position to his own.

But then Heidegger adds that for Hegel, "Experience designates the subject's subjectness. Experience expresses what '*being*' in the term 'being conscious' means—in such a way that only by this 'being' does it become clear and binding what the word 'conscious' leaves still to thought."[21] Thus, Hegel's notion of experience remains hostage to that fateful privileging of the subject that Heidegger found so distressing in modern metaphysics. This bias is revealed, Heidegger continues, because experience for Hegel involved the presentation of an appearance for a consciousness, a manifestation of being to a subject in the present. In fact, Hegel's dialectical method is itself grounded in a still subjective view of experience: "Hegel does not conceive of experience dialectically," Heidegger writes, "he thinks of dialectic in terms of the nature of experience. Experience is the beingness of beings, whose determination, *qua subjectum*, is determined in terms of subjectness."[22] The ultimate subject for Hegel is, of course, the Absolute Spirit. Thus, Heidegger writes that for Hegel, "experience is the subjectness of the absolute subject. Experience, the presentation of the absolute representation, is the *parousia* of the Absolute. Experience is the absoluteness of the Absolute, its appearance in absolving appearance to itself."[23]

Heidegger concedes that Hegel understood that natural consciousness lacks this more exalted, metaphysical notion of experience, because it ignores the deeper question of Being. But the way in which the Hegelian Absolute exteriorizes itself and re-collects itself at a higher level produces the questionable claim that the experience of consciousness lends itself to an ex post facto scientific recapitulation. Significantly, Heidegger points out, "experience" occupies the middle position between "science" and "consciousness" in the title "Science of the Experience of Consciousness," which indicates that for Hegel, "experience, as the being of consciousness, is in itself the inversion by which consciousness presents itself in its appearance. That is to say: in making the presentation, experience is science."[24]

Heidegger concludes by speculating on the reasons Hegel dropped this original title shortly before the book was published and substituted "phenomenology of spirit" instead. Noting that for Kant "experience" merely meant "the only possible theoretical knowledge of what is," he hazards the guess that Hegel found it too daring to restore an earlier meaning: "a reaching out and attaining, and attaining as the mode of being present, of εἶναι, of Being."[25] Perhaps because of this failure of nerve, Hegel had not quite attained the level of insight into Being that Heidegger ascribed to his own thought. Heidegger's sympathetic interpreter, Robert Bernasconi, summarizes the essential differences between the two thinkers in the following terms: "'Experience' in Heidegger does not have the sense of a progressive development as it has in Hegel. For Heidegger, experience almost always takes place in the face of a lack ... For the phenomenological thinking of Heidegger, a lack or default gives access to Being ... The difference between Hegel's concept of experience and Heidegger's is that the former is tied to the rule of presencing and the latter commemorates it. Phenomenology for Hegel is a *parousia*, whereas for Heidegger it is letting the nonapparent appear as nonapparent."[26]

Commemorating what has been lost—the oblivion of Being in Heidegger's case—rather than celebrating presence as the cumulative realization of a successful dialectical process is reminiscent of Benjamin's critique of Hegelian memory as *Er-innerung*, a too harmonious re-membering in the present of what had been sundered in the past. A commonality between Heidegger and Benjamin might also be found in the shared recognition of the etymological link between *Erfahrung* and *Gefahr*, the danger that must be encountered in the perilous journey that is experience (which has the Latin *experiri* in its root, giving us as well the English word "peril"), a danger in the modern period perhaps best revealed in the context of technology with its destructive as well as emancipatory potential. And both thinkers were arguably at one in their dissatisfaction with Hegel's contention that knowledge or science *(Wissenschaft)* can be perfectly reconciled with experience, an assumption that rests, as Hans-Georg Gadamer was to claim in *Truth and Method*, on the solipsistic nature of the Hegelian subject that ultimately absorbs the object into itself, and never really has an encounter with what is truly different and alien to it.[27]

Such an encounter was, of course, also the earmark of Adorno's *Negative Dialectics*, which sought to avoid Idealism's coercive sublation of difference and to preserve the nonidentity of subject and object. Adorno's own interpretation of Hegel's notion of experience was designed, however, to resist the ontological interpretation of Heidegger's *Holzwege* and brush Hegel against the grain, finding in him what both Heidegger and Benjamin had claimed he denied. Adorno deliberately began the essay entitled "The Experiential Content of Hegel's Philosophy," first published in 1959 and included in the 1963 collection *Hegel: Three Studies*, by distancing himself from Heidegger's reading:

> The concept [of experience] is not intended to capture phenomenological 'ur-experience'; nor, like the interpretation of Hegel in Heidegger's *Holzwege*, is it intended to get at something ontological ... His thought would never have ratified Heidegger's claim that 'The new object that arises for consciousness in the course of its formation' is 'not just anything that is true, or any particular being, but is the truth of what is true, the Being of Beings, the appearance of appearance.' Hegel would have never called that experience; instead for Hegel, what experience is concerned with at any particular moment is the animating contradiction of such absolute truth.[28]

If experience for Hegel is more than the presubjective "event" or "appropriation" (*Ereignes* in Heidegger's special lexicon) of Being, it is also not the unmediated sense perception assumed by empiricists like Hume. Experience is not for Hegel something undergone by the isolated individual, but entails the interdependency of subjects with each other and with the world. Nor—and this is even more important—is it equivalent to the science of knowledge, the *Wissenschaft* that was its tombstone: "by no means does the experiential content of Idealism simply coincide with its epistemological and metaphysical positions."[29] Tacitly respecting the limits on knowledge placed by his predecessor Kant, even as he ultimately hoped to overcome them, Hegel identified experience precisely with the obstacles to full transparency presented by the contradictions in reality, not merely in thought. According to Adorno, Nietzsche's claim that "there is nothing in reality that would correspond strictly with logic"[30] captures Hegel's notion of experience better than attempts, such as those of orthodox dialectical materialists, to impose dialectical reason onto the world without remainder. In fact, it is the recognition of contradiction in society, the idea of antagonistic totality, that allows Hegel to move beyond absolute Idealism.

Hegel, to be sure, had wrongly thought his philosophy could encompass the whole and reveal its truth. But, Adorno argued, "even where Hegel flies in the face of experience, including the experience that motivates his own philosophy, experience speaks from him ... the idea of a positivity that can master everything that opposes it through the superior power of a comprehending spirit is the mirror image of the experience of the superior coercive force inherent in everything that exists by virtue of its consolidation under domination. This is the truth in Hegel's untruth."[31] Another unintended truth, one with a very different implication, is revealed in the tension between Hegel's desire to work entirely with concepts adequate to their objects and the linguistic medium through which he necessarily expressed them.[32] That is, "in Hegel the expressive element represents experience; that which actually wants to come out into the open, but cannot, if it wants to attain necessity, appear except in the medium of concepts, which is fundamentally its opposite ... The whole of Hegel's philosophy is an effort to translate intellectual experience into concepts."[33] But the medium of its expression inevitably interferes with this goal, for "thought, which necessarily moves away from the text, from what is said, has to return to it and become condensed within it. John Dewey, a contemporary thinker who for all his positivism is closer to Hegel than their two alleged standpoints are to one another, called his philosophy 'experimentalism.' Something of this stance is appropriate for the reader of Hegel."[34]

Adorno's surprising reference to Dewey, whose pragmatism the Frankfurt School often disparaged, suggests a certain countercurrent in Adorno's thought to the lament about the virtually complete withering of experience, for Dewey was cautiously optimistic about the possibilities of genuine experience at the present time. Adorno, to be sure, resisted Dewey's identification of experiment with its scientific variety, preferring instead the literary essay, which "invests experience with as much substance as traditional theory does mere categories."[35] But that substance, he claimed, involves an opening to what is new, rather than a ratification of what has been: "What Kant saw, in terms of content as the goal of reason, the creation of humankind, utopia, is hindered by the form of his thought, epistemology. It does not permit reason to go beyond the realm of experience which, in the mechanism of mere material and invariant categories, shrinks to what has always already existed. The essay's object, however, is the new in its newness, not as something that can be translated back into the old existing forms."[36]

If Adorno shared with Dewey a belief that some sort of experimentation pointing toward the renewal of experience was possible even in the totalizing system of domination that he saw as the sinister reversal of Hegel's dictum that the "whole was the true," Adorno also agreed that aesthetic experience in particular was its privileged laboratory. In such works as *Art and Experience* of 1934, "the unique and truly free John Dewey," as Adorno once called him, had ruminated on the significance of aesthetic experience as a model for a more general mode of unalienated existence.[37] Although it has sometimes been argued, most notably by Hans Robert Jauss,[38] that Adorno's own understanding of aesthetic experience was too negatively ascetic and lacking an appreciation of the communicative function of art, even in the present "administered world," it is clear that he shared with Dewey an appreciation of the utopian moment in that experience.

This is not the place to attempt a full-fledged analysis of what Adorno meant by aesthetic experience, but several points warrant emphasis.[39] First of all, it should be understood that contrary to the image of him as a mandarin elitist, Adorno never considered aesthetic experience, even that engendered by the most advanced modernist art, as if it were an entirely protected sphere in which the horrors of modern life were somehow successfully kept at bay. As he once wrote in an essay on the great nineteenth-century realist novel *Lost Illusions*, "Balzac knows that artistic experience is not pure, official aesthetics to the contrary; that it can hardly be pure if it is to be experience."[40] Aesthetic experience, at least in this usage, which one might term descriptive rather than normative, is necessarily impure, because it is damaged by the changes outside art mentioned above: modern warfare, the replacement of narrative by information, alienating technology, and capitalist industrialization. By itself, it cannot bring back the world of Benjamin's storyteller. Its truth content, Adorno always emphasized, thus had to be brought out by an accompanying philosophical cum social theoretical analysis that provided the critical discursive tools that art inevitably lacked.

But it is also the case that for Adorno, aesthetic experience, however maimed, can preserve a certain trace of what existed before, that which somehow has not been completely obliterated. Here he employed "experience" in an explicitly normative sense. Proust, Adorno claimed, was able to provide an almost Hegelian model of that preservation, for in his work, "undamaged experience is produced only in memory, far beyond immediacy, and through memory aging and death seem to be overcome in the aesthetic image. But this happiness achieved through the rescue of experience, a happiness that will not let anything be taken from it, represents an unconditional renunciation of consolation."[41]

As Stendhal, Nietzsche, and Marcuse argued, genuine experience, experience worth rescuing from the damaged variety of modern life, is thus closely tied to the memory of happiness, whose faint promise to return is what art is able to offer. Significantly, in *Neg-

ative Dialectics, when Adorno answered his own question "What is metaphysical experience?," he fell back on Benjamin's argument about an Adamic, prelapsarian language of mimesis before the fall into arbitrary language:

> If we disdain projecting it upon allegedly primal religious experiences, we are most likely to visualize it as Proust did, in the happiness, for instance, that is promised by village names like Applebachsville, Wind Gap, or Lords Valley. One thinks that going there would bring the fulfillment, as if there were such a thing ... To the child it is self-evident that what delights him in his favorite village is found only there, there alone and nowhere else. He is mistaken; but his mistake creates the model of experience, of a concept that will end up as the concept of the thing itself, not as a poor projection from things.[42]

Although necessarily a semblance of such a mimetic paradise and not the real thing—indeed precisely because it is such a semblance and knows itself as such—art gestures toward the happiness of genuine metaphysical experience, which is precisely what the current world denies and which the merely epistemological concept cannot even envisage. It does so paradoxically through its mimesis of the other, which resists reduction to subjective constitution.[43] Experience, as many commentators have used the term, comes only with an encounter with otherness in which the self no longer remains the same. Adorno would add that to be undamaged, that experience must treat the other in a nondominating, nonsubsumptive, nonhomogenizing manner.

Can such an encounter, however, be with what Benjamin called "the absolute" in his earliest writings on colors? Certainly, some of the pathos of that claim clings to many of Adorno's statements about experience and its decay, which are written from what the famous last aphorism in *Minima Moralia* called "the standpoint of redemption."[44] We have already noted the claim in *Negative Dialectics* that resistance to the world of exchange "is the resistance of the eye that does not want the colors of the world to fade." As a result, some commentators have ignored Adorno's attempts to distance himself from "allegedly primal religious experiences," and decried what they see as the "mystical" underpinnings of his concept of experience.[45]

But what perhaps indicates the inadequacy of such a reading, and by extension suggests that Adorno was not entirely happy with Benjamin's formulation of the problem, is Adorno's unwillingness to go all the way toward "experience without a subject," that moment of equiprimordiality prior to the split between self and other. Giorgio Agamben has noted in his essays on the destruction of experience, *Infancy and History*, that "in Proust there is no longer really any subject ... Here the expropriated subject of experience emerges to validate what, from the point of view of science, can appear only as the most radical negation of experience: an experience with neither subject nor object, absolute."[46] Adorno, as we have seen, may have approvingly invoked Proust's preservation of childhood happiness through memory, but he did not, I want to argue, embrace this notion of absolute experience in which neither subject nor object was preserved. As his disdain for Heidegger's appropriation of Hegel's "science of the experience of consciousness" for Heidegger's own project of the recollection of Being illustrates, Adorno was loath to short-circuit a negative dialectic that preserved some distinction between the two. The unsublatable dialectic of art and philosophy, like those between mimesis and construction or concept and object, suggest that even the most metaphysical of experiences for Adorno could not be reduced to perfect reconciliation or the restoration of equiprimordiality. Thus, even the Benjaminian rhetoric of a child's perception of color is inadequate to his position, for color is precisely that aspect of visual experience that resides in the subjective response to objects, not in material objects in themselves. Despite his occasional mobilizing of the rhetoric of Adamic names, as in the passage cited from *Negative Dialectics* above, Adorno never relied on mimesis alone to provide the model of realized utopia.

But such an acknowledgment still does not answer the question we posed at the beginning of this paper: is there a crisis of experience that can be understood in historical terms, involving a loss of something that once actually existed? Ruminating on the work of Benjamin more than Adorno, Agamben presents a challenge to the implied assumption that such a condition has ever really occurred in some prior Golden Age. He notes that a robust notion of experience, which puts one in touch with the absolute and is prior to the alienations of damaged life, ultimately derives from a fantasy of recovered infancy, which he defines as the period of human existence before language and before history. "In this sense," he writes, "to experience necessarily means to reaccede to infancy as history's transcendental place of origin. The enigma which infancy ushered in for man can be dissolved only in history, just as experience, being infancy and human place of origin, is something he is always in the act of falling from, into language and into speech."[47] That fall is the source of the split between subject and object, because only grammar produces a strong sense of the autonomy of the first person singular, the "I" who is apart from the world. If this is true, then authentic experience, at least as a metaphysical possibility, was not destroyed by the depredations of war or the reifications of capitalism, but was always already undone by the fall into language, the primal alienation that defines us as human. The alleged "memory" that we have of a lost happiness is thus of a condition that can never be regained short of the death that reunites us with a mute world prior to our insertion into language. Even as sympathetic a reader of the Frankfurt School tradition as Albrecht Wellmer could extend this skeptical conclusion beyond Benjamin, claiming that Adorno too, "like Schopenhauer, conceives aesthetic experience in ecstatic terms rather than as a real utopia; the happiness that it promises is not of this world."[48]

However, what may allow us to salvage a less impotent reading of Adorno's lament about the loss of experience is the recognition of his subtle movement away from the more intransigently absolutist position of Benjamin and the Heidegger of *Holzwege*. For Agamben's rebuke only draws blood if one understands his description of absolute experience, prior to the fall into language, anterior to the split between subject and object as, in fact, converging with what is normally understood as experience's most charged antonym: total innocence. Although Adorno does have positive things to say about childhood and the memory of happiness, he shows little real nostalgia for any historical time of alleged prelapsarian grace, as in the following passage from *Negative Dialectics:*

> The meaningful times for whose return the early Lukács yearned were as much due to reification, to inhuman institutions, as he would later attest it only to the bourgeois age. Contemporary representations of medieval towns usually look as if an execution were just taking place to cheer the populace. If any harmony of subject and object should have prevailed in those days, it was a harmony like the most recent one: pressure-born and brittle. The transfiguration of past conditions serves the purpose of a late, superfluous denial that is experienced as a no-exit situation; only as lost conditions do they become glamorous. Their cult of pre-subjective phases, arose in horror, in the age of individual disintegration and collective regression.[49]

In his studies of Hegel, it will be recalled, the experience he claims shines through the *Phenomenology* is that of the inability of life to be subsumed entirely under concepts and the extent of the present order's totalizing power to compel a social equivalent of that outcome. It is the tension between these two insights, which Adorno called Hegel's depiction of the antagonistic totality, that is forgotten in Idealism and *Lebensphilosophie*. Despite his borrowing of Benjamin's rhetoric of loss and decay in the passages cited at the beginning of this paper, Adorno understood, as he put it in *Negative Dialectics*, that "the concept of metaphysical experience is antinomical, not only as taught by Kantian transcendental dialectics, but in other ways. A metaphysics proclaimed without recourse to subjective experience, without the immediate presence of the subject, is helpless before the autonomous subject's refusal to have imposed upon it what it cannot understand. And yet, whatever is directly evident to the subject suffers from fallibility and relativity."[50]

In short, redeemed experience, undamaged experience, authentic experience, if indeed such a condition can ever be attained, would not mean a restoration of innocence before the fall into language or a harmonious reconciliation in a utopian future, but rather a nondominating relationship between subject and object. Paradoxically, it would retain at least some of the distinctions felt as alienated diremptions by what Hegel had called "the unhappy consciousness," but now in such a way that they no longer frustrate the subject's desire to master the world through conceptual and practical activity. Instead, the experiential happiness that is promised by works of art restores one of the fundamental senses of "experience" itself: a passive suffering or an encounter with the new and the other, which moves us beyond where we, as subjects, were before the experience began. It is for this reason, as J.M. Bernstein has noted, that "the image of life without experience is finally the image of life without history, as if the meaning of life were in its eternal cessation: death. There cannot be historical life without experience; only lives articulated through experience can be fully and self-consciously historical."[51] Here precisely the opposite conclusion is reached from Agamben, who identifies history with the fall out of the pure experience that is prelinguistic infancy or postlinguistic death.

I have to admit in conclusion that Adorno himself never fully sorted out the welter of denotations and connotations that cling to the numinous word "experience." At times he expresses an apparent nostalgia for a lost undamaged experience; at others, he mocks romanticizations of an alleged state of prelapsarian bliss. While invoking the rhetoric of a progressive loss, he only vaguely hints at the existence of an actual historical time before the decay. Accepting Benjamin's critique of empiricist or Kantian notions of experience, he nonetheless resists accepting the maximalist notion of absolute experience that also infuses, as shown above, Heidegger's reading of Hegel in *Holzwege*. Looking for traces or prefigurations of undamaged experience in aesthetic experience, Adorno clearly knows that semblance is not reality and that a gap looms large between works of art and redeemed life, which may never be as close to the absolute as Benjamin in his more metaphysical moods had hoped. In short, the experience of reading Adorno on experience is itself one of nonidentical refusals of easy consistencies, producing the realization that experience is an openness to the unexpected with its dangers and obstacles, not a safe haven from history, but a reminder of the encounters with otherness and the new that await those who, despite everything, are willing and able to embark on the voyage. In this sense, it may be premature to write the epitaph of experience as such, for it will only paradoxically be when the crisis itself ends and a deadly calm settles over the world that the perilous journey that is experience will no longer be a human possibility.

Notes

1. This essay appears courtesy Cambridge University Press. The essay will be published in *The Cambridge Companion to Adorno* (Cambridge: Cambridge University Press, forthcoming fall 2001).
2. Theodor W. Adorno, "The Position of the Narrator in the Contemporary Novel," *Notes to Literature*, vol. II, trans. Shierry Weber Nicholsen (New York: Columbia University Press, 1992), 31.
3. Theodor W. Adorno, *Minima Moralia: Reflections from Damaged Life*, trans. E.F. N. Jephcott (London: New Left Books, 1974), 54-55.
4. Walter Benjamin, "The Storyteller: Reflections on the Work of Nikolai Leskov," *Illuminations*, ed. Hannah Arendt, trans. Harry Zohn (New York: Schocken, 1968), 84.
5. There is, in fact, a considerable discussion in German of Adorno's concept of experience. See, for example, Hans-Hartmut Kappner, *Die Bildungstheorie Adornos als Theories der Erfahrung von Kultur und Kunst* (Frankfurt am

Main: Suhrkamp Verlag, 1984); Peter Kalkowski, *Adornos Erfahrung: Zur Kritik der Kritischen Theories* (Frankfurt am Main: Suhrkamp Verlag, 1988); Anke Thyen, *Negative Dialektik und Erfahrung: Zur Rationalität des Nichtidentischen bei Adorno* (Frankfurt am Main: Suhrkamp Verlag, 1989).

6. Adorno, *Aesthetic Theory*, eds. Gretel Adorno and Rolf Tiedemann, trans. Robert Hullot-Kentor (Minneapolis: University of Minneapolis Press, 1997), 31.

7. Adorno, "Presuppositions: On the Occasion of a Reading by Hans G. Helms," *Notes to Literature*, vol. II, 101.

8. Adorno, "Theory of Pseudo-Culture," *Telos* 95 (Spring 1993): 33.

9. Adorno, *The Jargon of Authenticity*, trans. Knut Tanowski and Frederic Will (Evanston, Illinois: Northwestern University Press, 1973), 99. Whether or not Adorno was accurate in characterizing Heidegger's notion of experience in these terms is debatable.

10. Adorno, "Charmed Language: On the Poetry of Rudolf Borchardt," *Notes to Literature*, vol. II, 205.

11. Howard Caygill, *Walter Benjamin: The Colour of Experience* (London: Routledge, 1998). For references to earlier literature on the question and my own attempt to make some sense of it, see "Experience without a Subject: Walter Benjamin and the Novel," in Martin Jay, *Cultural Semantics: Keywords of Our Time* (Amherst, Mass.: University of Massachusetts Press, 1998).

12. The relevant essays are now available in Benjamin, *Selected Writings*, vol. I, 1913-1926, eds. Marcus Bullock and Michael W. Jennings (Cambridge: Harvard University Press, 1996).

13. Caygill, *Walter Benjamin*, 23.

14. Benjamin, "A Child's View of Color," *Selected Writings*, 50.

15. Caygill, *Walter Benjamin*, 8.

16. Theodor W. Adorno, *Negative Dialectics*, trans. E.B. Ashton (1966; New York: Continuum, 1973), 405.

17. The relevant section is translated as Martin Heidegger, *Hegel's Concept of Experience* (New York: Harper & Row, 1970). For a suggestive commentary, see Robert Bernasconi, *The Question of Language in Heidegger's History of Being* (Atlantic Highlands, N.J.: Humanities Press, 1986), chapter 6.

18. All of Benjamin's recorded reactions to Heidegger were critical; Heidegger seems to have been unaware of Benjamin's work. Nonetheless, similarities between Heidegger and Benjamin were first stressed by Hannah Arendt in her controversial introduction to Benjamin, *Illuminations*. For more recent attempts to see parallels, as well as some distinctions, see Howard Caygill, "Benjamin, Heidegger and the Destruction of Tradition," and Andrew Benjamin, "Time and Task: Benjamin and Heidegger Showing the Present," in *Walter Benjamin's Philosophy: Destruction and Experience*, eds. Andrew Benjamin and Pete Osborne (London: Routledge, 1994). For discussions of the differences between the two, see Richard Wolin, *Walter Benjamin: An Aesthetic of Redemption*, 2nd ed. (Berkeley: University of California Press, 1994), 102; and Beatrice Hanssen, *Walter Benjamin's Other History: Of Stones, Animals, Human Beings, and Angels* (Berkeley: University of California Press, 1998), 2.

19. Heidegger, *Hegel's Concept of Experience*, 112.

20. Heidegger, *Hegel's Concept of Experience*, 114.

21. Heidegger, *Hegel's Concept of Experience*, 114.

22. Heidegger, *Hegel's Concept of Experience*, 119.

23. Heidegger, *Hegel's Concept of Experience*, 120-21.
24. Heidegger, *Hegel's Concept of Experience*, 139.
25. Heidegger, *Hegel's Concept of Experience*, 143.
26. Bernasconi, *The Question of Language in Heidegger's History of Being*, 83-85.
27. Hans-Georg Gadamer, *Truth and Method* (New York: Crossroad, 1986), 318-319.
28. Adorno, *Hegel: Three Studies*, trans. Shierry Weber Nicholsen (Cambridge: MIT Press, 1993), 53.
29. Adorno, *Hegel: Three Studies*, 61.
30. Cited in Adorno, *Hegel: Three Studies*, 76.
31. Adorno, *Hegel: Three Studies* , 87.
32. Adorno, "Skoteinos, or How to Read Hegel," in *Hegel: Three Studies*.
33. Adorno, "Skoteinos, or How to Read Hegel," in *Hegel: Three Studies*, 138.
34. Adorno, "Skoteinos, or How to Read Hegel," in *Hegel: Three Studies*, 144.
35. Adorno, "The Essay as Form," *Notes to Literature*, vol. I, 10.
36. Adorno, "The Essay as Form," *Notes to Literature*, vol. I, 21. In this passage, Adorno seems to forget the redemptive notion of experience he inherited from Benjamin and uses the term instead to refer only to the epistemological synthetic a priori judgments of Kant's first *Critique*.
37. Adorno, *Aesthetic Theory*, 335; John Dewey, *Art as Experience* (New York: Minton, Balch & Company, 1934).
38. Hans Robert Jauss, *Aesthetic Experience and Literary Hermeneutics*, trans. Michael Shaw (Minneapolis: University of Minnesota Press, 1982), 13-22.
39. For helpful recent discussions, see Shierry Weber Nicholsen, *Exact Imagination, Late Work: On Adorno's Aesthetics* (Cambridge: MIT Press, 1997), and Thomas Huhn and Lambert Zuidervaart, eds., *The Semblance of Subjectivity: Essays on Adorno's Aesthetic Theory* (Cambridge: MIT Press, 1997).
40. Adorno, "On an Imaginary Feuilleton," *Notes to Literature*, vol. II, 33. In *Aesthetic Theory*, he makes a similar point: "no particular aesthetic experience occurs in isolation, independently of the continuity of experiencing consciousness ... The continuity of aesthetic experience is colored by all other experience and all knowledge, though, of course, it is only confirmed and corrected in the actual confrontation with the phenonmenon." Adorno, *Aesthetic Theory*, 268-69.
41. Adorno, "On Proust," *Notes to Literature*, vol. II, 317.
42. Adorno, *Negative Dialectics*, 373.
43. I have attempted to explore some of the implications of mimesis in his work in "Mimesis and Mimetology: Adorno and Lacoue-Labarthe," in *The Semblance of Subjectivity*, eds. Huhn and Zuidervaart.
44. Adorno, *Minima Moralia*, 247.
45. Kalkowski, *Adorno's Erfahrung*, 110-11.
46. Giorgio Agamben, *Infancy and History: Essays on the Destruction of Experience*, trans. Liz Heron (London: Verso, 1993), 42.
47. Agamben, *Infancy and History*, 53.
48. Albrecht Wellmer, *The Persistence of Modernity: Essays on Aesthetics, Ethics, and Postmodernism*, trans. David Midgely (Cambridge: MIT Press, 1993), 12.
49. Adorno, *Negative Dialectics*, 191.
50. Adorno, *Negative Dialectics*, 374. Translation emended.
51. J.M. Bernstein, "Why Rescue Semblance? Metaphysical Experience and the Possibility of Ethics," in *The Semblance of Subjectivity* 203.

Chapter 3

Mega Melancholia

Adorno's Minima Moralia

Eva Geulen

[A]nd the pious girl thought: the night is dark, so nobody will see you and thus you may give up your shirt as well, and she gave it away. And as she stood there and had nothing left at all, the stars suddenly fell from the sky and all were hard, shiny pieces of silver, and though she had given away her shirt, she had a new one on and it was of finest linen. Therein she collected the silver pieces and was rich for the rest of her days.

— Brothers Grimm, "Die Sterntaler" [1]

I

"On re-reading one of Anatole France's meditative books, such as the *Jardin d'Epicure*, one cannot help feeling embarrassed (*ein Gefühl des Peinlichen*) ... His mode of delivery contains, beneath the poised humanity, a hidden violence: he can afford to talk in this way because no-one interrupts him." [2] A similar sense of embarrassment manifests itself when rereading Adorno's own meditative book *Minima Moralia*, whose grand pretensions are at odds with its minimalist title, its vow to theoretical chastity strangely mismatched with the range of its claims. This feeling is exacerbated by the temporal distance that has rendered many aspects of the *Minima Moralia* anachronistic—its now somewhat distant fame has turned into something more akin to shame. But shame, Adorno writes in this very book, is the expression of things having outlived themselves: "It is to be explained not only by mere temporal distance, but by the verdict of history. Its expression in things is the shame *(Scham)* that overcomes the descendant in face of an earlier possibility that he has neglected to bring to fruition ... Only what failed is outdated" (93/104). Accordingly, if Adorno's book has come to be considered a failure, then Adorno himself would suggest that shame is its proper mode of reception because failure—one's own or that of others—results not in guilt (which is associated with transgression), but rather in shame.[3] One could say that the question or the impulse lurking behind today's critical derision of *Minima Moralia* is something like: "Why are you not ashamed (to issue such judgements)?"; or "Shame on you (to elevate your existence to a normative measure)!"

Failure and shame may be appropriate critical angles on *Minima Moralia*, but the book was never intended to be a success; what presents itself in the subtitle as "Reflections from Damaged Life" can only fail. The critics' somewhat embarrassed responses, however, aim at the premeditated nature of this failure, its elevation to a categorical imperative that demands: Fail![4] According to *Minima Moralia's* concluding passages, the world has to be presented in the state of its failure, "with its rifts and crevices, as indigent and distorted as it will appear one day in the Messianic light" (247/283). And yet the attempt to *present* the world in such a perspective cannot but be of this world and is therefore necessarily disfigured, "marked ... by the same distortion and indigence which it seeks to escape" (247/283). Consequently, it is always possible and necessary to read the book's distortions, its discrepancies, contradictions, and disproportionality—in short, its failings—as the mark, seal, and scar of damaged life. But just this, dialectics' self-immunization against failure through failure, has become problematic today. Its more subtle failure is dialectics'—even and precisely negative dialectics'—failure to ever fail.

The image of the world laid bare, its "rifts and crevices" exposed, dictates *Minima Moralia's* methodological approach: the world is subjected to a physiognomic gaze that does not so much read as recognize according to classifications and types, which the physiognomist sometimes posits and sometimes claims to have found established. This perspective reduces what the physiognomist encounters to the truncated stereotypes populating this book, such as the beautiful woman, the "tough guy," the intellectual, the emigrant, the hostess, etc. Adorno even claims, quasi-platonically, that for every person "there is an original (*Urbild*) in a fairy-tale [sic], one need only look long enough. A beauty asks the mirror whether she is the fairest of all, like the Queen in Snow White ... Another went out into the world as a lad to seek his fortune, got the better of numerous giants, but had to die all the same in New York ... yet another undresses for lovemaking with the same childlike immodesty (*kindlich schamlos*) as the girl with the starry silver pieces (*Sterntaler*)" (87-88/98). Adorno's unequivocal critique of any taxonomic and classifying method, whose last stage, he writes, will inevitably be "the medical examination to decide between labor camp and liquidation" (131/149), appears to leave cynicism as the last resort for justifying the physiognomic method: "Where everything is bad, it must be good to know the worst" (83/94), reads the epigraph to *Minima Moralia*'s second part, dated 1945. Here again Adorno's dialectical negativity should immunize against troublesome, potentially shameful methodological moves.

But willfully turning incidental traits into features of universal abnormality—in the hope that "consummate negativity, once in full view *(einmal ganz ins Auge gefaßt),* delineates the mirror image of its opposite" (247/283)—still relies on the very ideal of physiognomy that suggests seeing is knowing and vice versa. Where utopia itself turns on physiognomy and turns out to be like a face, physiognomic studies cannot be relegated to a means in the service of cynical caricature or satire. The fact that any description of the world remains of this world should render uncertain any and all criteria for physiognomic judgements of the kind that Adorno passes without hesitation. Yet, Adorno charges Anatole France and Karl Kraus with precisely this lack of modesty or deliberation: "no witticism of Karl Kraus wavers over the decision who is decent and who a scoundrel, what is intelligence and what stupidity, what is language and what journalism ... Just as, in their instantaneous grasp of the matter in hand, no question holds them up, so they admit no question" (210-11/240). Because of this reminder of the role that doubt *(Zweifel)* plays at the core of Adorno's ethos of despair *(Verzweiflung),*[5] *Minima Moralia* appears so outrageously, embarassingly immodest.

According to Adorno, psychoanalysis is only true when it exaggerates (49/54). It suggests a relatively straightforward explanation

of the books shameful immodesty. In his essay "Mourning and
Melancholy," Freud argues that one significant difference between
mourning and melancholy consists in the lack of any shame in the
case of the latter, who exhibits rather the "feature of an obtrusive
talkativeness" *(Zug einer aufdringlichen Mitteilsamkeit).*[6] The paradox of self-shaming self-denigration, and the shamelessly exhibi-
tionist display of these very emotions lends Adorno's *Minima
Moralia* the character of "Mega Melancholia."

Where nature, which once served to confer validity on physiognomic judgements, is nothing but the "scar *(Wundmal)* of social
mutilation" (95/107), the only realm left in which to ground justification for physiognomy is history—but history, according to
Adorno, has turned into the continuum of a "terror without end."
In the absence of historical change, ephemeral traits have solidified
into physiognomic constants, "as if the reified, hardened plaster-
cast [sic] of events takes the place of events themselves" (55/61).
When subjectivity has become entirely exteriorized, when individuality has become but a standard, pathological aberration or has
become the universal norm, and perception "attains merely the
socially pre-formed plaster-casts [sic] of things" (236/270)—then
what exists can in fact *only* be read as a physiognomist reads a face,
for everything has become face, bare and exposed. In a world ruled
by "naked brutality" (42/46), everything is obscenely obvious.
Physiognomic treatment marks and remarks the very unintelligibility and obscene transparency of the world and seals the fact that all
hermeneutic projects of understanding, interpreting, representing,
and criticizing have been rendered absurd.[7] Any search for meaning
is finally senseless when "senseless[ness] is blatant" (34/37). Physiognomy is not only possible but unavoidable, since "total unfreedom
can be recognized, but not represented" (144/165). By displaying
the dialectic that has invaded and eroded the distinction between
the visible and the invisible, physiognomy sets out to discover the
obvious that escapes the view. Even lingering doubts regarding the
legitimacy of physiognomic techniques of representations still conform to a physiognomic code that functions like hieroglyphic scrip-
ture: "Every thought ... bears branded on it the impossibility of its
own legitimization *(bleibt wie ein Mal die Unmöglichkeit seiner
vollen Legitimation einbeschrieben)"* (81/91).

Since physiognomy's circumscribed field of investigation is the
body in general and the face in particular, Adorno's inclination

towards this particular mode of reading is, however, also due to the privileged status that the body—and for Adorno, always the sexual, erotic body—holds in his thought: "No intention exists, nothing 'spiritual' that would not somehow be founded in bodily perception and sought bodily fulfillment" (242/277). One of the most striking phrases in this regard states: "He alone who could situate utopia in blind somatic pleasure, which, satisfying the ultimate intention, is intentionless, has a stable and valid idea of truth" (61/68). The same erotic affectivity adheres to the image of the "world laid bare, its rifts and crevices" exposed.[8] The body is the very site where the quasi-theological elements in Adorno's thought enter into a vexed relationship with its materialist, somatic tendencies.

What marks this intersection in *Minima Moralia* is the very phenomenon that has long regulated economies of covering and uncovering, self-exposure and self-effacement: shame and its dense cluster of correlates such as shameful/bashful and shameless (*schamlos, unverschämt*). Firmly at home only in theology, shame has otherwise lived uneasily in the margins of a number of discourses, including physiognomy and ethics, perhaps because it is the category of uneasiness pure and simple.[9] Already in Aristotle's *Nicomachean Ethics*, shame is marginalized, relegated to a mere disposition towards ethical behavior, a quasi-virtue at best. Physiognomy, in turn, also excluded shame from its registers, as too much in it is elusive affect and thus too fleeting for physiognomic consideration. Theories of affect, finally, cannot accommodate shame for the inverse reason that it is not quite a genuine affect, its purity compromised by the fact that it presupposes and is directed towards sociability. Until very recently, theorizations of shame seemed to bear a primary characteristic of shame—self-effacement.[10]

In *Minima Moralia*, however, shame and its correlates (such as "*Schmach*" and "*Schande*") take center stage, as if shame, this marginalized and shamefully avoided hybrid of affect and ethics, this displaced and, under the conditions of modernity, strangely anachronistic phenomenon, constituted the last remaining residue, the bare minimum of morality that the book's title alludes to—and alludes to shamelessly, in the sense that Adorno positions it as a direct descendant of Aristotle's *Ethica Megala*, and shamefully at the same time, since all he has to offer now are "small" ethics.

Adorno's recourse to shame seeks to delimit a sphere located between the interiority of the subject and the exteriority of socia-

bility, between involuntary bodily innervation and socially determined norms of behavior. In this regard he resists the dominant
models that conceptualize the elusive category of shame, which
either elevates it to an anthropological constant or anchors it exclusively in the workings of social injustice.[11] Like the skin that
blushes, shame in Adorno functions as a membrane in which oppositions such as nature and culture are constituted in the first place;
it is the medium of their simultaneous association and dissociation.

If it can be shown—and whether shame can at all be shown,
exposed, or theorized without turning into something other than
shame is indeed a question—that *Minima Moralia* contributes to
current efforts to re-examine the notion of shame, then the reconstruction of Adorno's logic of shame may also hope to bear upon
certain well-known problems of Adorno's criticism, where frus-
trations with the dead ends of negative dialectics run deeply.
Albrecht Wellmer, for example, pointed out the uneasy and untenable coexistence of theological and sensualist motifs in Adorno's
thought. In order to compensate for the perceived lack of intersubjectivity in Adorno's notion of aesthetic experience, Wellmer
proposed to sunder the two currents and, after surrendering the
theological dimension altogether, to short-circuit the sensualist
motifs with a Habermasian notion of communicative reason. The
very presence of shame in *Minima Moralia*, however, not only
marks the inseverable nexus of theology and so-called sensualism,
but also might point the way to account for a dimension of intersubjectivity in Adorno that need not revert to the dogma of communicative reason.[12]

II

Together with tact and taste, shame belongs to a type of "unconscious inervations [*sic*] which, beyond thought processes, attune
individual existence to historical rhythms" (139/158). They are by
definition intersubjective, the very exteriority in which subjectivity
can develop in the first place, "the delicate connecting filigree (*das
feine Gefädel*) of external forms in which alone the internal can
crystallize" (41/45). All three share the definition that Adorno gives
of tact: "the discrimination of differences (*eine Differenzbestimmung*)" (37/40). Just as tact proves itself by deviating ever so

slightly from what the norm requires, taste is truly tasteful only where it suspends its own requirements: "Taste is the most accurate seismograph of historical experience. Unlike most other faculties, it is even able to register its own behavior" (145/165). This capacity for self-recording or self-reflection is—and Adorno is thoroughly Hegelian in this respect—nothing other than taste's capacity for self-contradiction or self-dissociation: "Reacting against itself, it recognizes its own lack of taste" (145/165). Tact and taste are therefore *"Differenzbestimmungen"* in a double sense: they can mark a difference to the norm they represent because they are capable of self-differentiation, and they are capable of self-differentiation because their formation depends not on any self, but on the external forces of social control that enforce individuality as they also seek to oppress it. As functions of traditions, tact and taste—even though they are codified power relations and precisely because they are internalized—have, however minimally, a chance to offer sites of resistance: "The individual is so thoroughly historical that he is able, with the fine filigree *(das feine Gefädel)* of his late bourgeois organization, to rebel against the fine filigree of late bourgeois organization" (145/156).

From such *"Gefädel"* leads a red thread to the burning experience of shame. Shame is also a *"Differenzbestimmung"* but it differs from tact and taste because shame is not a capacity at all. One does not "have" shame the way some people have tact or taste. In a strict sense, tact and taste are properties and as such the exclusive property of a class that can afford the luxury of deviating from norms. Shame is democratic, not because it belongs to all but because it does not belong to anyone or at all. Yet shame appears to inhabit the spaces in which tact and taste also thrive, in environments protected by the very obsolescence of their codes of behavior. Such spheres provide something like ecological niches in which impoverished experience finds temporary refuge and in which notoriously overtaxed morality has a chance to succeed albeit at the price of irrelevance, perhaps even banality: "The subject can measure up to these minute traits of the mistaken or the correct and pass muster as capable of right or wrong actions ... the minimal offences are so relevant because in them we can be good or evil without smiling over it, even if our seriousness is a little delusive. Through them we get the feel of morality in our very skin—when we blush—and assimilate it to the subject, who looks on the gigantic moral law within himself as helplessly as at the starry sky of which the former is a poor imitation" (180-81/205).

Adorno's examples of such minimalist morality are indeed so negligible, microscopic, indeed so invisible that they seem no match for the sublime power of abstract Kantian ethics that Adorno sets out to critique. Yet he insists: "The thought of particular indelicacies (*Taktlosigkeiten*), however, microorganisms of wrongdoing, unnoticed perhaps by anyone else—that at a social gathering one sat down too early at table, or at a tea reception put cards with the guests' names at their places, though this is done only at dinners— such trifles can fill the delinquent with unconquerable remorse and a passionately bad conscience, and on occasion with such burning shame that he shrinks from confessing them even to himself" (180/205). Shame marks a deviation at once too great and too small to be restored by the internal dialectics of taste and tact. The very disproportionality of cause and effect finds expression in shame— and perhaps shame has never been anything else but this experience of disproportionality. Shame does not express anything, but it is the experience of the disproportionality that determines the temporal lag sustaining tact and taste. That the social norms of formal etiquette have long lost their binding force, but that the accompanying affect still lingers, is the precondition for Adorno's appeal to tact, taste, and other forms of tradition that have outlived themselves: "The precondition of tact is the convention no longer intact yet still present" (36/39). To the extent that shame is, or at least has become, the experience of a disproportionality of cause and effect, it provides a translation of the historical modality of anachronicity into an affective structure.

Since shame is also and perhaps always to the shame to be ashamed, it does not possess the dialectical power to dissociate itself and recognize itself as "other" in the way tact and taste do. Rather, shame's only capacity, if it can be called a capacity, is the power to outlive itself as the shame of being ashamed. In this sense it is the agent that makes the minimally empowering anachronicity of tact and taste possible in the first place. This privilege of shame over taste and tact is reflected in the unique position this phenomenon comes to assume in Adorno's book. For the only positive instruction Adorno offers in *Minima Moralia*—which otherwise strictly observes its infamous, self-imposed taboo of categorically denying any right life in the wrong life (39 /43)—pivots around shame:

"There is no way out of entanglement. The only responsible course is to deny oneself the ideological misuse of one's own existence, and for the rest to conduct oneself in private as modestly, unobtrusively, and unpretentiously as is required, no longer by good upbringing, but by the shame of still having air to breathe, in hell" (27-8/29). Thus concludes a section entitled "Antithesis," which reflects precisely on what we perceive today—if not with shame then at least a certain embarrassment—as Adorno's rather immodest and certainly pretentious claim to render "his own life in the frail image of a true existence" (26/27). Prior to this conclusion, the section describes only the social inevitability of what would have to be considered shameless behavior if those orders of social distinctions that once conditioned the very notion of shame, in Greek society for example, had not been leveled: "We shudder at the brutalization of life, but lacking any objectively binding morality we are forced at every step into actions and words, into calculations that are by humane standards barbaric, and, even by the dubious values of so-called good society, tactless" (27/28). Given the irreversible disintegration of all those social structures that sustained themselves through the dynamics of shame, given the absence of a binding ethos and the ridicule of so-called good upbringing, what can possibly represent the standard by which to live "modestly, unobtrusively, and unpretentiously"?

The passage's very aim, and *Minima Moralia*'s stated intention, is to unmask any attempt to institute a borderline between public and private spheres as an ideological maneuver to cover up their fatal identity. In the name of shameful behavior, however, Adorno insists on an asceticism that gives both realms their due and gains sight of the possibility of living rightly in the wrong life. The only reason for this deviation from the norms of negativity is that shameful behavior is a priori threatened by and exposed to the possibility—acted out on every page of this enormously immodest book—of being nothing but false shame or even the very opposite of shame, namely, shameless or, more precisely, "*unverschämt.*" This intrinsic possibility seems sufficient to endow shame with the ability to mark, however tentatively and insecurely, a border. The social state of affairs, Adorno seems to suggest, has brought to light the very aspect of shame responsible for its persistent marginalization: the questionability of its criteria and the fluctuating nature of its manifestations. Since Adorno believes that affects, like everything else, are deformed and have been replaced by plaster-cast simulacra, shame, which is by definition exposed to the possibility of being fake shame and thus of being inauthentic, is the last remaining genuine affect.[13]

Adorno's final sentence in this passage insists on this status as genuine affect once more. For what demands and even dictates the canon of bashful behavior is not an institution, not even a last, minimal (even if anachronistic) base of moral standard or social consensus, but rather shame: "the shame of still having air to breathe, in hell." When shame dictates shameful behavior, shame has split to occupy two incompatible positions at once. As a response to the hellish life, shame is the very powerlessness that empowers turning shame into a site of resistance.

Adorno's notion of shame here appears closely related to what has come to be known—perhaps wrongly so—as survivor guilt: at issue here, however, is the very impossibility of guilt, "shame over the participation in universal injustice." The failure to feel guilt induces shame. But this failure, the passage suggests, is the result or effect of a more profound and paradoxical failure: not to have died. With this survival logic, Adorno inverts Hegel's argument that shame is an effect of love. Lovers feel shame, Hegel argued, because their "immortal" love is exposed as a failure by the fact that they have to die after all: "this anger over individuality is shame."[14] In Adorno, it is death itself that has been survived and the failure in question is shame's own failure to perish. If shame in Hegel is in effect a reminder of love's mortality and thus its particularity, then for Adorno it is a remnant. For what is truly shameless is shame's refusal to die along with the world to which it belonged. Shame is shame over the embarrassing presence of shame in a shameless world ruled by "naked reproduction" (27/28). Not a reminder of Hegel's inevitable finitude, shame is an infinite remainder, a remnant that lives on and survives its own impossibility.[15] That shame survived in a world of universal shamelessness disrupts that very totality. Yet, that shame cannot manifest itself other than as shamelessness seals that very totality. In this untenable position, if it can be called a position, shame persists and eludes.

The risk run by Adorno's exposure of an economy of shame under the conditions of its anachronicity—that is, the potential dangers of prying open the secretive workings of shame—is precisely the very overexposure that makes *Minima Moralia* so immodest, obtrusive and pretentious. Its readers respond to such indecency with—shame that is hastily cloaked as critique and channeled into critical inroads.

III

Adorno did not simply abandon or sever the Hegelian nexus of love and shame. Rather, in accordance with Nietzsche's dictum that "'the degree and kind of a man's sexuality extends to the highest pinnacle of his spirit'" (122/138), he intensified the nexus to a point where shame and love turn out to share an analogous structure. Underscoring the constitutive complementarity of shame and love, virtually all of the examples of shame-inducing experiences and microorganisms of injustice, such as a hand kiss at the wrong time or the conclusion of an illicit affair, belong to the sphere of sexual contacts and conflicts. So akin are shame and love that they can even coalesce into one and the same phenomenon: "in love with propriety *(Verliebtheit ins Geziemende)"* (181/206). Love and shame are bound to each other because their necessary exposure to others defines them as modes of constitutive or originary self-alienation. As it is an element of sexual utopia not to be oneself, so shame supplies an analogous experience that, moreover, corrects any overestimation of blissfully losing one's self. The reasons for these intimate relations between love and shame are rooted in their common natural history.

Like Freud, Adorno claims that lust is always the sublation of earlier *"Unlust,"* and therefore a "late acquisition, scarcely older than consciousness" (90/101). The origins of shame involve a similar structure of sublating one experience in its opposite. The very section dedicated to the potentially productive implications of shameful reactions bears the title "Just hear how bad he was *(Und höre nur wie bös er war).*" This truncated verse from *Struwwelpeter* actually continues, *"er peitschte, ach, sein armes Gretchen gar"* (he even beat his poor Gretchen). In other words, at the beginning of the section on shame stands, unspoken, an act of rape and abuse of a woman who happens to bear the name of Adorno's wife. Unobtrusively, shamefully even, Adorno reminds his readers that before shame there was rape. Shame, the word and the experience, hands down the memory of this primordial event, and all shame is haunted by it as shame haunts all love. The primal scene of shame is rape as the primal scene of lust is *"Unlust"*: "Observing how compulsively animals couple, one recognizes the saying that 'bliss *(Wollust)* was given to the worm' as a piece of idealistic lying, at least as regards the females, who undergo love in unfreedom, as objects of violence ... The memory of the old injury persists, though the physical pain and the immediate fear have been removed by civilization" (90/101). As the princess in Goethe's *Tasso* puts it: "Willst du genau erfahren, was sich ziemt,/ so frage nur bei schönen Frauen ... Die Schicklichkeit umgibt mit einer Mauer/Das zarte, leicht verletzliche Geschlecht."[16] ("Do you want to find out exactly what is proper/only ask beautiful women ... the propriety surrounds with a wall/the tender, lightly wounded sex.") According to Adorno's implicit *"Urgeschichte"* of shame and lust, shame figures as "the lingering awareness of the ancient wound, in which lies hope of a better future" (66/74). Such assertions are, as Michael Theunissen among others has shown,[17] mythical to the core and therefore as dubious and problematic as the entire concept of *"Naturgeschichte,"* in which they are embedded. The question, however, is whether the dynamics of shame that Adorno has put into motion can indeed be contained by the quasi-historical narrative he provides, or whether, conversely, the logic of shame in the final instance also survives, outlives its history, and oversteps the conceptual place assigned to contain it.

Given their shared past, there can be no doubt at what point the common story of love and shame comes to rest: all of its paths lead straight into the heart of Adorno's aesthetic theory, to the notion of aesthetic experience. *"Höre nur wie bös er war"* has its correlate in a passage in which Adorno feels compelled to trace the archaic memory of primordial rape into the lofty heights of speculative idealism, "because even thought's remotest objectifications are nourished by the drives" (122/138): "Peasant greed, only with difficulty held in check by the threats of priests, asserts in metaphysics its autonomous right to reduce everything in its path as unceremoniously to its basic essence as do soldiers the women of a captured town. The pure unreflective act *(Tathandlung)* is violation *(Schändung)* projected on the starry sky above" (89/100). Opposed to this archaic and perpetually reenacted rape is the long and longing gaze of the voyeur, who shamefully abstains from direct contact and instead seeks the pleasures of intimacy in maintaining distance: "But in the long, contemplative look that fully discloses people and things, the urge towards the object is always deflected, reflected. Contemplation without violence, the source of all the joy of truth, presupposes, that he who contemplates does not absorb the object into himself: a distanced nearness" (89-90/100). The fundamental tenant of aesthetic theory—from Kant's disinterested pleasure to Benjamin's definition of auratic art as a distance, however near it may be—is condensed in this emphatic appeal to aesthetic experience as contemplative, shameful distance.

If aesthetic experience, however, can be said to satisfy the demands of shame towards humans and objects alike, it is by no means free from the violence it seeks to displace. The very unavoidability of this violence, in fact, is acted out in art itself. Adorno continues: "Only because Tasso, whom psychoanalysis would call a destructive character, is afraid of the princess, and falls a civilized victim to the impossibility of immediate contact, can Adelheid (!), Klärchen, and Gretchen speak the limpid, unforced language that makes of them an image of a pristine world (*Urgeschichte*)" (90/100-01). If shame carries the memory of rape for women, men like Tasso or Theodor are subject to the threat of castration; the cycle of violence does not leave the women unaffected even if they are spared the rape, for: "The sense of life radiated by Goethe's women was bought with withdrawal, evasion" (90/101). Their very shame undermines their liveliness and lends them the aura of death. Since Goethe's women and their language are an issue here primarily because they serve as emblematic instances of art in general— and that such allegorization presents in itself another violation goes without saying—Adorno feels compelled to add, rather enigmatically, "and there is more in this than mere resignation before the victorious order" (90/101). What is this incommensurate measure that renders shameful actions more, or other, than an affirmation of the powers that be?

What remains beyond question, however, is the recognition that Adorno's famous dialectics of "*Schein*" is, at bottom, a dialectic of shame: "Every work of art is a coerced malfeasance (*eine abgedungene Untat*)" (111/125). The paradox of art is the paradox of covering the shame of originary rape with shame and in that very act not redeeming but perpetuating such acts of rape. Such contradictoriness is, Adorno never fails to assert, "the vital element of art and circumscribes its law of development, but it is also art's shame (*Schande*)" (226/258). According to Adorno, aesthetic judgement preserves and maintains itself as shame "within immediate impulses every one of which, shamed in face of the culture industry, averts its eyes from the mirror image" (145/166). In the culture industry art encounters not its other or opposite but itself and its own shame, as it registers its failure as the very medium of its constitution and identity.

The response to this experience of shame is once more shame, which finds expression in art's self-imposed taboos of shameful distance. Not surprisingly, the list of taboos is headed by the restriction on any aesthetic display of eroticism: "In art since Expressionism the prostitute has become a key figure ... since it is only by portrayal of figures devoid of shame that sexuality can now be handled without aesthetic embarrassment (*ästhetische Beschämung*)" (145/166). This is obviously a key passage not only for the workings of shame in *Minima Moralia* but Adorno's theoretical edifice of aesthetic theory in general. Aesthetic shame characterizes Adorno's notion of art and suggests that the privilege accorded to the aesthetic is actually derived from the privilege of shame. Art offers and displays an experience of shame. The paradox on display in art is the paradox of self-exposing shamefulness. Adorno's hopes for resolving the paradox, arresting the dynamics of shame, was nothing short of magic, a fairy-tale happy end: "In the magic of what reveals itself in absolute powerlessness, of beauty, at once perfection and nothingness, the illusion of omnipotence is mirrored negatively as hope" (224/256). In short: *Sterntaler*.

But despite his preference for such endings and figures, the story of shame in *Minima Moralia* does not come to rest in art. It survived and outlived Adorno's own attempts to press it in the service of aesthetic theory and lives on in the performative paradox of this book which speaks so shamelessly of shame.

IV

One must speak shamelessly of shame, for shame itself does not speak. Like the tactful gesture, it belongs to the realm of the pre- or extralinguistic. Blushing or paleness mark the cessation of articulate language. Yet shame is like language in that it bears the traces of memory; as the word "shame" bears witness to the multiplicity of its meanings, language preserves "the traces of degradation" (86/97): "Words and phrases spoilt by use do not reach the secluded workshop intact. And the historical damage cannot be repaired there. History does not merely touch on language but takes place in it" (219/250). Language itself—and, given the allegorical powers with which Adorno often invests this word, one ought to say "language herself"—is subject to abuse, even rape, as Adorno suggests when he writes of the proletariats' dialect, "being forbidden to love it, they rape *(schänden)* the body of language" (102/115). Rape and abuse of language are unavoidable, no shame can protect her from it. The failure to protect language is as preprogrammed as the shame it will induce. This dictates the excesses and shortcomings of *Minima Moralia*'s language: "Linguistic quixotry has become obligatory, since the putting-together of each sentence contributes to the decision whether language as such, ambiguous since primeval times, will succumb to commercialism and the consecrated lie that is part of it, or whether it will make itself a sacred text by diffidence towards the sacral element on which it lives" (222/253). Adorno's discourse on shame is quixotry because it is doomed to fail and thus doomed to induce shame. But the line between false shame as "consecrated lie" and authentic shame as distant "diffidence" cannot be decided; it does not fall in language for language is the very medium of such oscillation, "ambiguous from primeval times." As shame exceeds the boundaries of art and oversteps the limits of prose, it becomes clear that it is, finally, not art but language, "passion for language," that retains the "dream of existence without shame" (86/97).

In a passage that takes its title from Hölderlin's verse "Dem folgt deutscher Gesang," Adorno articulates the goal of such passion, the magical transformation of shameful prose into the beautiful artwork: "Prose isolates itself so ascetically from poetry for the sake of invoking song (Asketische Abdichtung der Prosa gilt der Beschwörung des Gesangs)" (222/253). If this is *Minima Moralia*'s objective, then it failed, for this overwritten and overexposed book does not measure up to the dialectic of the aesthetic for which it strives.

"Dem folgt deutscher Gesang" belongs together with two similar excursions into national languages, entitled "On parle français" and "English spoken." In the name and, as it were, under the cover, of those two languages, the difference between shame as it relates to art and shame as it relates to language surfaces once more. In "English spoken" Adorno recalls a song by Brahms whose original German text by Heyse, "*O Herzeleid, du Ewigkeit/Selbander nur ist Seligkeit,*" reads in the most popular translation: "O misery, eternity/ But two in one were ecstasy." Adorno remarks: "The archaic, passionate nouns of the original have been turned into catchwords for a hit song, designed to boost it. Illuminated in the neon-light [sic] switched on by these words, culture displays its character as advertising" (47/53). The scene is once more art's shameful encounter with itself in the magic mirror of the culture industry. But the failure is neither that of the translation nor of the culture industry; it rests rather with the original, whose failure is that, as artwork, it is by definition exposed to kitsch, which the culture industry only confirms.

In "On parle francais," however, one reads conversely: "How intimately sex and language are intertwined can be seen by reading pornography in a foreign language. When de Sade is read in the original no dictionary is needed. The most recondite expressions for the indecent, knowledge of which no school, no parental home, no literary experience transmits, are understood instinctively ... It is as if the imprisoned passions, called by their name in these expressions, burst through the ramparts of blind language, as through those of their own repression, and forced their way irresistibly into the innermost cell of meaning *(Sinn),* which resembles them" (48/53). Whereas the chaste union with its medieval and religious overtones in Brahms and Heyse is unveiled as kitsch and lie, the pornographic obscenities offer the mystery of sudden revelation. Called by their name, the passions break through the walls of suppression in the service of social norms and like waves—unpredictable, irresistible, violent as the sudden flashes of shame—they enter the innermost cell of the body of language. Even the walls between the difference of meaning and sense/sensuality have collapsed in the word "*Sinn*," which resembles the sensuousness of passions and lends them meaning at the same time. It is here, far removed from the beautiful, in the realm of the affective potential of language, that shame in Adorno is truly at home.

One of the most touching—and in its very disproportionality somehow embarrassing—passages in *Minima Moralia* tells the story of this belonging: "One evening, in a mood of helpless sadness, I caught myself using a ridiculously wrong subjunctive form of a verb that was itself not entirely correct German, being part of the dialect of my native town *(Vaterstadt).* I had not heard, let alone used, the endearing misconstruction since my first years at school. Melancholy, drawing irresistibly into the abyss of childhood, awakened this old, impotently yearning sound in its depths. Language sent back to me like an echo the humiliation *(Beschämung)* and unhappiness *(Unglück)* inflicted on me in forgetting what I am" (110-11/125).

Misfortune literally overlooked Adorno when it spared the German Jew from the disaster. But this shame of the survivor is inseparable from the shame of the intellectual who chose to renounce and forget—along with the paternal dialect—the uneducated father, whose very name he erased from his own. Language can echo and send back such *"Beschämung"* because deep in the well of forgetting it retains the abuse it has suffered. That alone accounts for its historicity: the forgotten word is already distorted, misconstructed, a misnomer. When Adorno wrote that the expression in things that outlived themselves "is the shame that overcomes the descendant in face an earlier possibility that he has neglected," he added: "Only what failed *(mißlang)* is outdated, the broken promise *(das gebrochene Versprechen)* of the new" (93/104). What is a promise, a "Versprechen," but a misnomer, a *"Versprecher,"* a lapsus, a failure? What is *Minima Moralia*, dedicated to Max Horkheimer "in gratitude and promise," but a misnomer for "Mega Melancholia"?

Adorno's "pure image" of a broken promise is once again a fairy tale; not *Sterntaler*'s story of shame regained, but a fairy tale to end all fairy tales, the story of a survivor who gained her life at the cost of another and whose beauty bears the colors of shame, purity, and melancholy, namely, red, white, and black: "More perfectly than any fairy tale, Snow White expresses melancholy. Its pure image is the queen looking out into the snow through her window and wishing for her daughter, after the lifelessly living beauty of the flakes, the black mourning of the window frame, the stab of bleeding, and dying in childbirth. The happy end takes away nothing of this. As the granting of her wish is death, so the saving remains illusion" (121/137). The true image of true beauty is death, for "only death is an image of undistorted life" (78/87). Snow White, the living incarnation of her mother's desire for a beauty alive and dead at the same time, is therefore truly beautiful only when she is believed dead and lies as if sleeping in the glass coffin, offering the view her mother had of snow in front of the glass window. "For deeper knowledge cannot believe that she was awakened who lies as if asleep in the glass coffin. Is not the poisoned bite of apple that the journey dislodges from her throat, rather than a means of murder, the rest of her unlived, banished life, from which only now she truly recovers, since she is lured by no more false messengers?" (121/137-38). As her life was inscribed in death, her reawakening to life and love is the final death of the unlived life, her own and her mother's.

"And how inadequate happiness sounds: 'Snow White felt kindly towards him and went with him.' How it is revoked (*widerrufen*) by the wicked triumph over wickedness'" (121/137). Her happiness, her love, and life are restored but also, and in the same word, repudiated and denied, for the verb "*widerrufen*" echoes and recalls both meanings: "So, when we are hoping for rescue, a voice tells us that hope is in vain, yet it is powerless hope alone that allows us to draw a single breath" (121/137). That we breathe in hell, Adorno had said earlier, makes us ashamed; here what allows us to breathe in the first place is hope. "Truth is inseparable from the delusion (*Wahn*) that from the figures of illusion (*Schein*) one day, in spite of all, real deliverance will come" (122/137). Truth cannot be separated from delusion, life cannot be separated from death, beauty cannot be separated from illusion, recollection cannot be separated from denial, and shame cannot be separated from hope. For Adorno they belong together like the red and white parts of the poisoned apple.

As the romantic he undeniably was, Adorno believed, with Schlegel, that our failures are our hopes—which is to say, he failed to recover from the romantic leftovers lodged deeply in his thought. The survival of these remnants is embarrassing: "*es war als solle die Scham ihn überleben*" ("it was as if the shame should survive him").[18]

Notes

1. Brothers Grimm, "Die Sterntaler," in *Kinder- und Hausmärchen, Ausgabe letzter Hand*, vol. 2 (Stuttgart: Philipp Reclam, 1989), 269-70. My own translation—E.G.

2. Theodor W. Adorno, *Minima Moralia*, trans. E.F.N. Jephcott, 3rd ed. (London: New Left Books, 1985), 98-99. All subsequent page references are made parenthetically without abbreviation to this edition. The translation has been modified from the published translation where necessary. Page references to the German edition follow as the second page reference in the parenthetical citations; they refer to the edition of the text in *Gesammelte Schriften in zwanzig Bänden*, ed. Rolf Tiedemann, vol. 4 (Frankfurt am Main: Suhrkamp Verlag, 1997), here 111.

3. At least this is how psychoanalysis views the matter: Gerhart Piers and Milton B. Singer, *Shame and Guilt. A Psychoanalytic and a Cultural Study* (Springfield,

Illinois: Charles C. Thomas, 1953); Silvan S. Tomkins, *The Negative Affects,* vol. 2 of *Affect Imagery Consciousness* (New York: Springer, 1963); Gershen Kaufman, *The Psychology of Shame. Theory and Treatment of Shame-Based Symptoms* (New York: Springer 1996).

4. In one of the earliest reviews of *Minima Moralia,* the conservative Max Rychner sensed this as a weakness in his essay "Moral an Kleinigkeiten," in *Sphären der Bücherwelt. Aufsätze zur Literatur* (Zürich: Manesse Verlag, 1952), 235-42; more recently Michael Rutschky, "Erinnerungen an die Gesellschaftskritik," *Merkur* 38.1 (January 1984): 28-105; on the impasses of categorical negativity see Michael Theunissen, "Negativität bei Adorno," in *Adorno-Konferenz,* eds. Ludwig von Friedeburg and Jürgen Habermas (Frankfurt am Main: Suhrkamp Verlag, 1983), 41-65.

5. For an exposition of this ethics after ethics see R. Schurz, *Ethik nach Adorno* (Frankfurt am Main: Stromfeld Roter Stern, 1985).

6. Sigmund Freud, "Trauer und Melancholie," in *Studien-Ausgabe,* ed. Alexander Mitscherlich et al., vol. 3 (Frankfurt am Main: S. Fischer Verlag, 1989), 201.

7. According to Rüdiger Campe and Manfred Schneider this might well be the function of modern physiognomy in general. In the preface to their book on physigonomy they write: "Physiognomik, die jahrhundertelang als Wissen, in Kunst und Literatur, darum bemüht war, Zeichen zu bestimmen und Bedeutungen hervorzubringen, wird nun oftmals Wort für das, was 'Bedeutung' erst verständlich oder noch einmal möglich oder in ihrer Unmöglichkeit verständlich und ihrer Unanschaulichkeit sichtbar macht: weil es selbst aller Zeichenordnung und Codierung entgeht." In *Geschichten der Physigonomik. Text. Bild. Wissen,* eds. Rüdiger Campe and Manfred Schneider (Freiburg: Rombach, 1996), 12.

8. Since Adorno's book is in many ways indebted to Benjamin's *One-Way-Street,* one can safely assume that this image is the result of a desecularizing appropriation of Benjamin's rendition of the beloved woman's face: "He who loves is attached not only to the 'faults' of the beloved, not only to the whims and weaknesses of a woman. Wrinkles in the face, moles, shabby clothes, and a lopsided walk bind him more lastingly and relentlessly than any beauty ... Our feeling, dazzled, flutters like a flock of birds in the woman's radiance. And as birds seek refuge in the leafy recesses of a tree, feelings escape into shaded wrinkles, the awkward movements and inconspicuous blemishes of the body we love, where they can lie low in safety." Walter Benjamin, *Reflections,* ed. Peter Demetz, trans. Edmund Jephcott (New York: Harcourt Brace Jovanovich, 1978), 68.

9. Cf. the entry on "Scham," in *Historisches Wörterbuch philosophischer Grundbegriffe,* ed. J. Ritter et al, vol. 8 (Munich: Kösel Verlag, 1992), 1207-16. Instructive in this regard is an essay by Davide Stimilli, "Über Schamhaftigkeit. Zur historischen Semantik einiger physiognomischer Begriffe" in *Geschichten der Physiognomik,* 99-124.

10. This has recently changed, most notably of course with Hans Peter Dürr, *Scham und Nacktheit,* vol. I-III (Frankfurt am Main: Suhrkamp Verlag, 1985). While Dürr's discourse remains within the traditional boundaries of anthropology and ethnology, more recent attempts theorize the phenomenon of shame from different points of view and seek not only to analyze but to rehabilitate a notion of shame capable of providing a corrective to individualistic ethics in the

Kantian tradition. See Bernhard Williams, *Shame and Necessity* (Los Angeles: University of California Press, 1993); certainly the most influential and important contribution to this effort is Eve Sedgwick's essay "Shame and Performativity: Henry James's New York Edition Prefaces," in *Henry James's New York Edition. The Construction of Authorship*, ed. David Whirter (Stanford: Stanford University Press, 1995), 206-39 (thanks to Neil Saccamano for this reference). In the German context, see Irmgard Wagner, "Arbeiten am Schamdiskurs. Literatur der Nachkriegszeit in psychoanalytischer Perspektive," in *Die dunkle Spur der Vergangenheit. Psychoanalytische Zugänge zum Geschichtsbewußtsein. Erinnerung, Geschichte, Identität* 2nd. ed., eds. Jörn Rüsen and Jürgen Straub, (Frankfurt am Main: Suhrkamp Verlag, 1998), 375-396.

11. The tendency to elevate shame to an anthropological constant is particularly strong in existentialist philosophy, particularly Jaspers, Scheler, and Sartre. For the inverse approach see Sighard Neckel, *Status und Scham: Zur symbolischen Reproduktion sozialer Ungleichheit* (Frankfurt am Main: Campe Verlag 1991).

12. Albrecht Wellmer, "Wahrheit, Schein, Versöhnung. Adornos ästhetische Rettung der Modernität," in *Zur Dialektik von Moderne und Postmoderne:Vernunftkritik nach Adorno* (Frankfurt am Main: Suhrkamp Verlag, 1985), 9-47.

13. See Davide Stimilli, "Über Schamhaftigkeit," *Geschichte der Physiognomik*.

14. G.W.F. Hegel, "Frühe Schriften," in *Gesammelte Werke in zwanzig Bänden*, ed. Eva Moldenhauer and Karl Markus Michel, vol. 1 (Frankfurt am Main: Suhrkamp Verlag, 1971) 247.

15. It can be argued that Adorno's dynamics of shame is not an inversion of Hegel but only brings to light and intensifies certain aspects of shame already operative in the Hegelian text. Werner Hamacher writes on shame in the early Hegel: "shame marks ... like the sublated veil of the fetish a remnant within pure unity, of which it can be said neither that it is nor that it is not; a relic of totality which by the same token renders this same totality impossible, as it makes possible the conception of this totality." Werner Hamacher, *Pleroma*, (Stanford: Stanford University Press, 1998), 86. That shame is capable of disrupting the very Hegelian totality it makes possible is affirmed by Adorno where shame also disrupts the negative totality of shamelessness.

16. W. Goethe, *Hamburger Ausgabe*, ed. Erich Trunz, 3rd ed., vol. 3 (Hamburg: Christian Wegner Verlag, 1958), 100-01.

17. Michael Theunissen, "Negativität bei Adorno," in *Adorno-Konferenz*, esp. 51.

18. Franz Kafka, *Der Prozeß* (Hamburg: S. Fischer Verlag, 1960), 165.

Chapter 4

STUMBLING INTO MODERNITY

Body and Soma in Adorno

Andrew Hewitt

In a study of Adorno's reception in the United States—and on the effect of the United States on Adorno's thought—Martin Jay draws our attention to what might seem the nadir of Adorno reception in the USA.[1] In the *New York Times* obituary of 7 August 1969, Adorno is presented—by virtue of a single, rather obscure essay from 1941 that, nevertheless, rehearses the crucial arguments of the more famous essay on the fetish character of music—as a sociologist of popular dance, the jitterbug; to be more precise: "German Expert on Cultural Problems Also Served as Music Critic." Not that the obituary was altogether one-sided: "In addition to inquiring into the sociological implications of dancing," the journalist concedes, "Dr. Adorno looked into the constituents of authoritarianism."[2] In what follows, I will suggest that this seemingly impertinent obituary in fact isolates an important and central *Denkfigur* in Adorno's work. In fact, the figure of the Jitterbug surfaces at precisely those moments when Adorno himself stumbles at a certain threshold in his thinking about the body.[3] In assessing Adorno's writings on the body, rather than merely querying for what Adorno might "stand," one must pay attention to these stumblings.

In two important areas a reading of stumbling can reframe certain central categories in Adorno's thought. First, with respect to the language and logic of psychoanalysis, I shall elaborate a concept of the "parapractical body" as a historically determined category; and second, with regard to the syncopated choreography of the jitterbug, I shall consider the broader question of dance as an aestheticization of social order or tact *(Takt)*. The question of syncopation is crucial both aesthetically and sociologically in Adorno because it raises the issue of what we might call "the dialectic of tact." As a disruption of beat (or *Takt*), syncopation implies at least some kind of attack on the tact or social accommodation that renders social order possible. Given this potentially disruptive or resistant status, it is therefore essential to examine how and why Adorno chose to overlook the critical potential of jazz. The syncopated movements of the Jitterbug articulate two important aesthetic elements in Adorno's social thought. On the one hand, there is a moment of pause and rupture that Adorno consistently—and curiously—fails to valorize in this instance, and, on the other, there is a compulsion to repeat that he links to an atavistic play instinct.

It must strike any reader of Adorno how quickly references to the body or to somatic experience are transformed into something else—more often than not, into symptoms of the demise of the psychical subject in social, political, and aesthetic life. Even though Martin Jay has rightly pointed out how art, for Adorno, offers "a somatic prefiguration of a more generalized future happiness,"[4] he does so to demonstrate Adorno's belief that "psychology (though not psychologism in its reductive forms) was a legitimate bulwark against that subject's suppression in the name of an allegedly higher or more general subject."[5] Noting Adorno's presentation of "psychology as the best guarantor of the individual's right to genuine corporeal gratification," Jay's linkage of "psychological and sensual pleasure" is faithful to similar elisions in Adorno: the corporeal or somatic is consistently subordinated to the psychological. Certainly, even this provisional foregrounding of the body seems crucial, and Adorno's distinction between "a well-known, written history and an underground history" is, as Jay points out, an unacknowledged predecessor of subsequent work on the body by those like Foucault. Instead of assessing Adorno's putative contribution to a Foucaldian tradition, however, I wish to point out some of the limitations of discursive approaches to the body and to point toward rare moments in Adorno where other, potentially more productive ways of conceiving of the body emerge.

As I suggested above, Adorno's dialectical understanding of embodied experience always sublates the body at the last moment into something if not spiritual, at least—as exemplified by Martin Jay's presentation—psychological. The body comes to be identified with the subject in ways that beg the question of *how* bodies become subjects. In a nutshell: Adorno is better on how the subject is embodied than he is on how the body is subjected—and it is the latter question I treat here. This is not to say that he is insensitive to questions of physical and sensory suffering—such corporeal suffering is obviously a crucial category in his work . Rather, I would argue, the violence of the body's subjection *to* a (paradoxically objectified) subject-centered rationality is conflated with a violence inflicted *on* the subject itself. The subject shifts in Adorno from agent of violence to its victim. By trying to trace in Adorno fleeting moments of the sensual prior to its subjection, I wish to seek and elaborate a prehistory of the subject that is not entirely recuperable within an Oedipal framework.

This prehistorical investigation presents a challenge not only to Adorno, but also as an underlying structural problem that must be confronted in this study: that is, how to elaborate a discourse on the prediscursive? Adorno is useful for highlighting the question and for certain allusions to a solution that are to be found in his work. Terminologically, I will try to keep track of this problem by referring to body and soma.[6] By body, I mean the body in its already subjected form; the body of a subject; a body that serves, moreover, to trope the presence—however attenuated—of a subject in Adorno's writing. Such a body would lend itself to a variety of theories of discourse and discursive construction. Though it introduces a new conception of materiality into textual reading, this model nevertheless tends to assimilate the body to the possibility *of* reading—albeit within a retooled hermeneutic—and thus to relegitimate the institutionalization of the traditional interpretive endeavor. By soma, I wish to suggest the body in a form that predates the subject—though the temporal suggestion of "predating" is imprecise. We might refer instead to a soma that subtends the subject and upon which the experiences of the subject leave a trace, without that body, or soma, necessarily assuming an identity with those experiences. It is not, then, a pure state simply because it is presubjective: it is manifested through the nonidentity of body and subject rather than through their posited utopian identity.

Adorno's mistrust of what I have termed soma derives from two sources: first, from a dialectical fear of falling back into a Feuerbachian materialism of inert matter; and second, from an observation of how fascism tapped into and instrumentalized a certain romantic notion of somatic, nonalienated experience. In contemporary theory we face a third danger—one to which Adorno also makes us sensitive—namely, the danger of positing soma as the site of resistance. While we need to acknowledge the danger of relapsing into a predialectical, Feuerbachian form of materialism, we should also resist placing the body that confounds symbolization in the position traditionally reserved for the unrepresentable sublime. Soma is not sublime—though it is, possibly, subliminal. A romanticism of the body essentially retains the binarisms of Idealist philosophy while reversing the terms. As Adorno notes in "On the Fetish Character in Music and the Regression of Listening," "radical reification produces its own pretense of immediacy and intimacy."[7] Indeed, the invocation of such immediacy is not the least of fascism's many attractions.

Adorno, in fact, highlights the dangers of such romanticization of the body as a site of resistance. He observes elsewhere that "the romantic attempts to bring about a renaissance of the body in the nineteenth and twentieth centuries simply idealize a dead and maimed condition."[8] Indeed, one might say that for Adorno a valorization of a presubjective condition produces neither body nor soma, but the corpse that results from any attempt to transfigure this tradition in positive terms:

> The love-hate relationship with the body colors all more recent culture. The body is scorned and rejected as something inferior, and at the same time desired as something forbidden, objectified, and alienated. Culture defines the body as a thing which can be possessed; in culture a distinction is made between the body and the spirit, the concept of power and command, as the object, the dead thing, the *"corpus"* (*DoE*, 232).

One needs to note an extremely important chiasmatic slippage here. The traditional binary of body and Spirit is displaced onto the dyad body-corpse. The corpse, in Adorno, is the Spirit in its embodied form, or the body in its etiolated, spiritual form. As such, the corpse serves to trope both utopian physicality and the murderous results of any immediate political instantiation of the body. Adorno's elaboration of the corpse reflects his self-conscious sensitivity to the dangers of celebrating a presubjective corporeal condition as emancipatory.

In the overly schematic terms I have just outlined, it is my contention that the most interesting recent work on the body has demonstrated a shift from body to soma; from a concern with "textuality" to an attempt to confront the very conditions of materialism—dialectical or otherwise. One could cite the proliferation of recent work on hysteria, which originated in a concern for how women's bodies are read historically—and constructed discursively—and how their bodies might produce a language that confounds translation, which needs to be listened to rather than read.[9] Similarly, the reevaluation of the ontic in recent antimetaphysical thinkers promises not only an inversion of existing binaries, but also a re-inscription of a new politics and philosophy of the body. Such gestures are also to be found in the late work of Foucault himself, whom I have otherwise identified with the discursive model. Borrowing a phrase from a recent work by Hal Foster, we might think of these related phenomena—this shift in concern from body to soma—under the rubric of *The Return of the Real*.[10]

But what of that piece of historical realia, the gyrating Jitterbug? This figure is most lucidly elaborated in a passage from the chapter on the culture industry in *Dialectic of Enlightenment*. In this passage Adorno observes how "life in the late capitalist era is a constant initiation rite. Everyone must show that he wholly identifies himself with the power which is belaboring him. This occurs in the principle of jazz syncopation, which simultaneously derides stumbling and makes it a rule" (*DoE* 153). In a related passage from the essay on "On the Fetish Character in Music and the Regression of Listening," Adorno extends his familiar critique of jazz to include the forms of dance to which it gives rise: "They call themselves Jitterbugs, as if they simultaneously wanted to affirm and mock their loss of individuality, their transformation into beetles whirring around in fascination" (*FSR* 292). By focusing on the figure of the Jitterbug, one can confront the status of syncopation: is it to be thought of as an immediate translation of vital rhythms (which is the ideological claim for which Adorno critiques it) or as a disruption and deferral of the possibility of any such rhythm as a moment of vital presence?

Adorno's foregrounding of a choreographic moment as the key to understanding a prevailing social order resonates in interesting, ironic ways with an observation made by Schiller in a letter of 1793 to his collaborator Körner. Schiller writes:

> I can think of no more fitting image for the ideal of social conduct than
> an English dance, composed of many complicated figures and perfectly
> executed. A spectator in the gallery sees innumerable movements inter-
> secting in the most chaotic fashion, changing direction swiftly and with-
> out rhyme or reason, yet *never colliding*. Everything is so ordered that
> the one has already yielded his place when the other arrives; it is all so
> skillfully, and yet so artlessly, integrated into a form, that each seems
> only to be following his own inclination, yet without ever getting in the
> way of anybody else. It is the most perfectly appropriate symbol of the
> assertion of one's own freedom and regard for the freedom of others.[11]

What persists—from Schiller to Adorno—is the trope of dance as a
trope for social order. What has shifted is the assessment of that
order and/or the valorization of play—the free play of bodies in
space—as a model of freedom. Schiller's understanding of dance
immediately introduces an ethical and sociological perspective—
"one's own freedom and regard for the freedom of others"—that
lifts the observation out of any limited or immanently aesthetic
realm. Rather than simply underlining the anti-Schillerian thrust of
Aesthetic Theory , I would like to note some paradoxes in Adorno's
thought. Generally, his mistrust of Schillerian aesthetics turns on
Schiller's privileging of the ideal and sublimating moment in the
aesthetic experience. Adorno, by contrast, will stress the contingent, the part—indeed, on occasion, the somatic. In this instance,
however, Adorno's opposition turns on a mistrust of the *body* as it
falters, stumbles, and tumbles into ecstatic spasm.

   If one were to address the question of play as it presents itself in
Schiller and Adorno, one would soon find oneself returning to the
problem of soma, since Adorno's problems with the category of
play throughout the *Aesthetic Theory* relate to his conviction that
play is reducible to an atavistic and presubjective, repetition compulsion. Such a compulsion, indeed, is at the heart of his analysis of
the Jitterbug as well as a key theme in this *Aesthetic Theory*: "playful forms are without exception forms of repetition ... In blunt
opposition to Schillerian ideology, art allies itself with unfreedom in
the specific character of play."[12] The paradox of reading the Jitterbug anthropologically, of course, is that he marks precisely the
moment when the human slips below the threshold of the anthropological into the realm of the bug. Adorno's response to this problem is to return to what I will call "the parapractical body" that
perversely produces meaning in its failures and stumblings. This
parapractical body, I would like to suggest, is historically specific: it

marks an attempt to reconcile the demands of reading the body with the reality of a resurgent, illegible soma. It is historical, not only in that it clearly derives from Freud, but also—and here the argument is Adorno's not mine—insofar as the soma reenters the field of history in the late nineteenth century.

For Adorno, jazz—and jitterbugging—function anthropologically as a ritual of socialization whereby bodies are harnessed to dysfunctional (syncopated) social norms. If dance has always functioned to induct bodies into a social order and choreograph them as subjects, jazz differs by teaching its children to stumble, not to walk. It is a ritual of socialization in which the inductee apparently fails. What does it mean to stumble? The question might at first appear absurd in apportioning to a simple somatic failure any significance whatsoever. Since Freud, however, there is a language for talking of such signifiers: is stumbling, then, a parapraxis? Before turning to the significance of stumbling, however, I would like to follow Freud by insisting upon the *work* of signification or what I have termed the moment of (para)praxis. It would be wrong to simply ask what stumbling "means." Stumbling is a stumbling *into* meaning—a failure that inaugurates meaning. One needs to stress the moment of (para)praxis in order to pose the question of what stumbling *does*; in rhetorical terms, one needs to understand it epideictically as a performative act. This is what Adorno means by speaking of the "initiation rite," the action that acquires significance through its performance context.

So what does one "do" when one stumbles? Well, of course, one fails—one fails to walk. Something doesn't work. Something doesn't work—and yet work is being done. Something "is belaboring" us so that we become not the subject, but the object of a certain social labor. "Amusement under late capitalism," Adorno reminds us, "is the prolongation of work" (*DoE* 137). In jitterbugging, one might say, pleasure and play (fun) are defined in purely negative terms: play is the pleasure taken in (the fact of something's) not working. And yet, work *is* being done. When one stumbles one does not fall. Indeed, the fallen body—at its extreme, the corpse—might conceivably serve as a trope of the body at rest, as an experience of pleasure. Jitterbugging, however, figures a social order that does not bring one to one's knees, but, nevertheless, keeps one permanently unbalanced. When one stumbles, one neither falls and comes to rest, nor walks and progresses. Two central metanarratives of political modernity—progress and utopian rest—are dismantled by stumbling. Syncopation—and its aesthetic of stumbling as repetition—problematizes not only a historically specific set of aesthetic norms (as critics of Adorno would charge) but the very metaphysics of a certain historical thought.

In the movement from Schiller's English line dance to Adorno's American jitterbug, we trace, perhaps, the very dialectic of enlightenment itself—something gone wrong somewhere with dance as a model of social order. I will argue that at least two things have "gone wrong" in the tropological shift from Schiller to Adorno. First, there is the question of *Takt*—the rhythmic trope of social cohabitation that renders society possible; and second, there is the question of the body's loss of control over its own putatively expressive gestures. Both of these questions can be addressed through a consideration of Adorno's discussion of syncopation, a disruption of beat (or *Takt*). Though I wish to focus on the Jitterbug as a model for understanding the modern "somatic" body, I would first like to address, briefly, the historical question of dance and the decay of *Takt*.

As far back as the ancient Greeks, music has influenced the very possibility of social law: to learn to dance is to learn sociability. Music is measured and orderly—as society itself should be. What, then, does it mean to play with the beat *(Takt)* of music and to oblige unwilling feet to follow this tactless social order? In Adorno's lexicon, tact is a precious, though always already compromised term. In Goethe, he observes in *Minima Moralia*, tact is "the saving accommodation between alienated human beings. This accommodation seemed to him inseparable from renunciation, the relinquishment of total contact, passion, and unalloyed happiness."[13] Tact, in fact, arises from a relinquishing of the tactile. The acknowledgement of bodily relationality—our choreographed coexistence in space and time—arises from a sensory renunciation. This is an important distinction, for it means that when Adorno uses images of the body to figure the fate of the bourgeois subject, he is, necessarily, yoking together two antipathetic elements. The bourgeois subject can be figured by his body only on the ideological assumption that he is somehow identical with it— which he is not. Or, maybe, this is too simplistic: maybe, the very ability of the body to stand in for the subject already acknowledges its diacritical difference from that subject. Either way, the slippage from body to subject—from soma to psychology—is necessarily ideological. The body that can stand in for the subject is already an alienated body that has been made to "mean." I wish to destabilize—quite literally—the ability of the body to "stand for" the subject by elaborating elements of the body-subject nonidentity: the tropes of stumbling and steadfastness in Adorno.

Elsewhere, Adorno will refer to the spastic Jitterbug as an example of how social adaptation under late capitalism is bought at the cost of bodily motor coordination. When I dance, I stumble like everyone else: others deride my failure and in so doing instigate a derisive social unity. My apparent joy in dancing—the joy of the jitterbug—is but the internalized reflection of that derision. Derision is not joy gone bad; joy is the internalization of derision—in Adorno's terms "a medicinal bath." My joy at identifying with the social force that derides the failed choreography of my individuation is a joy at the possibility of (collective) identity beyond its (individual) failure. The irrepressible snigger at another's stumbling—the laugh that escapes us when someone falls, even when that fall causes serious injury—is, to say the least, tactless. But the stumble is also tactless. Between these two lapses of tact, however, there is a homology or synchronicity that reestablishes a social rhythm and reinstates *Takt*: one laughs (tactlessly) at the (tactless) Jitterbug, without missing a (tactful) beat. Not even laughter can be hypostatized as somehow a purely somatic eruption—it is itself the inauguration of a derisive community.

What appears to be a quibble—my concern that one not simply accept Adorno's idea of what stumbling "stands for" since, quite clearly, stumbling marks a failure to stand—is, in fact, a crucial element of my argument. Leaping, for a moment, from this particular *Denkfigur* to its possible parapractical implications in the broader reception of Adorno's aesthetics, I would argue that a sensibility to stumbling might allow us to free Adorno from certain reified aesthetic doxa. There is something in Adorno's modernist rigor akin to a rigor mortis. As if suspicious of the organicist perils of any vitalistic troping of the body, Adorno consistently moves negatively through images of arrestation and stasis. Thus he observes how "Hegel arrests the aesthetic dialectic by his static definition of the beautiful as the sensual appearance of the idea" (*AT* 51). I argue, however, that Adorno offers himself up for a similar fate when he claims that:

> The radically darkened art—established by the Surrealists as black humor—which the aesthetic hedonism that survived the catastrophes defamed for the perversity of expecting that the dark should give some-

thing like pleasure, is in essence nothing but the postulate that art and a
true consciousness of it can today find happiness only in the capacity of
standing firm. (*AT* 40)

Despite the valorizing of the contingent and the partial in Adorno's
aesthetic writings, art always seems to consist in a "standing firm."
This standing firm tends to lend itself to the antidialectical, to an aesthetic that engages in a curiously oxymoronic dialectical rigor. Can
the Jitterbug, as a parapractical body, cure Adorno's rigor mortis?

Adorno derides the Jitterbug because his stumbling figures both
a semiotic instability and the possibility of a somatic body that
questions the stoicism of an aesthetic "standing firm." Adorno's Jitterbug figures the demise of both an intersubjective tact and the
autonomous subject. More properly and more dialectically, the Jitterbug gives birth to a new order even as he or she performs the
death throes of an old one. This new order, Adorno suggests, is one
in which one's position in society is guaranteed not on the basis of
a successful individuation, but only on condition that one renounce
individuality. In a typical gesture, Adorno insists that the failure
implicit in stumbling *is* the initiation—that by failing one somehow
succeeds. As a choreographed stumbling, Jazz dance stands for (or
topples for, one might say, since I am talking here not about static
denotative significance, but about a performative parapraxis) a society that will accept only individual failure (or the failed individuation) as the mark of social adaptation. It is not "tactful" to maintain
a sense of rhythm that might resist syncopation. *Takt*, which used to
mean respect for the subjectivity of the other, now means a renunciation of one's *own* subject position. Even the purely codified subjectivity that is empowered and acknowledged by tact has been
surpassed. By renouncing a purely formalistic tact, however, one
does not reach a more "authentic" subjectivity, but merely loses the
last vestige of the only (purely formal) subjectivity left to us.

One needs to be careful of seeing in the act of stumbling a
somatic resistance to coercive or choreographed socialization: the
body, in other words, offering a resistance of which the psyche is no
longer capable. In stumbling it is important to see how the body
does not, in fact, fall—indeed, it fails to fall—but rather rights itself,
marking time to the syncopated beat, instilling temporal distortion
into the body itself. It is not a question of totalitarianism *or* individuality, but rather—in a parody of Schiller's fusion of freedom
and necessity in play—it is a question of totalitarianism creating

pseudo individuals and allowing them to stumble as they dance. In the essay "The Fetish Character in Music," Adorno obliquely forecloses any somatic or utopian reading of the Jitterbug. "Their ecstasy," he writes, "is without content":

> That it happens, that the music is listened to, this replaces the content itself ... Passion itself seems to be produced by defects. But the ecstatic ritual betrays itself as pseudoactivity by the moment of mimicry. People do not dance or listen "from sensuality" and sensuality certainly is certainly not satisfied by listening, but the gestures of the sensual are imitated ... The same jitterbugs who behave as if they were electrified by syncopation dance almost exclusively the good rhythmic parts. (*FSR* 292)

Finally, one needs to rule out any reading of this passage that would romanticize the body as a locus of sensual resistance to totalitarianism. For Adorno, the spastic vitality of the Jitterbug resembles nothing more than the muscular spasms of the recently deceased corpse—he locates them far from any emancipatory moment. Death has become the measure of life: and even in death there is no peace, but rather spasmodic movement. As Adorno observes in *Dialectic of Enlightenment*, "the body cannot be remade into a noble object: it remains the corpse however vigorously it is trained and kept fit" (*DoE* 234). Against Adorno's unilateral negativity here, I would like to suggest a kind of dancing in between, or rather both simultaneously, body and soma. What I am suggesting is not that one declare oneself for or against the signifying body or some resistant soma, but that one reacknowledge the implication of the somatic in the bodily, of the performative in the denotative.

Historicizing from jazz a certain brutalization of gesture, Adorno opens up a space from which his own critique might itself be problematized. He notes:

> Technology is making gestures precise and brutal, and with them men. It expels from movements all hesitation, deliberation, civility ... The movements machines demand of their users already have the violent, hard-hitting unresting jerkiness of Fascist maltreatment. Not least to blame for the withering of experience is the fact that things, under the law of pure functionality, assume a form that limits contact with them to mere operation and tolerates no surplus ... (*MM* 40)

In this passage, hesitation is the very space of the aesthetic insofar as it lingers, as opposed to mere mechanized operation. Surely, syncopation—a description of beat and therein *Takt*—is in some sense a hesitation or repetition, and therefore opens up its own aesthetic possibilities? In fact, Adorno is concerned with ways in which potentially subversive musical projects throw up their own dance forms that eliminate the reflective moment by choreographing a stumble to the very stumbling of the music. Whereas to stumble might be subversive in its tactlessness, to stumble in time to the beat is to acknowledge a social order from which even the minimal safeguards of tact have been eliminated. The hesitation in jazz is one in which reflection is displaced by mere mimesis: it is the mere ritual form of socialization without its content.

Adorno's stumbling, however, allows us to further elaborate the phenomenon of the "parapractical body" that I have been underscoring—and to trace its historical provenance. It is the parapractical body that allows us to continue in a regime of reading even at moments when the body seems to depart from its own script. In Adorno's binary one fails not only to walk, but to fall, to come to rest. The fallen body represents, for Adorno, a body that has come to rest in and with itself—the cadaver, remember, is the bodily cognate of soul, the soul as soma. Equally important in stumbling is that instinct causing us to right ourselves, a reality principle telling us that work must go on, that hesitation—and civility—are luxuries we cannot afford ourselves. At its most extreme, Adorno argues, this instinct urges us beyond walking. In a fragment entitled "More haste, less speed," he observes the disturbing phenomenon of a bourgeois running in the street: "Running in the street conveys an impression of terror. The victim's fall is already mimed in his attempt to escape it. The position of the head, trying to hold itself up, is that of a drowning man" (*MM* 162). As in the passage from *Dialectic of Enlightenment*, stumbling is the telos of the bourgeois gait, the fall that is "already mimed" in the fall guy's head. Indeed, walking, sped up to a terrified trot, becomes the very model of parapraxis for Adorno. It is precisely in the desire not to do something that one performs the gesture one sought to escape. Moreover, the notion that the fall has been "already mimed" robs the gesture of falling of its spontaneity.

This implication of the mimetic in parapraxis suggests a productive rereading of the prevalent interpretations of parapraxis, because it elicits a consideration of performance that destabilizes any purely denotative semiotic legibility. In stumbling, we encounter not an eruption of the somatic as resistance, but rather a return of the repressed. At the same time, however, the logic of stumbling is not so simple. Rather than figuring the fall as a repressed event, Adorno introduces his central category of mimesis to suggest that the fall is the *telos*—and at the same time only the *absent* origin—of the harried bourgeois gait. There is a curious *Nachträglichkeit* in the performance: one rushes toward the thing one sought to escape, thereby bringing it about. It is as if Adorno were foregrounding the moment of revelation in parapraxis rather than the moment of concealment. There is no original fall to dissemble. There will be more to say on this question of mimesis later. For now, I observe only the ways in which it opens up the possibility of other—parapractically performative, as opposed to pathographic—ways of reading the body, without reducing the gesture to symptom and the symptom to its (usually psychological) cause.

The second implication of this fragment from *Minima Moralia* is that we inhabit a parapractical society, one in which all gestures can be read as involuntary, and in which significance derives not from intention, but from the unintentionality of gesture. Indeed, one might argue that it is this observation that makes the very project of *Minima Moralia*—the isolation of *Denkfiguren*—possible. In fact, for Adorno the perambulatory stability of walking is historically obsolete: "the walk, the stroll, were private ways of passing time, the heritage of the feudal promenade in the nineteenth century" (*MM* 162). In the twentieth century, the ritual function of stumbling seems to have something to do with the erosion of the historical private sphere—stumbling, indeed, over the very threshold of the private into the realm of the public. In the public space of the modern city, the luxury of the leisurely promenade can no longer be afforded. It must be regulated and channeled by clearly identifiable—and not very tactful—markers: "Traffic regulations no longer need allow for wild animals, but they have not pacified running. It estranges us from bourgeois walking ... Human dignity insisted on the right to walk, a rhythm not extorted from the body by command or terror ... With the liberal era walking too is dying out, even where people do not go by car" (*MM* 162). Adorno further notes how the youth movements of the early part of the century "challenged the parental Sunday excursions and replaced them by voluntary forced marches" (*MM* 162). Simple walking seems so difficult; we are now obliged to march, or terrified into running. What Adorno is elaborating—as Martin Jay suggests in the essay I cited earlier—is the possibility of a historical reading of the body and its actions.

In a similar vein, the Italian philosopher, Giorgio Agamben, has argued in an essay on gesture from *Infancy and History: The Destruction of Experience* that "by the end of the nineteenth century, the gestures of the Western bourgeoisie were irretrievably lost."[14] This loss of gesture, however, might be seen instead as a loss of syntactical or legible gesture—the readable body-subject gesture—for in fact what seems to have happened, at least in Agamben's account, is an explosion of gesture. Charting the destruction of gestural experience from the clinical writings of Gilles de la Tourette at the end of the nineteenth century, Agamben notes how the wild gestures noted by Tourette (and captured in the films of Marey and Lumière) seemed to have gone underground, "until the winter's day in 1971, when Oliver Sacks, walking through the streets of New York, saw what he believed were three cases of Tourettism within the space of three minutes" (*IH* 137). This historical and bodily return of the repressed leads Agamben to conjecture "that beyond a certain point everyone had lost control of their gestures, walking and gesticulating frenetically" (*IH* 137). The fate of the gesture is interesting here. Precisely inasmuch as nonverbal languages have been subjected to a logocentrism, this subjection has led to a proliferation of unreadable bodily ejaculations that outstretch and complicate Adorno's binary of body-legible and corpsestatic. The repression of the body's (linguistic) movements has led to ever broader ranges of (uncontrolled) movement that Adorno reads, I suggest, in an exceptionally reductive manner.

Agamben's depiction recalls a paradigmatic Foucaldian play of repression and proliferation, in which the usual displacements of a sublimation have no place left. The body—the final resting place of the repressed in so many cases—cannot itself be displaced. It is as if we had nothing left for protection and camouflage but the techniques of condensation—the terse, condensed gestures of Tourettism. Of course, if one accepts the hypothesis that Agamben proposes and that one finds implicitly in Adorno also, the question of parapraxis—and the regime of reading on which it depends—becomes highly problematic. If the body's gestures have become spastic, one can no longer simply read back from them—even parapractically—to a putative subject. Furthermore, if the logic here is Foucaldian, it is precisely those discourses and technologies of the body that both silence and give voice to the somatic ejaculations. It is only from the perspective of such discourses that the somatic can be made to figure anything like a "natural language." This reformulation and romanticization is something I shall return to when considering Adorno on the fascist body. It is precisely the *refusal* to ground a discourse on the somatic that resists fascism, for fascism's appeal, according to Adorno, rests on its recognition of the importance of the body crafted from the somatic. Its ideological distortion rests on the false discourse it derives from that body.

One might think of stumbling—in Adorno—as the somatic correlative of Oedipus. For Adorno it is *the* rite of social initiation under late capitalism. What stumbling stumbles on, furthermore, are the very thresholds of public and private, nature and culture, soma and body. Once again, via alternate routes, one arrives at important reconfigurations of the somatic: specifically, it is *not* ahistorical, *not* a condition of utopian unity and dedifferentiation. Like the bourgeois who almost brings about his own downfall for fear of falling down, the fascist merely fears the prospect of bodily unity implied in free sexuality. And if bourgeois fear conjures up the very thing it seeks to escape—the dreaded fall—by implication, the fantasy of immanent bodily unity is likewise merely a conjuring trick of protofascist ideology. Reading Adorno's insistence, in *Minima Moralia*: "He alone who could situate utopia in blind somatic pleasure, which, satisfying the ultimate intention, is intentionless, has a stable and valid idea of truth. In Freud's work, however, the dual hostility towards mind and pleasure, whose common root psychoanalysis has given us the means for discovering, is unintentionally reproduced" (*MM* 61).

If the soma does not ground a discourse—there is no original fall to the ground—it nevertheless operates in and through it parapractically ("intentionless") or performatively. Furthermore, Adorno's invocation of an "intentionless" soma foregrounds the aesthetic element within all discursive performance, enjoining a rhetorical—as opposed to symptomatic—sensibility in our readings of the body.

Rather than moving toward anything like a conclusion on the question of the body in Adorno, I wish now to consider three areas that might open up future work: namely, the consideration of the body of the Jew in the "Notes on Anti-Semitism," a presentation that

gives the lie to my notion that Adorno repeatedly averts his gaze
from the body; second, the analysis of fascism's response to the
alienation of bourgeois experiences of the body as an example of
how the soma can be rendered the ground of a discourse only in the
crassest ideological terms; and finally, the question of pornography,
insofar as it addresses the limitations of the body's passage into
script, while illuminating the latent sensual aspects of language.

It is not my intention to examine the details of Adorno's presentation of the body of the Jew in *Dialectic of Enlightenment*, but
merely to point out certain structural elements that offer the most
glaring exceptions to my assertion that Adorno averts his gaze from
the body. Two bodies are, in effect, at play in this section on anti-
Semitism. First, the body is distributed across the various senses—
most notably, the sense of smell, a body considered in its details,
almost anatomically dissected. Second, there is the cadaver: the
body as an image of natural unity, the body that—in a sense—
incites the project of the death camps because, for the Nazi, "the
victim represents life which has overcome the separation; it must be
broken and the universe must be mere dust and abstract power"
(*DoE* 236). This cadaver both realizes and scandalizes a certain idealist hierarchy. It has overcome the mere contingency of life to
become "all there is": it is effectively the thing into which Spirit has
retreated. By destroying it, the fascist reestablishes the binarism of
matter and Spirit—"dust and abstract power." The status of the
cadaver needs to be measured against that critique in which—para-
phrased by Martin Jay—"Heidegger's insistence on the ontological
meaning of death betrayed a covert sympathy for a totalizing identity theory that denied difference even as it purported to defend
it."[15] By the same token, a vitalistic insistence on the ontological
meaning of the vital impulse also rides roughshod over the contingent, suffering, worldly body.

In the presentation of the Jewish body as an amalgam of sensory faculties, however, one is immediately struck by how Adorno
can approach the body in this case only from the caricatural perspective of the Nazi. The body he describes is the body as perceived
in fascist propaganda. No matter what the Jews as such may be like,
"their image, as that of the defeated people, has the features to
which totalitarian domination must be completely hostile" (*DoE*
199). The limits of Adorno's presentation, however, are shown by
the focus on "the nose—the physiognomic *principium individuatio-*

nis, symbol of the specific character of an individual" (*DoE* 184). Does the Jew—with his big nose—represent the fleshly, corporeal, somatic, and contingent? Or is the hypertrophy of the nose the hypertrophy of the "*principium individuationis*," that is, of the very category of the subjects? While Adorno goes on to suggest the former—the identification of the Jew with the longed-for bodily immanence—he is consistently ambiguous on these questions. Is it the category of the subject that is being attacked or the possibility of a presubjective, immanently somatic experience? Of course, the ambiguity is the answer—the two cannot be divided: body and soma inhabit the same space. From the fascist perspective, the Jew is both self-identical (finally, as cadaver) and nonidentical, dissolved by the smells that permeate his nostrils. In either case, however, he is definitely identified. While it is easy to talk of a subject's experience of the body, or a body's experience of the soma, it is well nigh impossible to even envisage a somatic experience of the body, to envisage the somatic as an experience at all. This explains why Adorno is obliged to approach the body of the Jew—as a figure for soma—only from the perspective of a fascist mentality that disfigures and eventually destroys it. Figuring always disfigures.

Horkheimer and Adorno assert that "there is no anti-Semite who does not basically want to imitate his mental image of a Jew, which is composed of mimetic ciphers" (*DoE* 184). Of course, once the Jew has been reduced to ciphers, a mimetic approach to him becomes all the more possible. But the ambiguity of the Jewish body—replicated in the physical and verbal ambiguity of "smelling"—helps us understand the play of what I have been calling the parapractical performative within otherwise denotative discourses. "To smell" is both a transitive and an intransitive verb, and the caricatured Jew smells in both senses—he smells things and he "is smelly." But how does the fascist know the Jew is smelly? Simple, he smells him: "anyone who seeks out 'bad' smells may imitate sniffing to his heart's content" (*DoE* 184). The verb allows an accommodation of persecutor to victim, but the mimesis nevertheless retains difference. The Nazi smells as an activity, but the Jew also "is" smelly. Mimesis does not simply mimic an action, it distinguishes between what, in that action, is an ontological condition—the putative smell of the Jew—and what can be rescued as a realm of mimetic play. This would be the barbarous and atavistic aspect of the Schillerian play instinct. Furthermore, this question of smell is not unrelated to the foregoing consideration of walking, as Adorno and Horkheimer insist that "when man began to walk upright ... the sense of smell which drew the male animal to the female in heat was relegated to a secondary position" (*DoE* 233). There is clearly a double nostalgia in Adorno—both for the nineteenth-century promenade and for a posture more conducive to immanent sexual fulfillment. We need only to think of this hint at walking's relation to sexual repression in the context of *Minima Moralia*'s observation that "modern man wishes to sleep close to the ground, like an animal" (*MM* 38) to see how the body of the Jew, in fact, serves to figure the atavistic modern body, in general.

Meanwhile, what fascism offers is a return to the hidden body of the democratic political tradition. "In Western civilization," Horkheimer and Adorno point out, "and probably in all other forms of civilization, the physical aspect of existence is taboo" (*DoE* 233). Even "for the Greek rulers and in the feudal system," they insist, "the relationship with the body was still conditioned by personal strength as a requisite of rule" (*DoE* 233). The considerations of walking, stumbling, dancing, running are all, in the final analysis, the very rudiments of a political analysis, not simple tropes. In Greece, we read, "the gymnasium was a necessary aid to maintaining the individual's power, or at least as training for the *posture* of a ruler" (*DoE* 233, my emphasis —A.H.). It is not simply a countermodel to Western democracy that fascism offers, but rather a prototypical return to the body of politics. Racism, for example, offers a distorted vision of the body's immanent political instantiation: bodies shaping and determining discourse. Hence, Horkheimer and Adorno suggest, its attractiveness to social strata whose very self-definition derives from their bodily alienation in labor. Horkheimer and Adorno suggest that the fascist destruction of bodies marks an inarticulate revenge against the body-Spirit dualism. What it leaves as a remainder, however, is the corpse—which is merely a *figure* for body-Spirit reconciliation (the stumbling body as if it had fallen), while *being*, in fact, is the severance of all aspiration toward the spiritual.

While I have already argued that one needs to move beyond a radically textualized notion of the body in order to understand the workings of the soma, I have resisted romanticizing soma as that which annuls history and discourse, resisted installing it in the position of the unfigurable sublime or even—as cadaver—in the infinitely contracted space of Spirit. How is the soma something not merely constructed but still active in discursive and historical construction? Are we to understand its activity in the modal ambiguity of that verb—"to smell": as something that is active in its very passivity, as something that refuses to go away, something that lingers and permeates discourse?

Horkheimer and Adorno's assertion that "the Fascist present in which the hidden side of things comes to light also shows the relationship between written history and the dark side which is overlooked" (*DoE* 231) imposes on us the necessity of thinking not only of fascism's relation to the fantasies of democratic politics, but also the somatic functioning of the body politic. The *Dialectic of Enlightenment* allows us to understand fascism not as the return of the repressed, nor—and herein lies the obvious problem of an overzealous embrace of the book—as an historically specific political and ideological phenomenon, but rather as the meeting place for two embodied models of history. It is not simply "the dark side" nor, indeed, "written history," but rather the confrontation of the two. Such an insight returns us to my thesis: we are alerted not simply to the experience of an alienated subject with respect to its own somatic body, but also to the "experience" of that body—or soma—with respect to the category of the subject. Theory's insistent return to fascism as something other than a contingent historical phenomenon marks its attempt to find a place where two models of the body— and history—enter into dialogue, a dialogue that simultaneously moves beyond the subjected body's mere textuality, while also rendering discursive the formerly illegible somatic.

But what trace is there—and I use the term advisedly—of soma in Adorno? What space is left in his readings of the body for a resistance to textualization? I am aware of the paradoxicality of what I am suggesting—the possibility of an approach to the body that eschews textualization but is simultaneously mediated through language. Nevertheless, one needs to bear in mind that the soma is not the sublime: it is not unrepresentable, but operates within representation. In *Minima Moralia* Adorno at least intimates some such approach to the body. In the fragment "On parle français," he writes of reading Sade's pornography;

> How intimately sex and language are intertwined can be seen by reading pornography in a foreign language. When Sade is read in the original no dictionary is needed. The most recondite expressions for the indecent, knowledge of which no school, no parental home, no literary experience transmits, are understood instinctively … It is as if the

> imprisoned passions, called by their name in these expressions, burst
> through the ramparts of blind language as through those of their own
> repression, and forced their way irresistibly into the innermost cell of
> meaning, which resembles them. (*MM* 48)

This fragment is important for the ways in which it approaches and
yet problematizes the question of the somatic. The assertion that
"sex and language are intertwined" can all too readily be reduced
to the textual model of the body: sex as text, desire in signs, etc. But
it is something quite different Adorno is getting at here, an alternative model of reading that he intimates. Here we have a language
that has no need of translation, but which is, nevertheless, in a foreign language. This is the point: not the unrepresentability, but
rather the untranslatability or the supertranslatability of the somatic.
Adorno suggests here an alternate textuality, or discursiveness, of
the body, one tending to the somatic, a language that one does not
speak but that is spoken—"On parle." The grammatical complexity of the French passive voice is revelatory here: one has a similar
problem of active and passive that we found in the "smelling" of
the anti-Semite. In this case, it is not a question of a simple undermining of the psychic subject—a psychoanalysis in which "ça
parle." The impersonal locution of the sexual in pornography is not
subversive, but actually constitutive, of the abstract categorical subject—the "On." The somatic is aggressively and insistently active in
constituting the abstract subject (of language) rather than in simply
resisting discourse.[16]

    This is an example of the ways in which Adorno addresses
debates central to contemporary theory without being readily sub-
sumable within such theory. His critique of pornography reminds us
that soma should not be reduced to sex—which he calls "the lovemaking taken like medicine as 'sex'" (*MM* 62). More than this, however, this presentation of the somatic's eruption in language is heavily
ironic—for it occurs precisely in language's most nominalistic forms:
when sex acts are reduced to names and cataloged. Intuition replaces
the dictionary, both undermining and replicating a nominalist fantasy of language. This dialectical reconfiguration—the radically
nominal and the putatively prelinguistic operating in and through
each other—reminds us of the somatic ground of the subject while
refusing to somehow isolate soma as something that resists language.
It is the parapractical performative within the denotative I have
sought since the beginning. The most complex of symbolic systems

gives voice to the most resolutely somatic impulses. As Adorno notes in the fragment on *Die Räuber* from *Minima Moralia* "something of this sexual crudity, this inability to make distinctions, animates the great speculative systems of Idealism" (*MM* 89).

Before going on to draw some tentative conclusions about further analysis suggested by my observations, I wish briefly to touch on the status of the anthropological in Adorno. As I observed above, his presentation of jitterbugging as an initiation ritual depends on the fusion of a notion of social labor and the notion of play: play (dance) has become a medium of work. Adorno is famously suspicious throughout the *Aesthetic Theory* of the Schillerian tradition that foregrounds play as the basis of aesthetic freedom. The moment of syncopation in jitterbugging—the repetitive gesture enacted in stumbling—in fact makes explicit what was always, for Adorno, the principle of play; namely, an atavistic and barbaric—ultimately infantile—compulsion to repeat. In jitterbugging, Adorno is concerned with the barbaric and infantile, as well as with disruptions of the temporal order. Syncopation, ultimately, is work done upon time. The significance of this fusion of play and work in Adorno's anthropology is made explicit again by Agamben, who uses Levi-Strauss's notion of hot and cold societies to argue that cold societies enlarge the sphere of ritual over and against the realm of play. Hot societies, on the other hand, are those in which play takes over from ritual. Yet both, in a way, are aiming for the abolition of history by folding it into one of the extremes. Agamben argues that: "we can hypothesize a relation of both correspondence and opposition between play and ritual, in the sense that both are engaged in a relationship with the calendar and with time, but this relationship is in each case an inverse one; ritual fixes and *structures* the calendar; play, on the other hand, though we do not yet know how and why, changes and *destroys* it."[17] Extrapolating from his sources, Agamben hypothesizes that "In play, man frees himself from sacred time and 'forgets' it in human time."[18] His argument is that play takes up the material of ritual and reworks it. He quotes Benveniste on the difference of ritual and myth:

> The potency of the sacred act resides precisely in the conjunction of the *myth* that articulates history and the *ritual* that reproduces it. If we make a comparison between this schema and that of play, the difference appears fundamental; in play only the ritual survives and all that is preserved is the *form* of the sacred drama, in which each element is re-

enacted time and again. But what has been forgotten or abolished is the myth, the meaningfully worded fabulation that endows the acts with their sense and their purpose.[19]

This distinction between myth and ritual is important for our consideration of Adorno because it locates "meaning" in the mythic and textual element that play refuses to acknowledge, that play abolishes in the moment of performance. The binaries of play and ritual—or play and myth—are, I have been suggesting, fused in Adorno's figure of the Jitterbug, where the work of play and the play of meaning can be parsed out only by undoing a unitary understanding of what the body is and operating with the heuristic terms of body and soma. Just as the Jitterbug suggests both subjected body and sub-/supersubjective soma, it also contains both ritual and play.

This work on history seems the most important direction in which we can take our consideration of body and soma in Adorno. I have argued that recent shifts in theories of the body—from text to soma—map the route one might need to follow. More pressing, however, is a formulation of a theory of language in Adorno that moves beyond the pre- and postlapsarian dichotomy that is replicated in many psychoanalytically-inflected theories of language. In regard to the question of foreign words and translation, I am struck by the tone of Adorno's fragment "On the Use of Foreign Words" in *Notes to Literature*.[20] Here we find him insisting that "a determined defense of the use of foreign words ... is valid only where it works toward a definite stand" (*NL* 286). And yet in the very next sentence—as if by a dialectical twist—we read that "in doing so it oversteps the bounds of defense." This definitive stand that simultaneously oversteps itself stumbles into a veritable explosion of the foreign within and against language: such is the linguistic operation effected by the somatic. Stumbling—if it is to have any significance at all—must be read as resistant to any historical or linguistic narrative organized around the moment of the Fall.

Much work could be done on Adorno's various pieces on the foreign word—with their curious ability to "operate beneath the sphere of culture but without fusing with the body of language" (*NL* 290), an attribution recalling the ambiguous status of soma qua body; or the essay "Wörter aus der Fremde" with its shift from a precocious homosocial friendship to a heterosexually eroticized "Exogamie der Sprache" (*NL* 112).[21] In "On the Use of Foreign Words" we could not be further removed from prelapsarian fantasies of a natural body or soma—as Adorno observes: "The customary defense of foreign words shares with purism the notion of language as something organic, despite the fact that each measures the life of language by a different rhythm. It was the nineteenth century that first consciously, with syncopation, interrupted that rhythm itself under the pressure of the individual and his autonomous expression … Now one can no longer trust in an organic growth of language that would continually assimilate foreign words" (*NL* 287). To return to the body, to stumble over foreign words, is not to hypostatize the organic or natural language. Bodies are never more bodily than when they are foreign, like the "foreign bodies assailing the body of language" (*NL* 288). Adorno's defense of the foreign word as a rupture in the ideology of the organic is directly linked to the development of "syncopation" in this passage—as if in acknowledgment of the, at least, latent critical possibilities of jazz as a musical form.

Just as Adorno and Horkheimer isolated the relationship of two types of body to two modes of history—"written history and the dark side which is overlooked"—so the foreign word demonstrates "two spheres of language" (*NL* 290) and a "sphere of culture" that resists "fusing with the body of language" (*NL* 290). The kind of body I have been trying to move toward is one that has not been fused. Somewhat uncharacteristically, perhaps, Adorno perceives its voice in "political jargon" and in "the slang of love … in which we may see the contours of a language to come that cannot be understood either in terms of the idea of the organic or in terms of education" (*NL* 290). In the end, then, the elaboration of a nondiscursive body—or soma—in Adorno, nevertheless returns us to language, a language that can contain—or expand to entertain—both. Finally, the two orders of history, and the two bodies, need to be thought alongside Adorno's "two spheres of language." Thus, an attentiveness to the somatic body by no means necessitates a turn away from the problematics of language; merely a resistance to the glib subjection of the body to the regime of discourse. The question, of course, is whether we possess the language necessary for thinking these new relations of body to language.

Notes

1. Martin Jay, "Adorno in America," *New German Critique* 31 (Winter 1984): 157-82.
2. Obituary, *New York Times*, Thursday, August 7, 1969.
3. I shall be using the capitalized form of [J]itterbug to denote the person dancing the jitterbug and the lowercase form to denote the dance itself.
4. Martin Jay, *Adorno* (Cambridge: Harvard University Press, 1984), 113.
5. Jay, *Adorno*, 88.
6. I use the terms rather loosely both to suggest and to hold at bay links to other discourses on the body—namely, Foucault, Lacan, Deleuze and Guattari. For a detailed consideration of these and other competing theories of the body, see Leslie A. Adelson, *Making Bodies, Making History* (Lincoln: Nebraska University Press, 1993).
7. Theodor Adorno, "On the Fetish Character in Music and the Regression of Listening," in *Frankfurt School Reader*, eds. Andrew Arato and Eike Gebhardt (New York: Continuum, 1988), 270-99, esp. 282. Subsequent references are made parenthetically in the text as *FSR*.
8. Max Horkheimer and Theodor W. Adorno, *The Dialectic of Enlightenment*, trans. John Cumming (New York: Continuum, 1987), 233. Subsequent references are made parenthetically in the text as *DoE*.
9. Works in this field are too numerous to note. Perhaps the most compelling in relation to the arguments advanced here is Monique David-Ménard, *Hysteria from Freud to Lacan: Body and Language in Psychoanalysis*, trans. Catherine Porter (Ithaca: Cornell University Press, 1989).
10. Hal Foster, *The Return of the Real: The Avant-Garde at the End of the Century* (Cambridge: MIT Press, 1996).
11. Schiller to Körner, Jena, 23 February 1793, *Schillers Briefe*, ed. Fritz Jonas, vol. iii (Stuttgart: Deutsche Verlagsanstalt, 1892-96), 285. Translated in F. Schiller, *On the Aesthetic Education of Man,* ed. and trans. Elizabeth M. Wilkinson and L.A. Willoughby (Oxford: Clarendon Press, 1967), 300.
12. Theodor W. Adorno, *Aesthetic Theory*, eds. Gretel Adorno and Rolf Tiedeman, trans. Robert Hullot-Kentor (London: Athlone, 1997), 317. Subsequent references are made parenthetically in the text as *AT*.
13. Theodor Adorno, *Minima Moralia: Reflections From Damaged Life* , trans. E.F.N. Jephcott (London: Verso, 1974), 36. Subsequent references are made parenthetically in the text as *MM*.
14. Giorgio Agamben, *Infancy and History: The Destruction of Experience*, trans. Liz Heron (London: Verso, 1993), 135. Subsequent references are made parenthetically in the text with *IH*.
15. Jay, *Adorno*, 52.
16. At this point we rejoin the dialectic of *Takt* outlined earlier. Thus, Adorno writes—in *Minima Moralia*—of an understandable social reaction against the hegemony of tact: "Individuals begin, not without reason, to react antagonistically to tact: a certain kind of politeness, for example, gives them less the feeling of being addressed as human beings, than an inkling of their inhuman conditions, and the polite run the risk of seeming impolite by continuing to exercise politeness as a superseded privilege. In the end emancipated, purely individual tact becomes mere lying ...." (*MM* 37). Likewise, it is precisely at

those textual moments where the operation of a prelinguistic desire becomes noticeable in and through language that the emergence of an abstract "On" becomes oppressively apparent also.

17. Agamben, 69.
18. Agamben, 70.
19. Agamben, 69-70. The footnoting in the English edition of *Infancy and History* is incorrect. Agamben is quoting from Benveniste's "Le jeu comme structure," *Deucalion* 2 (1947): 161-67, esp. 165.
20. Theodor W. Adorno, *Notes to Literature*, ed. Rolf Tiedeman, trans. Shierry Weber Nicholsen, vol. 2 (New York: Columbia UP, 1992), 286-91. Subsequent references are made parenthetically in the text with *NL*.
21. Theodor W. Adorno, "Wörter aus der Fremde," *Noten zur Literatur*, vol. II (Frankfurt am Main: Suhrkamp Verlag, 1961), 110-30, esp. 112. The implicit sexual history of this essay clearly invites comparison with similar yet radically different systems offered in writers such as Kristeva, for example.

Chapter 5

AESTHETIC POLITICS TODAY
Walter Benjamin and Post-Fordist Culture[1]

Lutz Koepnick

There should be little doubt that one of the most enduring legacies of Critical Theory is its inquiry into the aesthetic dimensions of power. In particular Walter Benjamin's notion of aesthetic politics—formulated as a critique of the spectacular fusion of modern technologies and antimodern ideologies in European fascism—has come to occupy a privileged place within the postwar pantheon of cultural criticism. Thanks to Benjamin, it has become a truism to say that one cannot speak of fascism without speaking about the role of the aesthetic, about the beautification of political infrastructures, and about the translation of decadent idioms of nineteenth-century art into a mesmerizing language of power. In fact, isolated quotes from Benjamin's artwork essay have been canonized not only to verify global claims about the nature of fascism, but also to indicate the way in which postfascist societies either replay fascism as myth and movie, or displace the disenchanted routines of procedural politics with captivating spectacles. According to this understanding, fascism is unthinkable without a formal language of seduction. As a Wagnerian drama of total synthesis, fascism explores aesthetic resources so as to promote a tyranny of decadent art over modern politics.

Unlike Max Horkheimer and Theodor W. Adorno, whose *Dialectic of Enlightenment* primarily stresses the manipulation of the masses by the agents of private capital,[2] Benjamin's aestheticization thesis intends to think through the more explicitly political dimensions of twentieth-century mass culture, how mass mediated diversion could play into the hands of state power, or, alternatively, offer resources to challenge the state's coordination of mass culture. In Benjamin's view, fascism shapes mass cultural practice for its own political ends. Relying on a state-controlled culture industry, fascism employs postautonomous art and distraction for its projects of national rejuvenation and total mobilization. On the other hand, what Benjamin—strangely ignoring the Stalinist variants of aestheticized politics—calls "communism" symbolizes an emancipatory version of industrial culture. Communism renders the popular a politically relevant site at which people can appropriate the symbolic materials of mass culture in order to articulate them into their everyday lives, to negotiate intersubjective meanings, and thus to partake actively of the construction of individual and collective identities.

In Benjamin's view, fascism interrupts the dialectics between aesthetic and popular modernism, between avant-garde art and industrial culture. It fuses premodern sentiments with modern machines in order to foil the democratic power of the popular and, ultimately, to eliminate whatever is potentially subversive about the avant-garde. Political aestheticization is the logical result of this double suspension. Aesthetic politics proposes to move the state beyond bourgeois-democratic codes of legality, morality, and political emancipation. Driven by the idea of pure politics, of "Great Politics," fascist aestheticization exploits modern mass culture in order to consolidate the state against the ever increasing diffusion of power, to decouple political action from normative debates, and to undo the emasculating effects of procedural politics. It seeks to redefine the political as the site at which nothing less than authenticity comes into being.

But, for Benjamin, to speak of aesthetic politics does not simply mean to address a shrewd stylization of political action, a seductive organization of public signs, meanings, and iconographies. Instead, aesthetic politics sets out to control the structures of modern sense perception, shattering the older bonds of solidarity and instating some new kind of sutured community. The fascist spectacle mobilizes people's feelings primarily to neutralize their senses, massaging minds and emotions so that the individual succumbs to the charisma of vitalistic power. Similar to the way in which the *l'art pour l'art*, in its protest against the commodification of nineteenth-century art, severed all links between art and social life, fascism aims to redefine politics as an autonomous realm of absolute self-referentiality that privileges cultic forms over ethical norms. Although explicitly directed against the institutionalization of multiple centers of domination in modernity, aesthetic politics in Benjamin's view thus pursues its own project of differentiation, autonomization, and modernization. Fascism marshals mechanical reproduction to sanctify resolute leadership as a self-sufficient force, an auratic presence. In its most extreme formulation, Benjamin's aestheticization thesis, in fact, suggests that fascism happens whenever postauratic cultures manufacture aura synthetically with the intention to discipline distraction, coordinate perception, and mystify power. Fascist aesthetics, in the concept's original meaning, is anaesthetic—it assaults and neutralizes the senses and denies the human body as an autonomous site of desire and corporeal pleasure.[3]

Seen from our own vantage point, Benjamin's taxation of Fordist visuality and the synthetic aura of fascism remains challenging and, to say the least, provocative. In our present era of global media networks, visual culture has already surpassed the task Benjamin envisioned as the utopian charge of postauratic culture, the assumption that mechanical reproduction—film and photography—would burst the spatial and temporal coordinates of experience "by the dynamite of the tenth of a second, so that now, in the midst of its far-flung ruins and debris, we calmly and adventurously go traveling."[4] For today's couch potatoes and Web surfers, Benjamin's shock of spatial-temporal displacement constitute a daily livingroom routine. Individuals, as much as nations today, articulate their agendas, memories, and identities in response to values and passions that are increasingly formed through far-traveled images. What Benjamin in 1936 associated with emancipatory and communist cultural practices has ironically transformed into a banality: ubiquitous audiences constantly consuming transnational commodities.

On the other hand, however, it is questionable whether the multiplication of viewing positions in our age of digital reproduction has really eliminated aura, a process Benjamin attributed to film and photography. Does one not observe ubiquitous attempts to resurrect—in Hans Jürgen Syberberg's words—"with the means of contemporary technology a new aura"[5]? Can one still rely on Benjamin's dichotomy of auratic and postauratic art if postmodern culture, while emphatically endorsing technologies of temporal fragmentation and spatial stretching, is obsessed with the recreation of auratic art in mega-exhibitions and spectacular traveling shows? Does the popular adoration of events such as Christo's *Wrapped Reichstag*,[6] the mythic temptations of an Anselm Kiefer,[7] or the orchestrated proliferation of aura as special effect in Hollywood films, such as Alex Proyas's *Dark City* (1998), represent a new strain of aestheticization? Or does this ironic triumph of aura over distraction relegate Benjamin's modernist critique of auratic revivals to the dustbin of intellectual history?

In what follows I hope to give some answers to these questions, thereby reconsidering what the current industry surrounding Benjamin often takes for granted: the actuality of the aestheticization thesis for postmodern consumer culture. Benjamin's original argument, I suggest, relied on a number of reductive theoretical assumptions and empirical observations, which undermine the viability of Benjamin's overall critique of aesthetic politics, modern or postmodern. Some of Benjamin's key categories, I shall argue, ignored the multifacetedness of modern culture while at the same time consummating, rather than critically depicting, the historical processes of Benjamin's own time. Yet, as I will also propose, it is precisely by both historicizing and dialecticizing Benjamin's notions of aura, perception, and modern mass culture, and by thus rearticulating latent aspects of Benjamin's own reflections, that the continued relevance of Benjamin's aestheticization thesis to our own age may be revealed. In order to do so, I shall first revisit Benjamin's theory of experience and film in light of the arguments of some of his most insightful critics. Second, I shall examine postmodern interfaces between technology, identity, and the popular dimension in order to better illuminate the altered function of auratic sentiments in contemporary culture. Finally, I shall indicate what contemporary criticism can still learn from the aestheticization thesis even if the relationships between politics, sense perception, and culture today fundamentally differ from the peculiar configuration Benjamin sought to identify during 1930s.

I

A term only inadequately captured by the English "experience," the category of *Erfahrung* is at the heart of Benjamin's entire critical program. It links his metaphysical work from the 1910s to his final theology of history in 1940. Explicitly opposed to instrumentalist, scientific, or positivistic definitions of experience, Benjamin elaborates his concept along both spatial and temporal vectors at once. Experience mediates an individual's perception to collective patterns of cognition and material modalities of production, transportation, and information; experience articulates conflicting temporalities, including those of utopian promises and historical memory, of conscious and unconscious acts of recollection and remembrance. In his early metaphysical phase prior to 1920, Benjamin at certain points seemed to imply that humanity's postlapsarian embrace of history, reflection, and language itself already marked the end of experience proper.[8] Only children retain something of the paradisiacal plentitude of experience, because only children can see the world without imposing intellectual cross-references and deadening distinctions; only children possess the uncorrupted imaginative activity that can see objects with "a pure mood, without thereby sacrificing the world."[9]

In the course of the 1930s, however, in particular in the artwork essay and the study on Baudelaire, Benjamin fundamentally rethinks and historicizes his earlier metaphysics of experience: he claims that the fundamental restructuring of temporal and spatial relations in modernity—i.e., the adaptation of the human senses to urban traffic and industrial modes of production—undermines the conditions for what he then terms auratic experience. Defined as a quasi-magic perception of an object invested "with the capability of returning the gaze,"[10] aura withers in modernity. Taylorism, industrial mass production, and urbanization render obsolete any spatial-temporal enchantment with a unique phenomenon, displacing auratic experience with the modern regimes of distraction.

Film, for Benjamin, is both symptom and agent of this transformation. It extends the thrust of social changes to the arenas of cultural exchange and aesthetic expression. Accordingly, the shock of cinematic montage emancipates cultural practices not only from auratic sentiments but from aesthetic experience altogether; it links cultural formulations—for (communist) better or (fascist) worse—directly to political projects. As a postaesthetic counterpart to the shifting grounds of collective perception, Benjamin's cinema, at first sight, no longer allows for moments of profane illumination, for the magic spell of the mimetic faculty, or for a reciprocal interaction between humanity and nature. A training ground for distracted modes of reception and cultural appropriation, Benjamin's cinema seems to offer not visual pleasure, but rather rational insight and critical debate, scientific examination and political self-representation. Cinema emancipates modern society from ritual, tradition, and the bourgeois cult of art at the cost of severing the individual from memory, nonintentionality, and playful mimesis, from the ecstasy of retrieving an unknown past, and from the bridging of the gap between subject and object that established spontaneous and noncoercive relations to the world.

It has often been observed not only that Benjamin overestimated the emancipatory potential of postauratic visuality, but also that his political appropriation of cinema remained pseudoradical because it assumed all-too close affinities between the modes of rationalized industrial production and the peculiar principles of mass cultural reception and experience.[11] A modality of experience after the end of experience proper, Benjamin's category of distraction, as a consequence, "elides—and all too readily surrenders—the regressive aspects of the cinema, its mobilizing of pre-rational mental processes, and thus unwittingly joins the long tradition of bourgeois rationality that asserts itself in the containment and exclusion of the other, of sensuality and femininity."[12] Benjamin's theory of modern disenchantment and visuality undermines the very position it seeks to emphasize. To the extent to which the category of distraction glosses over potential gaps between ideological uses of cinema mandated from above, and the often unpredictable ways in which actual viewers—positioned in historically contingent viewing situations—make use of the specific viewing event, Benjamin inhibits any thorough understanding of how a film makes its entry into the spectator's head and how cinema's symbolic materials might be consumed according to very different needs and agendas. In other words, Benjamin's celebratory use of the category of distraction impedes understanding cinema as a trading place of insight and articulation, as a proletarian public sphere that negotiates the concreteness of human experience across dominant demarcations of public and private. Though meant to offer a site of critical exchange and cultural empowerment, Benjamin's postauratic auditorium is populated by spectators who have nothing left to see or say. Denying the masses' auratic experience, aesthetic play, and sensual pleasure, Benjamin risks leaving the individual's emotional needs to be used and abused by the political enemies, a position paramount within the German Left circa 1930 and critiqued most forcefully by Benjamin's contemporary Ernst Bloch.

What is equally striking about Benjamin's theory of film is that Benjamin, though writing almost a decade after the introduction of the talkies, completely ignores how the advent of synchronized sound changed film exhibition, style, and consumption, how it permitted new patterns of identification and increasingly standardized perception. Part of a long-standing tradition of film scholarship, Benjamin's elaborations on film are exclusively image-centered; they disregard the way in which diegetic and nondiegetic sound can reinforce, complicate, or even subvert the work of a film's image track. Moreover, Benjamin's judgments about the power of moving images echo negative attitudes toward the visual, shaped in German intellectual life during the eighteenth century.[13] Benjamin favors Soviet montage cinema because montage allegedly disrupts the deceptive veneer of images and their appeal to merely emotive registers of reception. Montage transforms images into text. It keeps in check the affective force of the visual, renders it discursive, and thereby infuses our ways of looking with the critical—and, one might suspect, more respectable—power of hermeneutic reading. To avow—like "communism" in the artwork essay—distracted, readerly looking as the center piece of modern perception means for Benjamin to empower the collective to make history.

Given such curious short cuts in Benjamin's comments on film and aura, it should come as no surprise that even some of Benjamin's closest intellectual allies challenged the conceptual centerpiece of Benjamin's interlaced theory of film and the aestheticization of politics. Rigorously questioning Benjamin's radical dismissal of aura and aesthetic experience, Adorno insisted that auratic elements clearly survived the arrival of a full-fledged culture of mechanical reproduction in the twentieth century. According to Adorno, aura not only persists in the riddles of enigmatic modernism but also—in however perverted a form—in mass culture's ruthless unity of high and low, that is to say, in the culture industry's attempt to reconcile the fault lines of modern culture "by absorbing light into serious art, or vice versa."[14] Adorno and Benjamin clearly agreed that modern technology had moved art beyond its former magic and aura, but, contrary to Benjamin, Adorno insisted that modernist art, in spite of its anti-auratic impulses, remained aesthetic.[15] Challenging the ever-increasing standardization of cultural expressions under organized capitalism, the best works of aesthetic modernism, in Adorno's view, evidenced a dialectical relationship to both bourgeois art and industrial culture and therefore retained aspects of the very magical aura they sought to supersede. For Adorno, Benjamin's category of postauratic distraction, on the other hand, falsely and undialectically heroized fragmentation and commodity fetishism as strategies of cultural empowerment and subversion. Benjamin's distracted poachers of modern culture, Adorno believed, simply reproduce the culture industry's ideology of pseudoindividualization—that is to say, its "halo of free choice" on the basis of standardization itself.[16] In Adorno's view, Benjamin's account of film excluded any critical stance toward the commodification of cultural practices while Benjamin's praise of postauratic inattentiveness undercuts the possibility of conceiving of semantic unity as a repository of determined negation and resistance. Far from liberating humankind from the authority of tradition and ritual, distraction transforms disconnected parts into fetishes in front of which "consumers become temple slaves."[17]

Even during the last years of his life, when cautiously applauding the emerging New German Cinema for its disruption of hegemonic meaning, Adorno remained highly skeptical about Benjamin's optimistic denigration of auratic images and experiences. Experimental auteur directors such as Alexander Kluge, Adorno argued, might capitalize on the fact that the culture industry may itself contain antidotes to its own ideology, yet at the same time, such directors bring into focus the fact that Benjamin failed "to elaborate on how deeply some of the categories he postulated for film—exhibition, test—are imbricated with the commodity character which his theory opposes."[18] Benjamin's disenchanted realism—though dedicated to the enterprise of scientifically penetrating the phenomenal surface of the object world—remains a romantic endeavor. In contrast to modernist art's protest against universal commodification, Benjamin's postauratic representation fails to expose the reification that reigns at the bottom of reality and its mass cultural reproduction: "Every meaning—including critical meaning—which the camera eye imparts to the film would already invalidate the law of the camera and thus violate Benjamin's taboo, conceived as it was with the explicit purpose of outdoing the provocative Brecht and thereby—this may have been its secret purpose—gaining freedom from him."[19]

Adorno defended auratic residues against Benjamin's artwork essay because he resisted Benjamin's undialectical equation of auratic and autonomous art, of technological progress, and of the end of experience. Unlike Benjamin, Adorno in fact sensed a precarious complicity between, on the one hand, the philosophical denigration of auratic experience and, on the other, the industrial transformation of perception and the logic of commodity fetishism. In Adorno's perspective, Benjamin was pushing through a historical development that was still very much in dialectical process; he considered Benjamin's depiction of aura and cinema undialectical because Benjamin's key categories tried to consummate the historical process rather than depicting its constitutive tensions and ambiguities. Played out in the hermetic realm of autonomous art, mimetic experience and art's semblance of subjectivity were to lodge Adorno's desperate protest against the blunting of critical meaning and the disciplining of pleasure administered by twentieth-century mass culture.

In her recent Joyless Streets,[20] Patrice Petro has provided ample historical evidence in order to illustrate Adorno's critique of Benjamin's account of postauratic visuality. In contrast to Benjamin, Petro suggests that we should not—as Benjamin wanted to have it—understand the demolition of aura through cinema as an effect of cinematic technology per se, but rather of historically dominant film practices and the systematic marginalization of alternative forms of spectatorship. Petro argues that when Benjamin recasts modern experience and spectatorship as a paradigm shift from aura to distraction, he explains away the factual diversity of spectatorial practices in early cinema and thus ignores the historical manifold of modern culture. Most importantly, he completely elides the gender specificity of early cinematic forms of address and consumption— particularly the parallel existence of distracted and concentrated, industrialized and emotionally attentive modes of looking. While Benjamin's category of distraction might indeed encode the experience of those permitted to participate in the processes of social and cultural modernization since the middle of the nineteenth century, it obscures the structures of experience of those who, owing to given landscapes of power, remained at the margins of these processes, in particular women. Female spectatorship, especially during the 1920s, was often at odds with the kind of principles Benjamin presented as a universal ontology of cinematic communication. Highly popular in Weimar cinema as a "female" genre, the melodrama bears testimony to forms of spectatorship different from those described by Benjamin under the rubric of distraction and inattentive, detached appropriation. "For male intellectuals," Petro adds, "who experienced the demise of poetic forms with the advent of cinema, the film melodrama may have in fact entailed disinterestedness and detachment, but for female audiences, who were only just beginning to be addressed as spectators, the film melodrama almost certainly provoked an intensely interested and emotional involvement, particularly since melodramatic representation often gave heightened expression to women's experience of modernity."[21] In the context of the 1920s melodrama, then, mechanical reproduction also addresses those for whom distraction has not become the norm, whose "concentrated gaze involves a perceptual activity that is neither passive nor entirely distracted,"[22] and therefore those who desire what Benjamin would label the aura of contemplative identification and emotional intensity. Though increasingly eclipsed by the industry's attempt to shape a unified spectatorial subject, the "woman's film" demonstrates the historical possibility of an emancipatory or at least empowering aura on the grounds of mass culture itself, a nonantagonistic coexistence of mechanical reproduction and auratic perception.

Both Adorno and Petro agree that Benjamin's theory of experiential exhaustion in modernity cannot account for the survival or discontinuous return of aura in twentieth-century art and mass culture. Due to both theoretical and empirical overgeneralizations, Benjamin simplifies historical developments and thereby provides an inaccurate image of the multifaceted position of auratic experience in modern culture. Understanding cinema's role primarily as a functional agent and symptom of modern disenchantment, Benjamin not only undermines the very kind of categories that energize his overall criticism of modern culture, including his studies of surrealism, nineteenth-century flânerie, Baudelaire, and Kafka. As he inseparably mixes theoretical, historical, and normative lines of argumentation, Benjamin also implies all-too undialectical, and, hence misleading, links between the persistence of aura and the aestheticization of politics, between fascism and the resurgence of aesthetic experience in mass culture. Instead of understanding modernity in terms of a differentiation of competing modes of looking and cultural consumption, Benjamin—understandably eager to denounce the ways in which fascism musters aura and the irrational to engineer political homogeneity—fuses the complexity of modern spectatorship into a rather monolithic cast himself. In doing so, the artwork essay renders the effects of historical contingencies as "natural" facts; it mistakes a peculiar formation of visual culture and spectatorship for the ontology of the media.

Given these blind spots in Benjamin's theory of film and the politics of scopic pleasure, it appears timely to revisit the argument of the artwork essay and search for alternative or less monolithic accounts of auratic and postauratic visuality. After all, it is unlikely that Benjamin could have so drastically forfeited his self-proclaimed aim of dialectical thought without leaving behind numerous traces of containment or repression. Reading Benjamin against the grain of his iconoclastic posture, Miriam Hansen has shown that the artwork essay indeed contains a number of allusions to mimetic experience and auratic figuration. Suggesting that "the cinema's role in relation to experiential impoverishment could go beyond merely promoting and consummating the historical process,"[23] Hansen proposes that what are often seen as the essay's most pseudoscientific pronouncements contain building blocks for an alternative theory of vision in the age of mechanical reproduction. Benjamin's comments, on the one hand, about the tactile, ballistic, and hence, anti-illusionary thrust of film, and, on the other, about the photographic image's quasi-Freudian "optical unconscious," allow Hansen to reconsider Benjamin's wholesale denigration of aura. In doing so, Hansen not only helps to redialecticize Benjamin's key categories of aura and experience, she also discovers a more discrete evaluation of the differential gestalt of modern culture in terms of Benjamin's artwork essay itself—an evaluation which, I suggest, outrules any rash and ahistorical equation of postauratic aura and fascist aesthetics.

First of all, there is good reason to conceive of what Benjamin terms the tactile dimension of film as a mimetic figuration of the fragmented and atomized structure of modern existence and not simply as a catalyst of discursive insight and truth. "Being based on changes of place and focus which periodically assail the spectator,"[24] cinematic editing administers visceral shocks to the viewer, which allow for a sensuous, somatic relationship to what is seen on screen. A source of visual attractions and visceral astonishments, film results in a radical displacement of self in sentience; it takes us outside of ourselves like the ways in which a child "not only plays at being a grocer or teacher, but also at being a windmill or a train."[25] In the same way Kracauer endorses distraction as a sensuous "reflection of the uncontrolled anarchy of our world,"[26] Benjamin valorizes the ballistic qualities of film because they involve a mimetic component that clearly exceeds the bounds of Brechtian aesthetics of cognitive distantiation and discursive truth. Though hostile to the spatial dimension of auratic distance, Benjamin's cinematic image retains something of aura's temporality—it is powerful enough to actualize a prehistoric stratum of human practice. Film bestows upon the viewer the experience of quasi-magic, "primitivist" contact, a preconceptual and sensory form of knowing that resembles the infant's attempt to know an object by eating it.

Secondly, residues of auratic experience may also legitimately enter into postauratic film practice through the backdoor of what Benjamin calls the optical unconscious and the equipment-free aspect of the cinematic image. With the help of the optical unconscious, Benjamin admits dimensions into his theory of postauratic representation and spectatorship that clearly contradict his overall emphasis on presence, tracelessness, expertism, and radical distraction. Far from solely indicating an utterly disenchanting rationalization of vision, Benjamin's equation of camera work and Freudian psychoanalysis hints at film's capacity to authorize an unprecedented mimesis of technology and nature, "a thoroughgoing permeation of reality with mechanical equipment."[27] Because the camera pierces quotidian surfaces with its peculiar technologies of representation while tending to make its own work invisible, film is capable of ushering the spectator into the realms of profane illumination, into an arena of flashlike, nonintentional, and sensuous cognition similar to the one that Benjamin unearthed in the Surrealists, in Baudelaire, and in the context of his own experiments with drugs and intoxication. Cinema may, after all, allow for forms of reciprocity reminiscent of the experience of auratic phenomena: the optical unconscious rearticulates for the era of mechanical reproduction what in Romantic philosophy empowered nature to return the gaze.

All things considered, then, Benjamin's thesis about the visceral wonders of modern vision is more ambiguous and dialectical than it may at first seem. The advent of the filmic image does not elicit from Benjamin a condemnation of all auratic experience as complicit with authority, traditionalism, and political mystification.

Understood as an unsettling counterpoint to dominant film practices, a cinema that returns the gaze could also counteract the instrumental rationality and temporal fragmentation Benjamin's indicts all-too quickly and homogeneously as the signatures of modern life. While the surgical, permeating devices of film and the spatial-temporal displacements of mechanical reproduction clearly participate in the destruction of the aura of first nature, of the halo that surrounds natural presences and wonders, film's mimetic powers—its physiognomic mode of signification and its indebtedness to what Tom Gunning calls the cinema of attraction[28]—may at the same time map a second nature as a dimension of profane illumination. Therein they enable modes of spectatorship that escape the deadening grasp of reification Adorno saw at the bottom of Benjamin's theory of film: "If the mimetic capacities of film were put to such use, it would not only fulfill a critical function but also a redemptive one, registering sediments of experience that are no longer or not yet claimed by social and economic rationality, making them readable as emblems of a 'forgotten future.'"[29]

To bring into focus the artwork essay's discontinuous reinscription of aura and mimesis in and through film thus allows us to reconsider Benjamin's understanding of modern culture as differential and internally contested, as an ambiguous process rather than a finished product. Moreover, rectifying what both Adorno and Petro, from very different perspectives, vehemently oppose in Benjamin, Hansen's historicized and dialecticized notion of auratic experience makes it possible to demystify Benjamin's mysterious concept of aura itself. It allows one to free the aura from the suspicion that any return of auratic moments would inevitably result in a political coordination of perception and a concomitant mystification of power—that is to say, in aesthetic politics and fascism. If even Benjamin himself observes the survival of mimetic elements within postauratic visual practices, then it would be foolish to construe all rearticulations of aura and mimesis in the twentieth century as a replay of fascist media politics. To be sure, fascism elicits auratic experiences through postauratic means in order to relocate decadent aesthetic values to the arena of political action, to entertain the masses with the imagery of autonomous politics, and to provide a unifying product image for a heterogeneous ideological commodity; fascist mass culture appeals to utopian elements in auratic experiences in order to bond the individual to a charismatic project of national rebirth and pure politics. But because Benjamin's optical unconscious itself can offer valuable residues of auratic experiences, there is no conceptual reason why aura could not play a role in critical visual practices that challenge fascism's politicization of the bourgeois cult of art or the ever-increasing fragmentation of lifeworlds in modernity.

Aura, its decay, and its return are fundamentally ambivalent categories even in Benjamin's highly overdetermined philosophy of history and media aesthetics. The political value of aura therefore cannot be understood by means of universalizing theoretical or formalistic arguments. To suspect today that any postauratic return of aura would regress immediately to detrimental political effects is clearly off the mark. It would fall prey to the same kind of formalism and aestheticism Benjamin was so eager to overthrow, and it would also overlook the fact that postmodern culture involves circuits of cultural dissemination and strategies of consumption fundamentally different from the one at the core of fascist mass culture. Neither today's politics of commodification nor its commodification of politics directly duplicates what Benjamin sought to expose as the origin of fascist aestheticization. To discuss crucial differences, and thus to open up a framework in which it becomes possible to talk in a meaningful and differentiated way about the political uses and abuses of auratic experience under the condition of postmodernity, will be the task of the final two sections of this essay. If the preceding pages have sought to reconsider Benjamin's account of the politics of aura within Benjamin's own times, the following remarks shall ask whether a more discriminating understanding of Benjamin's formulas can also entertain the major historical shift from modern to postmodern culture. If the above pages have tried to reconstruct a more refined relationship between theory and historical process in Benjamin's work itself, the final sections of this essay shall inquire into the extent to which we can apply Benjamin's theory to our contemporary technoculture.

II

David Harvey has suggested that the postmodern represents a break with Fordist modes of standardized mass production and mass consumption, modes that were central to Benjamin's understanding of the role of aura in the age of mechanical reproduction. In Harvey's perspective, postmodernity introduces "flexible accumulation" as the hegemonic principle of capitalist reproduction; postmodern societies are "characterized by more flexible labour processes and markets, [by] geographical mobility and rapid shifts in consumption practices."[30] Inaugurated circa 1970, this new post-Fordist phase of capitalist accumulation brings forth the emergence of highly diversified sectors of production: unstable, heterogeneous markets and heated cycles of innovations. It also entails a new series of space-time compressions that shrink the temporal and spatial horizons of experience, and, in so doing, spread decision-making processes over an ever-more global, variegated, and accelerated space. As a result, post-Fordist societies observe the advent of new modalities of individualized and highly diversified commodity consumption. However ambiguous in nature, flexible accumulation cannot succeed without equipping individual consumers with a new kind of market authority that supersedes the standardized practices of Fordist mass consumption.

Fordist mass culture offered little choice between different media channels or offerings and thereby produced a relatively homogenous community of viewers or consumers, no matter how atomized they may have been. Fordist consumerism carried the burden of providing an always precarious mythology of social integration and democratic egality: it offered the image of a unified population pursuing the same goals and hunting for the same objects of desire. By way of contrast, post-Fordist culture is characterized by hybrid multimedia aggregates and diversified strategies of consumption. Confronted with technologically mediated processes of temporal and spatial stretching, the relatively predictable consumer of Fordist mass culture metamorphoses into a symbolic poacher who seizes heterogeneous materials from different times and spaces, takes position in multiple temporalities at once, and assumes protean positionalities. Post-Fordist technoculture grafts the principle of flexible accumulation onto the exchange and acquisition of symbolic materials. In so doing, it tends to nullify what allowed the individual to experience Fordist consumer societies as imagined communities. Cultural technologies such as VCRs or Walkmans, fast forward buttons or digital cameras, explode the assumptions about homogenous time and space that were central to the ideological effects of Fordist mass media; they point toward the arrival of a new kind of consumer whose continual selections result in a highly individualized (and commodified) use of an eminently diverse media landscape.

Benjamin understood Fordist mass culture as a catalyst for new forms of cultural authority: the newspaper boy who discussed the outcome of a bicycle race, for Benjamin, indicated the advent of a culture of experts thriving on Fordist mass media's satisfying of "modern man's legitimate claim to being reproduced."[31] In the age of the flexible accumulation of images, Benjamin's participatory utopia of cultural empowerment seems to have come to full fruition. Not only does one find oneself as an object of visual or digital reproduction, one also seems to be in greater control over some of technology and other means that allow cultural consumers to shape identities and self-representations. Expertism, in fact, has become a prerequisite of cultural survival today. Consumers need to know how to manipulate sophisticated technologies and traverse various media channels at once; they need to know how to reduce complexity and to forget about alternative offerings while consuming a specific options.[32] Yet, even if postmodern culture thus seems to require us to become experts in Benjamin's sense, it is not difficult to see that our contemporary life on screen fundamentally differs from the kind of images and identities Benjamin hoped to see expertly circulated on the screens of Fordist mass culture. Experts surfing the World Wide Web furnish their homes and network identities by fusing diverse materials, genres, styles, and idioms of expression into one intrinsically decentered and infinite hypertext. In other words, postmodern technoculture couples its new forms of cultural authority to a multiplication of identities and viewing positions that supersede the unified identity of Benjamin's newspaper boy fascinated with proletarian spectator sports.

Fordist concepts of cultural production, consumption, and reception, therefore, will no longer suffice in theorizing how individuals now make use of media channels and the pluralization of modes of expression. If the concept of postmodernism is meant to signify more than a new aesthetic paradigm, then it ought to bring into view precisely what is different about the conditions of individual experience and the institutions of cultural consumption today, i.e., to conceptualize the relationship between the emergence of highly strategic practices of symbolic appropriation, the progressive decentering and multiplication of identity, and the changes in the global economic system that make us live in a permanent elsewhere and elsewhen. Postmodern criticism, however, often overlooks possible complicities between, on the one hand, today's flexible accumulation of hybrid identities, and, on the other, the ways in which Western capitalism works on a global and local scale. Instead, it often heroizes the centrifugal force of post-Fordist societies as part of a subversive and "fantastic unbinding of cultures, forms of life, styles, and world perspectives,"[33] glossing over the fact that local acts of cultural empowerment do not necessarily result in inclusive articulations of experience or agency. One should keep in mind that no carnivalistic unbinding of fixed traditions, unified identities, or Fordist media practices per se will yield the emancipatory effects many theorists attest to technoculture's exploding of pre-postmodern space, experience, and meaning. If the multiplication of cultural identities should not lead to a cacophony of highly fragmented image bits and sound bites, but rather help enable politically relevant processes of collective will-formation, then what is needed instead is the formation of public and counter public spheres that mediate between the global and the local, between the by-no-means synchronized forces of cultural, political, and economic stretching. In other words, only if the post-Fordist refraction of culture is linked to a successful institutionalization of infrastructures that calibrate the conflicting dimensions of globalization,[34] only then will it be possible to safeguard forms of solidarity that can really empower individual and collective agents to master our kaleidoscopic age of digital reproduction.

It is interesting to note, in this context, that in many instances the contemporary desire for auratic experiences expresses nothing more than the hope for structures of mediation that negotiate the global and the local, that restore meaningful hierarchies to the exploded topographies of postmodern culture, that secure forms of individual agency and mimetic nonintentionality—and that thus remedy the loss of memory in our fantastically unbound culture of channel surfers. Whether cultivated in contemporary museum practices, the digital airlifting of nineteenth-century opera, or the wrapping of political monuments, postmodern aura suggests that the anarchic freedom of global poachers remains imaginary if they fail to develop an ethos of significance, i.e., individual and collective structures of valorization that allow situated subjects to distinguish among narratives, images, sounds, and symbols of lesser and of greater importance. While having been utterly absorbed into the circuits of commodified culture and digital information, aura today often signifies the thoroughly paradoxical quest for a return of the real,[35] a critical outcry against ever-more inclusive scenarios of simulation. As it aims at a transitory reenchantment of human perception and object relations, a discontinuous reinscription of aura can remind us of our deepest need for experience and sensuality in its most emphatic sense. It probes the economic and cultural hegemony of flexible accumulation, expressing residual opposition to the devaluation of objects under global commodification. At a time when post-Fordist capitalist relations simultaneously shrink and expand the spatial-temporal dimensions of our lifeworlds in an unprecedented manner, the reinvention of auratic experiences offers a "testing ground for reflections on temporality and subjectivity, identity and alterity."[36] Aura today may bring into focus that a life without memory and without the thick materiality of sentient experience is not a life at all. It can open our eyes for the fact that armchair voyages through hyperspace may ironically imprison meaning and freedom in an iron cage of false empowerment, which will provide a new form of pseudoindividualization. Resisting the dematerialization and detemporalization of experience in postmodernity, auratic residues remind us that radically heterogeneous spaces and conflicting temporalities will liberate us from oppressive traditions and monolithic identities, only, if we relate the symbolic material of diverse cultures to the experience of sentient bodies and the materiality of everyday practice.

III

Given the vicissitudes of auratic experience under the postmodern condition of flexible accumulation, then, there are good reasons to believe that Benjamin's critique of aura and the aestheticization of politics today no longer provides what it originally was meant to offer. As I have argued above, we cannot overlook radical changes in the organization of experience separating us from Benjamin's time and reasoning. Whether they concern transformations in the production and social function of auratic perception, the impact on today's media channels on the formation of cultural authority, or global capitalism's strategies of commodification, these historical differences, I would argue, should caution us not to draw any direct parallels between the role of aura in the 1990s and its contribution to what Benjamin called the aestheticization of politics, i.e., fascism. Thanks to fundamentally different modes of how one looks and of how one assumes subject positions in the fields of visual culture, a postauratic refurbishing of aura must result in quite different political effects than under the rule of Fordist mass culture. The point, however, is not to check Benjamin into the Grand Hotel Abyss of modernist theory,[37] but rather to investigate what can be redeemed of Benjamin for our own times—that is to say, how can we see ourselves in his critique of modern culture and how can we envision his role under the postmodern conditions of flexible accumulation. Is Benjamin's aestheticization thesis, then, still relevant? What exactly should the artwork essay teach us today?

According to Benjamin's peculiar understanding, historical materialism—as applied to the realm of aesthetic theory—inquires into the technical and economic conditions motivating our attitudes toward beauty.[38] What we consider beautiful is, Benjamin suggests, a matter of historical contingencies. It reflects changing structures of experience, of the modes in which technologies of reproduction inflect our ways of seeing, feeling, remembering, knowing, and dreaming. Benjamin's artwork essay theorized perceptions of beauty in an age of Fordist mass production and consumption. The aestheticization thesis was intended to analyze the political instrumentality of nineteenth-century conceptions of beauty as a means of integrating the Fordist masses into fascism. It hoped to conceptualize how fascism feeds on changing attitudes toward auratic and mimetic experience to carry out its counterrevolutionary projects of warfare and national rebirth.

Benjamin's materialist insistence on the historicity of aesthetic experience should alert us not to apply his terminology in an unmediated fashion to our post-Fordist age of flexible accumulation. Neither contemporary structures of sensual perception nor those of recollection are identical with those that Benjamin believed to be at the center of the fascist spectacle. To be sure, as I have argued earlier, Benjamin's notion of experience is clearly too narrow (and too gender biased) to count as fully valid even for the period he himself sought to examine. His original thesis about the decay of aura appears too monolithic to explicate the diverse and competing registers of seeing and experience that mark the modern condition.

But, in spite of such conceptual bottlenecks, it is precisely his emphasis on the historically specific organization of individual pleasure and collective perception that provides us with a strong argument to counter both revisionist reconstructions of fascist aesthetics as mere style, representation, or iconography[39] as well as to resist impetuous portrayals of contemporary visual culture and aura as uncanny relatives of the fascist public sphere. In many respects much more of a critical historicist than he was willing to admit, Benjamin himself urges us to understand notions such as fascist aesthetics and political aestheticization in their historical context. Instead of inflating Benjamin's conceptual apparatus and speculating about what else might be fascist besides fascism, one fares much better if one employs his tools of criticism for the purpose of better understanding what exactly was considered beautiful under fascism—and by whom.

Such cautionary use, however, is by no means meant to strip Benjamin of his actuality. Even if our structures of experience have undergone crucial changes since the 1930s, it is in Benjamin's emphatic insistence on experience and its historical indices itself that we may find the relevance of his reflections today. If one wants to follow Benjamin's lead indeed, then any meaningful analysis of the nexus of power and the aesthetic, of aura and domination, today needs to meet strong intellectual and methodological demands, and should transcend general remarks about the political as theater, the symbolic inventories of political representation, or the spectacular surfaces of pseudoevents. In critiquing the aestheticization of politics, Benjamin's aim was to show how political presentation interacts with historically contingent patterns of perception—and how imperatives of power and money may colonize the specific ways of what and how spectators see. Any theory of the stage-managing of politics today learning from Benjamin, therefore, cannot do without a strong ethnographic and phenomenological component, one that maps the symbolic spaces, modalities of perception, and cultural practices of everyday life. Benjamin teaches us that no discussion of the aesthetic moment of the political can assume any validity if it fails to account for how the self-stylization of power interacts with the historically specific topography of sense perception, how sentient bodies today maneuver their ways through the endlessly refracted spaces of culture in order to assume shifting positionalities that try to make and mark history.

Notes

1. A more extended version of the argument presented in this essay can be found in Lutz Koepnick, *Walter Benjamin and the Aesthetics of Power* (Lincoln: University of Nebraska Press, 1999). I am grateful to the University of Nebraska Press for allowing me to make use of previously published materials.

2. Max Horkheimer and Theodor W. Adorno, "The Culture Industry: Enlightenment as Mass Deception," in *Dialectic of Enlightenment*, trans. John Cumming (New York: Continuum, 1995), 120-67. Peter Uwe Hohendahl has provided ample historical material that illustrates that in Horkheimer and Adorno's model: "The relationship of the culture industry to the state is almost lost sight of ... Since Dialectic of Enlightenment is primarily concerned with mass culture in the United States, the description stresses the manipulation of the masses by the privately owned film and radio industries. This model would obviously not have applied to Germany under national socialism. To understand the origins of mass culture in Germany, one must examine more closely the importance of the state." Peter Uwe Hohendahl, *Building a National Literature: The Case of Germany, 1830-1870*, trans. Renate Baron Franciscono (Ithaca: Cornell University Press, 1989), 311.

3. Susan Buck-Morss, "Aesthetics and Anaesthetics: Walter Benjamin's Artwork Essay Reconsidered," *New Formations* 20 (Summer 1993): 123-43; Simonetta Falasca-Zamponi, *Fascist Spectacle: The Aesthetics of Power in Mussolini's Italy* (Berkeley: University of California Press, 1997), 119-47.

4. Walter Benjamin, *Illuminations: Essays and Reflections*, trans. Harry Zohn (New York: Schocken, 1969), 236.

5. Hans Jürgen Syberberg, *Vom Unglück und Glück der Kunst in Deutschland nach dem letzten Kriege* (Munich: Matthes und Seitz, 1990), 50.

6. Andreas Huyssen, "Monumental Seduction," *New German Critique* 69 (Fall 1996): 181-200; Lutz P. Koepnick, "Rethinking the Spectacle: History, Visual Culture, and German Unification," in *Wendezeiten—Zeitenwenden: Positionsbestimmungen zur deutschsprachigen Literatur 1945-1995*, ed. Robert Weninger and Brigitte Rossbacher (Tübingen: Stauffenburg Verlag, 1997), 151-70.

7. Andreas Huyssen, *Twilight Memories: Marking Time in a Culture of Amnesia* (New York: Routledge, 1995), 209-48.

8. For more on Benjamin's early metaphysics of experience, see Martin Jay's contribution to this volume.

9. Walter Benjamin, "A Child's View of Color," in *Selected Writings*, ed. Michael W. Jennings, vol I (Cambridge: Harvard University Press, 1996), 51.

10. Benjamin, *Illuminations*, 188.

11. Heide Schlüpmann, "Kinosucht," *Frauen und Film* 33 (October 1982): 45-52.

12. Miriam Hansen, "Early Silent Cinema: Whose Public Sphere?," *New German Critique* 29 (Spring/Summer 1983): 180.

13. Barbara Maria Stafford, *Good Looking: Essay on the Virtue of Images* (Cambridge: MIT Press, 1996), 20-41. For more on the iconophilia of European Enlightenment see Martin Jay, *Downcast Eyes: The Denigration of Vision in Twentieth-Century French Thought* (Berkeley: University of California Press, 1993), 21-148.

14. Horkheimer and Adorno, *Dialectic of Enlightenment*, 135.

15. Shierry Weber Nicholsen, "Adorno and Benjamin, Photography and the Aura," in *Exact Imagination, Late Work: On Adorno's Aesthetics* (Cambridge: MIT Press, 1997), 181-225.
16. Theodor W. Adorno, "On Popular Music," in *On Record: Rock, Pop, and the Written Word,* eds. Simon Frith and Andrew Goodwin (London: Routledge, 1990), 308.
17. Theodor W. Adorno, "On the Fetish-Character in Music and the Regression of Listening," in *The Essential Frankfurt School Reader,* eds. Andrew Arato and Eike Gebhardt (New York: Urizen Books, 1978), 280.
18. Theodor W. Adorno, "Transparencies on Film," *New German Critique* 24/25 (Fall/Winter 1981/82): 202.
19. Adorno, "Transparencies on Film," 202.
20. Patrice Petro, *Joyless Streets: Women and Melodramatic Representation in Weimar Germany* (Princeton: Princeton University Press, 1989).
21. Petro, *Joyless Streets,* 76.
22. Petro, *Joyless Streets,* 67.
23. Miriam Hansen, "Benjamin, Cinema and Experience: 'The Blue Flower in the Land of Technology'," *New German Critique* 40 (Winter 1987): 202.
24. Benjamin, *Illuminations,* 238.
25. Walter Benjamin, *Gesammelte Schriften,* eds. Rolf Tiedemann and Hermann Schweppenhäuser, vol. II (Frankfurt am Main: Suhrkamp, 1974ff.), 205.
26. Siegfried Kracauer, "Cult of Distraction," *The Mass Ornament: Weimar Essays,* trans. Thomas Y. Levin (Cambridge: Harvard University Press, 1995) 327.
27. Benjamin, *Illuminations,* 232.
28. The notion cinema-of-attraction, as developed by Tom Gunning, provides a valuable concept for describing modes of representation and address that precede the dominance of narrative in mainstream film; it conceptualizes modes of specularization that address the audience directly in order to elicit excitement and curiosity. See Tom Gunning, "The Cinema of Attraction(s)," *Wide Angle* 8.3-4 (1986): 63-70; see also Gunning's essay "An Aesthetic of Astonishment: Early Film and the (In)credulous Spectator," *Art & Text* 34 (1989): 31-45.
29. Hansen, "Benjamin, Cinema and Experience," 209.
30. David Harvey, *The Condition of Postmodernity: An Enquiry into the Origins of Cultural Change* (Oxford: Basil Blackwell, 1989), 124.
31. Benjamin, *Illuminations* 232.
32. See Gerhard Schulze, *Die Erlebnisgesellschaft: Kultursoziologie der Gegenwart* (Frankfurt am Main: Campus Verlag, 1992), 33-89.
33. Jürgen Habermas, "What Theories Can Accomplish—and What They Can't," in *The Past as Future,* trans. Max Pensky (Lincoln: Nebraska University Press, 1994), 119.
34. Anthony Giddens, *The Consequences of Modernity* (Stanford: Stanford University Press, 1990), 55-78.
35. Hal Foster, *The Return of the Real* (Cambridge: MIT Press, 1996).
36. Huyssen, *Twilight Memories,* 16.
37. Jim Collins, *Uncommon Cultures: Popular Culture and Post-Modernism* (New York: Routledge, 1989), 1-27.
38. Michael P. Steinberg, "The Collector as Allegorist: Goods, Gods, and Objects of History," in *Walter Benjamin and the Demands of History,* ed. Michael P. Steinberg (Ithaca: Cornell University Press, 1996), 107.

39. As, for instance, in the 1996 show "Kunst und Macht im Europa der Dikta-
toren 1930 bis 1945," put together by the Hayward Gallery in London for suc-
cessive exhibition in London, Berlin, and Barcelona.

Section III

IN THE WAKE OF JÜRGEN HABERMAS

Communicative Reason, Morality, and History

Chapter 6

CRITIQUE AND SELF-REFLECTION
The Problematization of Morality[1]

Christoph Menke

There is probably no subject matter about which the "first" and the "second" generations of Critical Theory are more deeply divided than the interpretation and assessment of morality. The first generation of Critical Theory regarded morality with a skeptical eye: first, in Horkheimer's writings of the 1930s, with the skepticism of Schopenhauer concerning the rational foundation of moral norms, and with the skepticism of Marx concerning the political efficacy of moral claims; second, in Horkheimer's and Adorno's writings of the 1940s, with the skepticism of Nietzsche concerning the consequences of morality for individual "persons." While this threefold skepticism—that of Schopenhauer, Marx, and Nietzsche concerning, respectively, the rational foundation, the political efficiency, and the personal consequences of morality—still forms the horizon for the treatment of morality in Adorno's later writings, the new beginning of the second generation of Critical Theory in the 1960s, Habermas and Apel in particular, can be understood as aiming at a new assessment of morality. If one follows Habermas' and Apel's account, the revaluation of morality in opposition to its skeptical treatment in older Critical Theory appears to have been the central motive and driving force behind the deep and far-reaching conceptual redefinition of language, reason, subjectivity, and

Notes for this chapter begin on page 137.

modernity, by which the younger Critical Theory generation tried to overcome what they interpreted as the impasse of its tradition.

All this is well-known. The reason I have recalled these facts from the history of Critical Theory is that this history determines the background of the rather systematic considerations that I will present in the following pages. The aim of these considerations is to develop and defend the project of a critical self-reflection of morality. I think of this project as a reformulation of the Schopenhauerian and Nietzschean skepticism towards morality in the first generation of Critical Theory. In this essay, however, I can only sketch the basic conceptual structure of such a critical self-reflection of morality. I must leave aside here the interpretative question of how Horkheimer's and Adorno's critique of morality would have to be reread in the light of these conceptual considerations.[2]

The central idea of those considerations can be stated by an initial thesis: that an adequate self-reflection of morality implies its questioning and, consequently, its limitation. By questioning and limiting morality, one considers it from the outside, as a necessarily restricted perspective within the totality of our lives. The questioning and limitation of morality could therefore be called its "external" reflection. At the same time, however, it would be wrong to understand the reflective questioning of morality merely as external (as "externalistic," as I shall say below), for it would then appear as a rejection or even a dissolution of morality. This misunderstanding arises when one overlooks the fact that—and the extent to which—the external reflection of morality is at the same time a *self*-questioning of morality: for the questioning of morality from outside is equally grounded in the internal effectuation of morality itself. Because an adequate determination of morality would be to define it as being internally self-reflective, it is precisely this internal self-reflection of morality that enables and justifies its external questioning and limitation with regard to its consequences for our lives. Being internally reflective, morality itself already entails its "other," which is then confronted from the outside. In Hegel's terms, one could describe such a structure as "dialectic." In other words, my thesis aims to grasp an aspect of morality that could be called its dialectics.[3]

This thesis demonstrates the general point I would like to suggest in this essay. But in order to make this point, I have to start somewhere else, namely, with the clarification of the concepts I have used in the formulation of this thesis: the concept of morality and its self-reflection (1). After these initial conceptual explanations, I shall attempt to present the basic argument of the thesis: that morality is in itself ("internally") self-reflective (2). Finally, I would like to show how this internal reflection of morality is necessarily connected with an external reflection that aims at questioning and limiting morality (3).

1. The Antinomy of Reflection

I use the term "moral" to designate a certain mode of behavior or behavior-oriented attitude. The basic characteristic of this mode of behavior or attitude consists in the idea of equality: "moral," as I am using the term here, means "egalitarian." Within the moral attitude, others are regarded as equals: the moral attitude is an attitude of equal respect. This is a familiar, perhaps even an everyday, understanding of the term "moral." At the same time, however, it is also a narrow use that has a double restriction: first, in my usage, the term "moral" refers only to modes of behavior vis-à-vis others and does not refer to the relation of the individual to him- or herself. Second, the term "moral" does not designate norm-guided behavior as such, but rather only modes of behavior that are guided by a specific norm, the norm of equal treatment.

As egalitarian, the moral attitude is reflectively constituted, for reflection—this is how Kant understood it in his explanation of the process of concept formation—means comparison. Reflecting on, or simply reflecting an object, means comparing it with other objects in order to find out "what they have in common."[4] In more precise terms, reflection for Kant is an intermediate between comparison, as a mere listing of differences, and abstraction, as a mere recording of commonalities under the "isolation of all by which the given representations distinguish themselves." Reflection consists in the "consideration of how different representations can be understood in a single consciousness." In that sense, also, reflection is comparison, yet a comparison that does not only record the differences, but aims at determining what they have in common, namely, their "unity." Such a reflective comparison—not in the process of object-determination but of self-determination—also takes place in the moral attitude: in the latter, I compare myself with others insofar as I set myself on a par with them and them on a par with me; I consider myself to be equal to the others, or I place myself amidst them as an equal.

In a certain sense, this reflection that constitutes morality could already be designated as "self-reflection." For if equality is the basic moral norm, then the moral treatment of others (as being equal to oneself) also amounts to viewing oneself differently, namely, as being equal to the others. But I speak here of self-reflection in another, more specific sense: not to characterize a reflection that has a particular object—namely, myself—but rather a particular constitution. Self-reflection is not a reflection on the "self," but rather a reflection that applies to itself, a reflection that reflects upon itself. Thus, I speak of a self-reflection of morality when (or where) moral reflection is not merely enacted, but rather when moral reflection itself becomes an object of reflection, an object of a removed beholding and critical examination.

Such self-reflection of morality comes mainly in two common forms. In both of these forms, "self-reflection of morality" means a reflection on moral reflection, in the basic sense of reflection mentioned above, namely, comparing different entities in view of their commonalities or relatedness. Self-reflection as a reflection on moral reflection means to relate comparatively moral reflection to something else, something not itself moral but morally relevant. The two common forms of this reflectively examined external relatedness of morality are, on the one hand, its relatedness to the grounds of morality (which are prior to it) and, on the other hand, its relatedness to the consequences of morality (which are subsequent to it). In each form, the reflective "comparison" of morality also has a different sense: the reflective examination of the relatedness of morality to its grounds serves the founding or justification of morality, whereas the reflective examination of the relatedness of morality to its consequences aims at questioning and limiting morality.

Both of these forms are familiar to us from the history of modern moral philosophy. Borrowing a phrase from Niklas Luhmann, one can designate modern moral philosophy—that is, since the eighteenth century—as a "reflection theory of morality,"[5] for modern moral philosophy is not just a form of articulating, but a theory, a (meta-)reflection of the moral attitude. In this attempt, the (historical and systematic) primary sense of self-reflection consists in the founding or justification of morality. Indeed, this is the only form of the reflection of morality that Luhmann—wrongly, as I will try to make clear in a moment—sees at work in modern moral philosophy. The foundation of morality with which the modern philosophical reflection on morality generally begins, is a foundation of the moral attitude in other, nonmoral interests, capabilities, or practices, such as the interest in one's own personal welfare (in contractualism) or the capacity for reasonable self-determination (in Kant). This attitude towards morality is taken up by the second generation of Critical Theory when Habermas and Apel try to derive the moral attitude of equal respect from the practice of communicative discourse.[6] "Foundation" or "justification" is here understood in a strong sense, as "deduction." Self-reflection as a founding of morality then means that something nonmoral can be located that is common to all human beings (being part of "human nature") and that from this nonmoral determination the moral attitude can be compellingly derived. Engaging and critiquing Kant and the tradition of moral philosophy following from him, I would like to argue that all such strong attempts at founding morality have failed; they are, as Ernst Tugendhat has written, "covertly circular."[7] The moral idea, i.e., the moral duty of equal treatment, cannot be derived from a foundation in nonmoral interests, capabilities or practices.

In opposition to this idea of the founding of morality stands a form of reflection that Friedrich Schiller, in his letters on aesthetic education, called the "anthropological evaluation (or assessment)" *(anthropologische Schätzung)* of morality. By this phrase Schiller understands an assessment of morality from the viewpoint of its consequences for human life as a whole, "in which, along with the [moral] form, the ['sensory'] content also counts and the living sensation has a voice."[8] The moral attitude appears in Schiller as one among, and alongside, other practical orientations that Schiller himself described in three different ways: ethically, as the desire to achieve a good life; instrumentally, as the interest for self-conservation; and politically, as the praxis of collective self-government. For Schiller, the history of revolution clearly demonstrated that the egalitarian moral attitude can yield harmful consequences for other, nonmoral orientations. This is why one must question reflectively, or even limit, the egalitarian moral attitude in view of these other orientations, and in three forms: namely (once again), the ethical, the instrumental, and the political reflection on equality. With this move, Schiller initiates a tradition of examining morality with

regard to the consequences it has for the individuals who are subjected to it, that is, for those who subject themselves to it. This tradition has been taken up in entirely different ways by Hegel and
Nietzsche. It leads then to the skeptical treatment of morality by the
first generation of Critical Theory and to contemporary versions of
the project of a self-reflective questioning of morality as diverse as
those of Michel Foucault, Charles Taylor, and Bernard Williams.

In view of these two strands one can speak of an "antinomy" in
the modern self-reflection of morality. Modern moral philosophy
develops the self-reflection of morality in two separate forms defined
by two opposing functions, i.e., as founding, on the one hand, and
as questioning and limitation, on the other. Thus, the contradiction
between the two generations of Critical Theory regarding morality
that I have recalled at the beginning refers in no way specifically to
that tradition, but is rather a contradiction that defines the modern view on morality as such. The founding of morality aims at a
deduction from an undeniable given in "human nature," in order to
demonstrate its absolute validity. On the other hand, the questioning of morality refers to an anthropologically undeniable claim, in
comparison to which morality—in the strongest conception of this
thesis—appears to be an oppressive and unjustified restriction. The
question then arises whether and how this antinomy in the reflection
on morality—in modernity's reflection on morality in general, and
between the two generations of Critical Theory in particular—can
be resolved. It cannot be resolved by giving up one of its two sides,
for both the justification and the questioning of morality possess
equal rights and equal necessity. Consequently, their antinomical
relation can only be resolved if (and when) each side can be understood and articulated in a different way than in their antinomical
configuration; that is, if the understanding of the founding as well as
the questioning of morality that leads to their antinomical opposition can be proved a misunderstanding.

I would like to term this misunderstanding of these two antinomical forms of reflection on morality their "externalistic" understanding. This is how the two traditions of moral philosophy
understand both the project of founding and of questioning morality, because they describe it as relating morality to an extramoral
dimension. According to such an externalistic understanding, the
founding of morality consists in its deduction from some nonmoral
feature of human nature, while the questioning of morality—in this

externalistic reading—consists in confronting morality from outside with its "other." In both ways, the moral attitude seems to be a simple phenomenon, one that is related to either grounds or consequences from the outside.

This externalistic approach, however, is a misunderstanding, for self-reflection is not just external to the moral attitude, but rather determines it internally. "Self-reflection of morality": this formula does not only mean—in the objective sense of the genitive case—an (exterior) reflection *on* morality. Rather, it also means—in the subjective sense of the genitive case—a process of reflection by and *in* (i.e., interior to) morality. Morality is self-reflective, not only in the examination of its relations to grounds and consequences; prior to this, morality was already self-reflective in the process of its internal determination or articulation—in the process of determining or articulating the basic moral attitude of equal treatment or respect. This reconsideration of morality as "internally self-reflective," which I will present in the following section, shall show why the externalistic self-understanding of the grounding as well as the questioning of morality—the self-understanding, that is, that leads to their antinomical opposition—is inadequate.

2. Internal Self-Reflection

Why is self-reflection required and what does it consist of within the moral sphere? In general, self-reflection consists in a bending-back-upon-itself—a referring back to itself of moral reflection that creates distance and enables critical scrutiny. Self-reflection in morality is thus required when simple moral reflection proves insufficient or wrong. Moral reflection tends towards blindness, and therefore one needs moral self-reflection.

This claim can be elucidated if one looks back upon the process of moral reflection. A reflection can be called moral, as I suggested above, when it consists of comparatively setting oneself on par with others. Equality of treatment or regard forms the normative content of the moral attitude or reflection. But this also presupposes equality, or likeness *(Gleichheit[9]),* in a descriptive sense. Equality of treatment means regarding others as equal. From this follows the idea that in moral contexts "equality" does not have a (primarily) quantitative sense; equality in treatment or regard is not necessarily equality in distribution. Rather, equality of respect frequently requires that I treat another differently from myself and others; here, it is precisely (and only) the different or deviant treatment that fulfills the requirements of equal moral regard. Thus, equality and difference are not absolute but rather perspective-relative terms, or more precisely description-relative terms: a treatment of others that, on one level of description, is marked by difference that can count, on another level of description, as equal, moral regard. From this it follows that to speak of moral, equal respect presupposes that the other can be described as equal to or like myself and others in certain, fundamental respects. Equality of treatment or regard demands equality (in the sense of likeness) of description—I can only regard others as equals if I can also describe them as being like me. Such descriptions indicate the respects in which others are to be regarded if one wants to regard them morally. Since these respects are those that concern the equality of treatment, they are necessarily general and abstract. That is why one says that, morally, one regards others as "persons." For a person is not a particular individual; the person is the mask taken on by equality, under which particular individuals step forth into the purview of the moral perspective. Only as persons, i.e., as descriptively alike in certain general and abstract respects, can others normatively count as equals.

This connection between a normative and a descriptive aspect, between equality in regard and likeness in characterization, indicates that in each act of morally-equal treatment, one presupposes a certain conception of what it is to be a person. Each moral deliberation, judgment, or action implies a concept of "person." Commonly, such concepts of person guide our understanding and judgments without becoming explicit and thematic. For usually, one just relies on a certain preunderstanding of what it is to be a person—that is, we rely on a certain preunderstanding of which features (desires and capabilities) of others are relevant to moral equality. This is the danger of blindness in moral reflection that I suggested above. Occasionally, however, this descriptive presupposition of our judgments does become explicit and thematic. This marks the step into moral self-reflection: self-reflection in the moral sphere implies a scrutiny of the descriptions of likeness *(Gleichheit)* upon which our treatment as equals *(Gleiche)* rests.

A concept of person applies to another in those abstract respects in which he or she is like myself (and like others, i.e., like "us"). A concept of person is thus formed by means of a process of abstraction. Or, following the Kantian terminology, the process of moral reflection is a comparison in the service of abstraction. That is why the act of a self-reflective scrutiny of the concept of person is tantamount to going through, that is, to repeating, this process of abstracting. Self-reflection means repeating a reflection or reestablishing the process of reflection against abstraction. For, following Kant, abstraction consists in an "isolation" (*Absonderung*) of commonalities from the differences, and the process, by which those differences were brought to commonality. The repetition of the process of abstraction that covertly underpins our common concept of a person means to execute it once again, starting from its beginning. The beginning of abstraction is "comparation," the grasping of the concrete and diverse. In the case of moral reflection, this means that one arrives at a concept of person only by starting from an understanding of individuals and their ever-variegated circumstances. Because moral self-reflection consists in scrutinizing the step of abstraction that leads to a concept of person starting from its beginning, this means that in moral self-reflection, one must—as a first step—seek to do justice to the other in his or her particularity. At stake in moral self-reflection is the revision of our apprehensions of persons in light of our understanding of individuals. Moral self-reflection aims at an adequate description of others as (abstract) persons, but it begins with an understanding that tries to do justice to others as (particular) individuals.

To do justice to the other as an individual is, not only in practice but also in its conceptual structure, not a simple thing. That is why attempts to clarify the processes of moral experience and comprehension make use of analyses of literary experience and comprehension—as can most impressively be seen in the works of Stanley Cavell and Martha Nussbaum. This should not amount, however, to a combined identification of moral and literary ways of comprehension. Literature is relevant to morality not as an exemplary embodiment of moral values (as in the traditional identification of the beautiful and the good), but rather because it poses and tries to answer the question of what it means and how it is possible to understand an individual, even, generally, what it means and how it is possible to understand.[10] Here, however, I would like to draw attention to one important aspect of doing justice in understanding. Such doing justice in understanding cannot consist in doing justice to the other "as such" or "in every respect."[11] An understanding of individuals that does not describe them as persons and in terms of equals cannot be a simple and inevitably infinite enumeration of their respective characteristics. This would only be an external, and thus objectifying, understanding. That would mean that the other would precisely not be done justice to, for this would overlook the distinction between good and bad, and, in the domain of the good, between important and less important things, even between the indispensable and that which can be disregarded—distinctions by means of which this other, as does everyone, orients him- or herself in his or her life. These distinctions must also orient our under-standing of his or her life: to do justice to the other is to do justice to the distinctions drawn by the other. These distinctions are dis-tinctions of value, and together they form a conception of the good. To do justice to the other in understanding him or her as an indi-vidual is thus to attain an adequate understanding of his or her con-ception of the good.

The understanding of others by means of which one does justice to them as individuals, forms the point of departure for the self-reflective scrutiny of their description as persons. As self-reflection, this scrutiny is part of the moral attitude. Consequently, the moral attitude cannot be completely characterized as just equal treatment of others—this is merely its basic aim. In order to realize this objec-tive, therefore, the moral attitude must continually pursue another goal. In fact, to bring about the moral goal of equal treatment, one must strive for the nonmoral objective (which, to be sure, is not an immoral objective) of doing justice to others understood not as (abstract) persons, but as (particular) individuals. For it is only on the basis of an understanding that does justice to the individuals considered in their diversity—and in relation to this understand-ing—that one is able to describe the persons in a way that is likely to guarantee their effective equal treatment.

How exactly do the two aims of equal treatment of persons and doing justice to individuals interact within the moral attitude? How do they play together and against one another? At stake in the moral attitude is the equal treatment of others, which presupposes a description of them as persons in terms of likeness. While one commonly takes these descriptions for granted, in fact they are the result of processes. Earlier, I described these processes as processes of abstraction. It appears that their self-reflective repetition is in fact a shortened description. The abstracting processes of forming the concept of "person" only revise a prior concept. That is to say, concepts of person are never simply given nor are they the simple result of abstraction on the basis of "concrete" determinations of the particular individuals. Rather, they are made through acts of a reflective scrutiny of prior concepts of persons—a reflectivity that is then forgotten but can be remembered and reactivated in situations of conflict or dispute.

Let me give an example from the history of political ethics by indicating how the much-told story of the emergence of the modern constitutional state would have to be reinterpreted in light of the idea of moral self-reflection. In this perspective, what enables the modern constitutional state to overcome the disastrous consequences of confessional civil war is its revised conception of what it means to be a person. This new description of others as "persons like us" consists in no longer viewing these others as heretics, infidels or Satan worshippers, but instead to describe them as "religious believers." It is only this new concept of "religious believer" in a neutral, nonconfessional way—a concept which was not available before—which allows for the respect of others as equals beyond confessional differences. One is now able to view the follower of a different belief as equally a believer, even though the content of his or her belief is considered to be wrong. In this respect, he or she deserves equal treatment. At the same time, however, such a new description is not final (or complete); its abstracting move must always be repeated anew in the moral attitude. Indeed, the determination of the person achieved by such a description is abstract, yet by no means empty: it still comprehends what makes up the concept of person in a certain, determinate, or substantial sense. In the example under consideration, the concept of person is understood as someone who has a religious belief, no matter what this belief may be. Determinate or substantial, each concept of person, once discovered and put into use, can be subject to objections. These objections form the motor for the concept's reflective scrutiny and revision.

These objections, so crucial to moral reflection, are always made in the name of what a certain, determinate concept of person means for the individuals who attempt to live in accordance with their idea of the good life. The starting point, and thus the "material," for the reflective scrutiny of a concept of person, comprises the experiences of individuals to whom this concept is applied. That is why moral self-reflection, constantly revising the step from individuals to abstraction—the step in which a concept of person is formed—should begin with the understanding of those individuals. In our example, it might begin with an understanding of the individuals who claim that they do not fall under the newly-discovered determination of personhood of being a religious believer because they subscribe to no religious beliefs whatsoever. At that point, one requires a revised description—another abstraction into concept— of different individuals as equal persons, namely, one in which the characterization of persons is located in a "conscience" that is no longer marked out by "religious" factors that, in a further step, will appear to some individuals as a narrow and exclusive understanding that stands in need of reflective scrutiny and revision. In other words this process can (and must) be repeated indefinitely. In moral practices, one is continually confronted with others who not only demand equality in accordance with current standards of moral equal treatment, but who also experience these moral practices— these very processes—of equal treatment themselves as unjust, for the current concept of persons contains descriptions that they cannot integrate into their self-descriptions unless they surrender their conceptions of the good. In such situations, one must undertake once again the abstracting process that leads from individuals to persons; one must once again scrutinize it self-reflectively.

3. External Reflection on Morality

Let me return to the two forms of an external reflection on morality that constitute the "antinomy" of modern moral philosophy. As I have shown, this reflection on—not (with-)in—morality encompasses two opposing functions: one that founds morality and one that questions and, as a result, limits morality. In the two lines of the tradition of modern moral philosophy that I have outlined, these processes of reflection have mostly been understood in an "externalistic" way. And it is this shared externalistic misinterpretation of the externality of the founding, as well as the questioning reflection on morality, that is responsible for their antinomic relation in modern moral philosophy.

One can elucidate this misinterpretation by distinguishing between two different ways of understanding the external character

of these forms of reflection—a correct and an erroneous understanding. The founding as well as the limiting reflection on morality are rightly called "external" insofar as they both represent an
outside perspective on morality, and thereby present morality itself
as a (particular) perspective among others. For in the founding and
the limiting of morality, one thematizes that which one takes for
granted in the moral perspective, that is, the principle of equal treatment and respect. Thus, in founding and limiting morality one
explicitly refers to the basic constitutive assumption—the "principle"—of the moral perspective itself, which, being basic and constitutive, never becomes visible in the moral perspective. What
constitutes a perspective is at the same time the blind spot of that
perspective—it can only be observed and, thus, reflected upon from
outside.[12] This indicates why—and to what extent—it is appropriate to conceive the founding and the limiting reflection on morality
as being external: in the external reflection of founding and limiting
one ceases to enact the moral perspective—rather, one interrupts the
enactment of morality by regarding its principle from outside.

This externality, however, only refers to the way, or rather the
perspective, of seeing, not to the elements that are seen. This is precisely what the traditional understanding of the reflective founding
and limiting of morality overlooks—and what leads to the antinomic interpretation of their relation. According to this understanding, in founding and in limiting morality, one reflectively relates
("compares") the moral perspective to something external to it:
prior grounds or subsequent consequences. But as our description
of the self-reflection within morality should have made clear, this is
a misunderstanding. For it becomes clear that in its internal self-
reflection, the moral perspective itself already refers to what seems
to be external to it—the particular perspective of individuals. The
moral perspective is not—and cannot be—exclusively defined by
the idea of equality. Being internally reflective, the moral perspective
is also internally divided and double. It entails its "other." Contrary
to their "externalistic" self-misunderstanding, the grounding as well
as the questioning of morality must, thus, be understood as reflectively relating the basic principle of the moral perspective not to
something external but, rather, to the "other" which this perspective already entails. More concretely: contrary to their "externalistic" self-misunderstanding, the grounding as well as the questioning
of morality must be enacted as reflectively relating the principle of

equal treatment of persons to their understanding as particular individuals. The understanding of individuals which takes place in the internal self-reflection of morality represents, at the same time, the point of reference of the founding and the limiting of morality in its external reflection.

This is why the founding and limiting of morality is neither purely external nor purely internal to it. It is not purely external, as the "externalistic" misinterpretation holds, because in founding and limiting we reflectively relate morality to the idea of individuality, which is already built into its internal self-reflection. Neither is it purely internal because, in the founding and limiting of morality, we refer to the idea of individuality in a way that is radically different from the internal self-reflection of morality: we use the idea of individuality to thematize the moral principle of equality itself.

In what follows, I shall try to explain in a little more detail this double relation between the external and the internal reflection of morality, particularly in relation to the questioning of morality in terms of its consequences for individuals. I would first, however, like to make a brief remark concerning the founding of morality. One can use the word "founding" in relation to morality in two ways: first, in relation to the justification of a specific interpretation of the principle of equality; or, second, in the sense of founding this principle itself. The first type of justification is related to the internal self-reflection of morality. But how is a justification of the very principle of moral equality possible? Such a justification cannot consist in a deduction of morality from nonmoral interests, capacities, or practices. In that sense, a strict external founding of morality is impossible. But this does not mean that there can only be an internal justification of morality. Rather, the difference between "internal" and "external" here is altogether insufficient. The justifications that I have just called "internal" to morality—since they are given in the moral attitude in respect of specific interpretations of the principle of equality—are never purely internal. They possess the force not to found, but to justify the principle of equality as well. For in such internal justifications one shows that the concept of person on which a specific interpretation of moral equality is based is appropriate in relation to our understanding of individuals. In this respect, these internal justifications imply a justification of the principle of moral equality itself. By showing that a certain understanding of moral equality is right, because it is founded on a concept of person that can be maintained in light of a comprehension of individuals which does justice to their conception of the good, one also justifies implicitly the principle of equality itself. For one demonstrates therein that there is at least one interpretation of moral equality that is compatible with doing justice to individuals and their conception of the good. This does not, however, necessarily imply a strong external foundation *(Begründung)* but just a weak justification *(Rechtfertigung)* of the principle of equality. First, it does not produce a direct foundation of the principle of equality, but only an indirect justification of that principle in a specific interpretation. Second, it does not show the absolute validity of the principle of equality, but defends it in a relative way, namely, in relation to individuals and their conceptions of the good.

Given this relation between the internal and external reflection of morality, one can now say that the external or founding reflection of morality at the same time follows from and goes beyond its internal reflection. The external or founding reflection of morality follows from its internal reflection insofar as it refers to the very elements that constitute the internal reflection of morality: both relate moral equality and the act of doing justice to the individuals. But the external or founding reflection of morality also goes beyond its internal reflection because it concerns the principle of equality itself which cannot be reflected upon in the moral attitude.

I would now like to turn to the other dimension of an external reflection of morality indicated at the original antimony, that of its questioning and limitation. Above, I briefly described this type of reflection with reference to Schiller's project and the subsequent tradition of an "anthropological" evaluation of morality. Such an external assessment is a questioning and a limitation of morality in relation to its consequences. These are consequences that the moral attitude has for individuals and their other, nonmoral orientations that determine their conception of the good. The above consideration of the self-reflective constitution of the moral attitude allows for a closer determination of, first, why and, second, how the problem of its consequences arises.

Why does the problem of the consequences of morality for individuals arise at all? That is to say, why does this problem arise, *after* we have already observed and assessed the consequences of actions in the moral attitude under the aspect of equal treatment? One answer is that in the moral attitude one relates not to individuals, but rather to persons, and therewith to others under an abstract description. But why is this tied up with a problem for individuals? A case involving such a problem has become evident in the example drawn from political ethics, for it can and does repeatedly occur that the concept of person upon which a practice of equal treatment is based does not do justice to certain individuals. This, however, does not answer the question either. For in this case, as was shown in the example, one adjusts the concept of person in a process of self-reflective scrutiny. Apparently, self-reflective scrutiny leaves no room for a problematization or even limitation of the moral attitude from outside, on the basis of its consequences for individuals. The consequences for individuals appear not to be problems for morality, but rather, problems in morality (thus, problems with which one deals in moral self-reflection and deliberation).

Nevertheless, this conclusion is false. When morally equal treatment—operating with a certain concept of a person—fails to do justice to individuals, then it does not necessarily lead to a new formulation of the concept of a person. For in some cases, it is impossible to frame a new (that is, a better) concept of a person. When the regard for others as equal persons does not do justice to certain individuals, it does not necessarily mean that something is wrong with the presupposed concept of a person. Rather, equal treatment as a person may mean that someone is done an injustice as an individual without a moral wrong being done to them. For it may be that what befits someone morally, as a person, does little for him or her as an individual. To regard another as a person morally, and to do justice to another as an individual, are distinct aims. They need not coincide, and they can be separated and even stand opposed to one another. The difference, the continual tension, and the occasional conflict between morally equal treatment and doing justice to someone as an individual is thus not a difference external to the moral attitude.[13] The distinction is to be found within the moral attitude itself. In the moral attitude, one returns to doing justice to individuals when one self-reflectively scrutinizes one's concept of a person and one abstains from doing justice to individuals when one treats oneself and others as equals. That is why even a "correct" form of morally-equal treatment, a treatment that evaluates and describes correctly, can have consequences for individuals. This poses a problem, at least to those individuals: namely, that their morally-equitable treatment does not do justice to them as individuals, that is, that it gives insufficient room for the realization of their idea of the good.

With this elaboration, however, I have only said of what the problem of the consequences of morality for individuals consists; I have not yet shown how it presents itself, that is, how it arises as a problem *for morality* (and not merely for the individuals concerned). Answering this question will allow us to come back to the problem of the "externality" of the problematization of morality. At first, the matter allows of a negative formulation: the problem of its consequences for individuals does not arise in the moral attitude as a problem that the moral attitude poses to itself, i.e., a problem regarding the equal treatment of persons. On the other hand, the problem of the moral attitude's consequences for individuals is also not simply external and foreign to the moral attitude. It is not a problem with which the moral attitude must be confronted from outside, that is, from the perspective of a critique or even rejection of morality, which Nietzsche tends to believe. For the relatedness to individuals—an understanding that seeks to do justice to individuals—belongs to the moral attitude itself. As I have shown above, this relatedness is immanent to its intrinsic self-reflection. Such self-reflection serves, above all, through the scrutiny of the concept of a person, to lead toward a better interpretation of moral equality. Self-reflection in morality, however, cannot be restricted to that. Insofar as it necessarily involves doing justice to individuals, morality in its self-reflection is also already implicitly confronted with the consequences that it, itself, has for individuals. This is the moment when self-reflection in morality, when performed consistently, has to become reflection *on* morality. I already have indicated the ambiguous character of the "externality" of the—either founding or limiting—reflection on morality. Accordingly, the move from a reflection in morality to a reflection on morality can be described in two ways: as transgression and as radicalization. In its move from "in" to "on," reflection transgresses the moral perspective, because it is no longer a self-reflection that serves to realize the moral goal of equality better, but instead questions the moral attitude from outside, from the perspective of the individual itself. At the same time, this same move can be termed a radicalization of the self-reflection that is intrinsic to morality because the perspective of the individual, in the name of whom morality is problematized from "outside," can already be found within the moral self-reflection itself.

The "anthropological" evaluation of morality corresponds in Schiller's thought to the project of observing morality from outside, that is, of confronting it with the inner or personal perspective of the individuals to which it applies. This project was later carried out more extensively and subtly and foremost by Nietzsche. Nietzsche, though, was also responsible for a misunderstanding of this project of an anthropological evaluation of morality that still makes it easy—too easy—to reject it: the misunderstanding of this project as a fundamental critique of morality, directed against the very ideal of equality. For Nietzsche, the project of a "problematization"—of a reflective questioning and limiting of morality—amounts to a destruction, at least a definitive rejection and overcoming of morality. The belief in the dangerous truth of this Nietzschean identification marks the starting point for the discourse on morality in the second generation of Critical Theory. Thus, for Habermas and Apel the only legitimate form of an external reflection on morality is its deduction from the idea of rationality. Such a stance definitively separates the second from the first generation of Critical Theory. When the late Adorno spoke of a "critique of morality,"[14] the term "critique" did not mean "rejection" but rather "distinction." Accordingly, for Adorno, criticizing morality first of all means to become aware of its internal division or "dialectic." With this, Horkheimer and Adorno dissolve the Nietzschean identification of questioning and rejecting morality that Habermas and Apel take for granted. To question morality does not mean to reject it from outside but, rather, to consider morality from the perspective of the individual who is already internal to it.

In this essay, I have tried to systematically reconstruct this basic claim of Adorno's in terms of the interplay between two forms of reflection. In questioning or problematizing we reflect on morality from outside, but this external form of reflection is only possible on the basis of a process of reflection within morality. For, in considering morality from outside, the questioning of morality refers to the very same elements whose interrelation make up the internal reflection of morality, namely, equality and individuality. The external questioning of morality does not speak in the name of the "other," but rather (with)in morality. This is why the external reflection of morality can also be described—as I have done before—as a radicalization of its internal self-reflection. Obviously, this does not mean that (reflectively) to enact and (reflectively) to question morality amount to the same. Rather, it shows that the questioning of morality in the name of its negative, hindering consequences for individuals can only be a problematization of (the application of) morality in certain specific and individual cases, not the rejection of morality as such. For while the moral attitude in its self-reflective enactment already entails the perspective on individuality, the application of the moral attitude in certain situations can nevertheless hinder, even oppress, individuality because it regards individuality in a necessarily restricted way, restricted by the idea of equal treatment and respect. This shows that, contrary to what Nietzsche hoped for and Habermas fears, the problematizing awareness of its negative consequences for individuality cannot shake or defeat morality, nor should it. However, it can and should "relativize" the moral attitude precisely by putting it in relation to its (internal) other. This is the fundamental meaning of self-reflection: the dissolution of the appearance of absoluteness, including the absoluteness of moral equality.

Notes

1. The author would like to acknowledge the translation kindly provided by Marie-Noelle Ryan.
2. For such a reading see my "Critical Theory and Tragic Knowledge," in *The Handbook of Critical Theory*, ed. David Rasmussen (Oxford: Blackwell Publishers, 1996), 57-73.
3. Following Hegel's Encyclopedic logic, I understand "dialectic" (*dialektisch*) here as "negative-rational" (*negativ-vernünftig*), but, contrary to Hegel, I understand the negative dialectic as being "speculatively" insurpassable. Another word for that is "tragic." Cf. Christoph Menke, *Tragödie im Sittlichen. Gerechtigkeit und Freiheit nach Hegel* (Frankfurt am Main: Suhrkamp Verlag, 1996), chap. 1.
4. See Immanuel Kant, *Logik*, in *Werke*, ed. W. Weischedel, vol. 5 (Frankfurt am Main: Suhrkamp Verlag 1977), 524 ff.
5. Niklas Luhmann, *Paradigm Lost. Über die ethische Reflexion der Moral* (Frankfurt am Main: Suhrkamp Verlag, 1990).
6. This is the program of a "*Letztbegründung*" of morality which Habermas has begun to modify and even criticize in the 1990s; cf. his *Erläuterungen zur Diskursethik* (Frankfurt am Main: Suhrkamp Verlag, 1991), 185 ff.

7. Ernst Tugendhat, *Vorlesungen über Ethik* (Frankfurt am Main: Suhrkamp Verlag 1996), 71.

8. Friedrich Schiller, *Über die ästhetische Erziehung in einer Reihe von Briefen*, in *Werke*, ed. Fricke and Göpfert, vol. 5 (München: Hanser, 1980), 577.

9. In German, *Gleichheit* can be used in both a normative and a descriptive sense. See R. Dworkin, *A Matter of Principle* (Cambrigde: Harvard University Press, 1985), 190

10. Christoph Menke, *The Sovereignty of Art: Aesthetic Negativity in Adorno and Derrida* (Cambridge: MIT Press, 1998), 29 ff.

11. This seems to be the presupposition underlying Derrida's claim that "to address oneself to the other in the language of the other is, it seems, the condition of all possible justice, but apparently, in all rigor, it is ... impossible (since I cannot speak the language of the other except to the extent that I appropriate it and assimilate it according to the law of an implicit third)." Jacques Derrida, "Force of Law: The 'Mystical Foundation of Authority'," *Cardozo Law Review* 11. 5-6 (July/August 1990): 949.

12. On this basic dialectic of "blindness and insight" (Paul de Man) as the law of reflection, see Niklas Luhmann, *Soziale Systeme: Grundriß einer allgemeinen Theorie* (Frankfurt am Main: Suhrkamp Verlag, 1984), chap. 11.

13. Cf. Menke, *Tragödie im Sittlichen*, chap. 6.

14. Theodor W. Adorno, *Negative Dialektik* (Frankfurt am Main: Suhrkamp, 1977), 281.

Chapter 7

DIALOGICAL RATIONALITY AND THE CRITIQUE OF ABSOLUTE AUTONOMY

Brian Jacobs

Subject autonomy is one of the most tenaciously nagging ideas of the Enlightenment tradition, at once indispensable and obscure. Kant's initial employment of the term seemed to provide a parallel "Copernican revolution" for systematic moral and political theory as the *Critique of Pure Reason* had provided for epistemology.[1] But it remained in critical philosophy a tentative experiment, and, as I shall later explain, a practical intervention in a problem that Kant himself did not think he had resolved. His comment toward the end of his life that "all philosophy is autonomy" already suggests the extent to which this concept had remained a life-long concern.[2] In Critical Theory—from Horkheimer to Adorno, Marcuse to Habermas—the appropriation of subject autonomy, a Kantian term, appears in its various shades as the basis of rational resistance to social and political domination; it may itself be the product of such coercive institutional systems, but the possibility always remains open to appropriate it for emancipatory ends.

For contemporary Critical Theory, a consideration of the status of autonomy is a means by which one can evaluate not only the internal integrity and coherence of the project, but also crucial aspects of the debates between it and "postmodern" criticisms of Enlightenment subjectivity. As Peter Dews has recently argued, one important point that is often overlooked, in the debates between Habermas and his opponents, is that they do share considerable philosophical assumptions. And not least among these is the view that, in Dews' words, "the era of the philosophy of the subject, which is also the culminating era of metaphysical thinking, is currently drawing to a close."[3]

Much of both the shared assumptions and the debate, however, concerns views about self-consciousness: there is a general agreement that the "classical" model of reflection, the paradigm of what Habermas calls the "philosophy of consciousness," is exhausted; the question, of course, is whether it is to be replaced or abandoned altogether. When it appears in these debates, the concept of autonomy is usually viewed as an appendage to a theory of self-consciousness: if one has a coherent view of how one knows oneself *as oneself*, then it follows that one can know that one's actions in some sense also "belong" to oneself, and hence, that they occur because one chooses them by and for oneself.

I would like to suggest, however, that the issues of self-consciousness and individual autonomy pose considerably different kinds of problems. An account of individuation, or of the formation of selfhood, cannot by itself provide the justification for why we ought to ascribe to ourselves the authority, or, more precisely, the "self-legislative" control over any particular act. Given, in other words, a defensible form of self-consciousness (whether one conceives of it through reflection theory, linguistic intersubjectivity, or some other way), one is still left with this question: why should one view those acts, opinions, and beliefs that one considers his or her own as particularly "autonomous"? This question is central for Critical Theory, and yet it remains without an adequate response.

In this essay I would like to consider both the contemporary critique of Kant's theory of absolute autonomy as well as the attempt to reconstitute a more limited form of self-determination under the aegis of dialogical rationality. What I wish to defend is not so much Kant's solution to the problem of autonomy, but his conception of the problem itself. For if a psychoanalytic-linguistic defense of autonomy is inadequate—a position I shall take —a psychoanalytic-linguistic critique does not sufficiently capture the extent of the problem either. What I wish to defend, then, is the Kantian view that the concept of autonomy is far more *tenuous* in experience than our contemporary prejudices perhaps allow, and that an adequate account of this experience leads us ineluctably back to (at least a modest form of) metaphysics. But metaphysics in this sense may mean nothing more than what Kant took it to mean: a repository of practically necessary ideas that experience can neither confirm nor deny. What seems to me inescapable, with regard to subject autonomy, is that there is an inextinguishable element of *Glaube* (belief or faith) in positing it. Kant accepted this, but emphasized that it is not religious *Glaube* but *Vernunftglaube*, a reason-belief, or a belief of reason, that leads us to it; *Vernunftglaube*, as Kant sees it, is the compass that provides our orientation in thinking.[4]

With the notable exception of Dieter Henrich, Manfred Frank, and a few others, however, one would be hard pressed today to find metaphysical defenses of subjectivity, much less of subject autonomy. When Kant appropriated the term in 1785, metaphysics was also rather out of favor, relentlessly attacked by counter-Enlightenment theologians and clerics, on the one side, and by Enlightenment skeptics and propositivists, such as Voltaire, on the other. Kant coined the term "indifferentism" to refer to these latter, who, he thought, were either unable or unwilling to recognize the metaphysical assumptions implicit in their philosophical standpoints. Indifferentists, as he stated in the first *Critique*, are those who speak in a popular tone against school philosophy, but who fall "unavoidably back into metaphysical assertions for which they have nonetheless professed so much contempt."[5] It may be that our professedly "postmetaphysical" age also suffers from this indifferentism.

This essay proceeds in two parts: first, I consider elements of the critique of absolute autonomy that contemporary figures in Critical Theory have adopted and turn to Habermas' alternative formulation of a dialogical model (whose antecedents lie already in the third *Critique* and in the early Fichte), viewing it partially as a response to this critique. In the second part, I take up Kant's appropriation of the term and discuss what is distinctive about it. And perhaps most importantly, I emphasize Kant's view of the "heteronomous" world to which such a concept is meant to stand against—which, it turns out, eliminates, and I think rightly so, the idea of an experiential form of autonomous selfhood.

I

Although Habermas had already made clear in his *Philosophical Discourse of Modernity* that he accepts the principle Foucauldian objections to the "philosophy of consciousness"—namely, that there is no mediation possible in the relationships of the transcendental and empirical egos as they appear and reappear in modern thought—Axel Honneth and Albrecht Wellmer have recently suggested a result of this position for subject autonomy. Honneth suggests that two "intellectual currents" challenge the "classical concept" of subjectivity."[6] The first current consists of Freud and his precursors in early German Romanticism as well as Nietzsche: "By pointing to the consciousness-eluding, unconscious driving forces and motives of individual action, it demonstrates that the human subject cannot be transparent to herself in the manner claimed in the classical notion of the subject."[7]

As Wellmer argues, after these criticisms, both the unity and the "self-transparence" of the ego must be viewed as a "fiction"[8]: "The 'de-centered' subject of psychoanalysis, in other words, is an intersecting point of psychic and social forces rather than the master of these forces; a stage for a series of conflicts rather than the director of a drama or the author of a story."[9] The radicalization of this model follows, according to Wellmer, in a second step with Horkheimer and Adorno's *Dialectic of Enlightenment*. Although also essentially a psychological (or intentionalist) argument, this "critique of discursive reason as *instrumental* reason"[10] nevertheless departs significantly from Freud insofar as it emphasizes the violence, rather than an "act of autonomous self-positing,"[11] that stands at the origin of the ego's constitution.

The second intellectual current that challenges the concept of subjectivity exists in the form of the later Wittgenstein as well as Saussure and his followers (although Honneth only elsewhere suggests Derrida explicitly). Honneth argues: "By pointing to the dependence of individual speech on a pregiven system of linguistic meanings, it shows that the human subject cannot constitute or exhaust meaning in the manner presumed primarily in transcendental philosophy."[12] Wellmer suggests that this development—rather than the psychoanalytic critique—constitutes the most radical challenge. For unlike Nietzsche, Freud, Horkheimer, or Adorno, this linguistic critique breaks with the "model of a meaning-constituting subject which posits itself in transcendental singularity against a world of objects."[13]

According to Honneth and Wellmer, particularly Wittgenstein introduces a new form of skepticism that, Wellmer points out, "puts into question even the certainties of Hume or Descartes."[14] For now the questions are "How can I know of what I speak? How can I know what I mean?"[15] According to Wellmer, this critique begun by Wittgenstein means the destruction of the "subject as author and as last judge of his meaning intentions."[16] Honneth thinks that the "philosophically decisive problem" concerns the conclusions that one must draw from these two currents: that "the human subject is no longer to be grasped as one completely transparent to herself or as a being in command of herself."[17]

Psychoanalytic and linguistic criticisms have certainly sharpened our awareness of some of the elements that undermine autonomous rational action. But, as I shall discuss shortly, this account of the "classical" view of the subject misunderstands, and indeed idealizes, the problem as Kant saw it. Before turning to Kant, however, I want to consider how the Habermasian model attempts to deal with these challenges.

As is well-known, Habermas is committed to naturalizing the Kantian model of transcendental philosophy by shifting from a paradigm of subject/object relations to one of "linguistically generated intersubjectivity."[18] Instead of considering ourselves from the perspective of an observer, this shift allows the ego to relate to him- or herself as a participant in an interaction from the perspective of the other. George Herbert Mead's contribution in particular, according to Habermas, provides the basis of a plausible theory of social individuation. In this case, the individual appears not in the independent and isolated singularity of a subject, but as a social being who gains one's self-understanding simultaneously with the understanding of others through communicative practice.[19]

To the inward possessiveness of an isolated subject, Habermas would oppose "the self of an ethical self-understanding." Instead of self-possession, the constitution of the self begins with a naturalized form of recognition: "Because others attribute accountability to me, I gradually make myself into the one who I have become in living together with others."[20] The I, in this case, "retains an intersubjective core because the process of individuation from which it emerges runs through the network of linguistically mediated interactions."[21]

The I, then, is not one's "own" and, somewhat paradoxically, subject autonomy lies "outside" of the subject. I am autonomous and individuated because, as a speaker that raises claims, others hold me to be so. I learn my individuality, autonomy, and spontaneity from others who expect as much from me.

Following Mead, Habermas wants to reverse the classical relationship between the spontaneous ego and the socially-constructed "me."[22] The "me" that emerges from discursive recognition, he suggests, recalls "the exact memory" of a still hidden spontaneous I: "The self that is given to me through the mediation of the gaze of the other upon me is the 'memory image' of my ego, such as it has just acted in the sight of an alter ego and face to face with it." But as "the reflected self-relation of a subject speaking with itself," Habermas admits, it still presupposes an "*originary* self-consciousness."[23] Like Mead, Habermas thinks that, as a speaker, one always does presuppose this, and must necessarily. Whereas Kant, as I shall suggest, projects the spontaneous "I" forever forward onto a kingdom of ends, Habermas and Mead project it forever backward, as an historical trace, a "shadow" that is always a step behind the subject's awareness of itself: "The self of self-consciousness is not the spontaneously acting 'I'; the latter is given only in the refraction of the symbolically captured meaning that it took on for its interaction partner 'a second ago' in the role of alter ego."[24]

Although Habermas thinks that this moves us beyond a metaphysical view of spontaneity (since it appears to be "communicatively-generated"), Mead, to be sure, sees himself posing another question altogether—one that does not deny the metaphysical content of the spontaneous ego so much as suspend it: "I do not mean to raise the metaphysical question of how a person can be both 'I' and 'me,' but to ask for the significance of the distinction from the point of view of conduct itself."[25]

Habermas, of course, recognizes that the paradigm shift would hardly be complete unless it includes an answer to precisely the question that Mead avoids. The intersubjective view of individuation and autonomy responds to the critique of "the classical subject," then, by avoiding the problem of monological self-reflection: there is no need for one to posit one's self either as "completely transparent to him- or herself or as a being in command of him- or herself" since the processes of acquiring autonomy are not one that a person determines alone. Since one comes to recognize one's indi-

viduation and autonomy through social relations, the claims that
one raises regarding individuation and autonomy is always open-
ended and testable: others, in other words, can challenge one's sense
of self-clarity and self-directed action.

What I would like to emphasize here is that such a suggestion
rests upon a considerable reduction of the claim of autonomy in two
related ways. First, insofar as it is constituted through social relations,
autonomy has no meaning apart from its employment in communicative practice. "External" normative expectations alone provides
the basis on what Habermas calls the "autonomization of the self."[26]
Correspondingly, "heteronomy" takes on a similarly socialized form:
it appears as "the dependence on existing norms."[27] Just as social
relations provide the possibility of autonomy, so too, it seems, can
these relations alone undermine it.

Second, insofar as it is a historical concept, autonomy is always
contingent upon specific conditions. Autonomy, Habermas argues,
"can be reasonably expected *(zumutbar)* only in social contexts that
are already themselves rational in the sense that they ensure that
action motivated by good reasons will not of necessity conflict with
one's own interest."[28] Or, as he puts it elsewhere, "Any universalistic morality is dependent upon a form of life that *meets it halfway.*
There has to be a modicum of congruence between morality and the
practices of socialization and education."[29] But the problem of historical contingency, and with it a theory of history, drop out. There
is no way to account theoretically for the historical conditions that
would allow for the possibility of this kind autonomy: it must
appear as an accident and be judged better than another alternative
only from the standpoint of the contingent relations themselves.

I hope it will become clear as I turn now to Kant's model, that
Habermas' dialogical view of autonomy is not so much an alternative to the Kantian formulation as it is a suspension of a metaphysical content that is always already supposed. As I shall suggest, there
is nothing particularly incompatible with Mead's theory of social
individuation and Kant's view of the empirical self.

II

Kant approaches the problem of autonomy, as he does moral philosophy generally, with the concern of a "natural philosopher" who

believes that science, or more precisely the reigning "natural history" of the day, seems to be eliminating the possibility of human freedom. This view of experience leads Kant to suggest in the first *Critique* that all empirical events (including all human activity) could, in principle, be traced back to their determinate causes: "If we could probe all the appearances of [people's] will back to their basis *(Grund),* there would be not a single human action that we could not with certainty predict and recognize as necessary from its preceding conditions."[30]

The notion that human experience unfolds according to natural-historical laws of causality sets up the basic problem of autonomy. In the *Groundwork of the Metaphysics of Morals*, the text that introduces the autonomy concept, natural-historical causality appears in the form of "heteronomy": the totality of natural forces that shape who and what we are. And it is significant here that, as opposed to Habermas, Kant sees social-cultural relations as the *effect* of this heteronomy rather than a cause.

If Kantian autonomy must be seen first as a moral concept, then one must nevertheless also consider that Kant's response to the problem of human uniqueness within the perspective of natural history is essentially a moral one. Autonomy as it appears in the *Groundwork* ought to be seen as a practical or political intervention that intends to rescue the concept of freedom by conceiving of it as inaccessible to human reason. As Kant suggests toward the end of the work, "Where determination according to natural laws ends, however, there ends also all *explanation*. And what remains is nothing other than *defense*, that is, the expulsion *(Abtreibung)* of reproaches of those who claim to have looked deeper into the essence of things and then unabashedly explain freedom as impossible."[31]

The task of the *Groundwork*, as Kant makes clear, is not to show how autonomy is possible (much less that it actually exists), but rather to demonstrate that active moral life must necessarily assume autonomy as an unverifiable, and hence metaphysical, idea.[32] Indeed, the *absolute* opposition between the "mechanism of nature" and freedom,[33] along with Kant's deep skepticism that one can ever distill an autonomous action from the subjective "interests" that otherwise cause people to act,[34] led Kant to think that one can *never* know whether an autonomous act has occurred in experience.

And yet it is precisely this mystery that secures the space where autonomy is at least possible as an idea. Since human understanding does not have the capacity to isolate autonomy as an experiential property, neither can it justifiably reduce all human action to natural causality simply because nature alone constitutes our experience of the world. One might recall here Kant's comment in the *Critique of Judgment*: "Perhaps nothing more sublime has ever been said, or a thought ever been expressed more sublimely, than in that inscription above the temple of *Isis* (mother nature): 'I am all that is, that was, and that will be, and no mortal has lifted my veil.'"[35]

The "true self"[36] that Kant posits as a necessary ideation stemming from this cognitive limit creates a peculiar situation: precisely to the extent that it is purely rational, a "true self" could not be conceived as a particularly *human* one. Already, then, in the conception of the true self as purely autonomous rational action, one confronts the antecedent to the "intellectual intuition" of the third *Critique* that would prove so decisive for Fichte, Schelling, and Hegel: for it is this notion of disembodied rational activity that unites both all rational beings with one another and with nature.

Since attributes that make up the notion of human nature or character are always based on experience, there is no way for Kant to connect directly the true self—as autonomous agent—with human beings. Indeed, there is good reason to think that Kant did not conceive of this rational being as necessarily a human one. In the early work *Universal Natural History and Theory of the Heavens*, for example, Kant suggests not only that rational beings probably inhabit other worlds, but that human beings (along with the inhabitants of neighboring Mars) might merely constitute a middle position on the scale of "moral constitution" that would correspond to their planetary position:

> Does not a certain middle position between wisdom and unreason belong to the unfortunate capacity that enables sin? Who knows? Are not consequently the inhabitants of those most distant world bodies too sublime and too wise to lower themselves to folly which is set in sin, while those however who live in the lower planets are too firmly fastened to matter and provided with far too few capacities of mind (*Geist*) so that the responsibility of their actions must be dragged before the tribunal (*Richterstuhle*) of justice? ... In fact, both planets, Earth and Mars, are the most middle members of the planetary system, and a middle position in both physical and moral constitution may be easily supposed, perhaps not with improbability, of their inhabitants.[37]

Accordingly, what would distinguish these rational beings from one another is not the rationality itself (which is universal) but the particular empirical characteristics that make up the nature of such beings and the degree to which they are "fastened" to these qualities. The true self, as a nonmaterial self, is, presumably, potentially at home on any planet and in any body.

Where does this leave the material, corporeal self—the only self to which one has access, the "classical" self that subsequent theoretical insight has done so much to undermine? Kant makes it very clear that he does not think we can ever really know ourselves, much less command ourselves as empirical beings. He argues in the *Groundwork*, for example, that "through the knowledge that [he—*sic*] has through his inner sensation, [man] may not presume to recognize how he is in himself. For since he does not, as it were, create himself and [since he] obtains his concept [of himself] not a priori but rather empirically, so is it natural that he can also only collect knowledge *(Kundschaft)* of himself through the inner sense and accordingly only through the appearance of his nature and the way his consciousness is affected."[38]

Our knowledge of ourselves consists, rather, of sensuous affectations and this is tenuous knowledge at best. The empirical Kantian self, as the Nietzschean self, is *Schein* (appearance), both to itself and to others. It is, in other words, precisely the "decentered self" that Wellmer argues is the "intersecting point of psychic and social forces." But Kant's skepticism on self-knowledge seems to me still deeper than these views that would undermine the classical model: for Kant's idea of a lack of self-control is constituted within a natural-historical model rather than a social one; humans lack self-determination not simply because they have not mastered language or have not a better understanding of ourselves as psychic entities, but more fundamentally because we are natural-historical beings subject to the same kind of causality that are all living beings.

The opacity of this self, its utter lack of transparency, is captured in Kant's notion of "obscure representations." The phrase, which comes by way of Descartes and Leibniz, appears in the first *Critique* as a means by which one can distinguish different degrees of consciousness. An "obscure representation" here is one that exists in some way in the mind, but that consciousness cannot clarify for itself. In the lectures on anthropology, however, Kant suggests that "The field of sensuous intuitions and sensations of which we are not conscious, although we can doubtlessly conclude that we have them, that is, obscure representations in man (and so also in animals), is immeasurable."[39] Kant then suggests that human consciousness is like a huge map that contains many points: the very few that are illuminated are clear representations; the rest—which make up most of consciousness—remain obscure. This self-opacity, moreover, is the very basis on which human beings appear to act.

What is remarkable about Kant's view of the human subject is not that he views it as transparent to itself or in command of itself—he definitely does not. What is remarkable rather is that, given precisely this "decentered" view of the subject, Kant nevertheless defends the idea of autonomy. One might offer the objection that subjectivity for Kant consists solely of the pure-thought activity of the transcendental ego; the empirical ego is utterly passive and could not be viewed as an agent. But this objection introduces a strict dualism that I do not think Kant held. The "form" or "way of representation," Kant thinks, is twofold, but not the "material (content)."[40]

Habermas suggests that intersubjective autonomy "takes into account that the free actualization of the personality of one individual depends on the actualization of freedom for all."[41] But quite mistakenly, he assumes that such a view is at odds with the Kantian version. Indeed, this is precisely the idea behind a projected "kingdom of ends," where autonomous agents would universally respect each other as such. Like Habermas, Kant too thinks that the concept of autonomy is socially-historically contingent: it is contingent upon what he calls the "civil condition" of a juridical state, upon proper pedagogy, as well as upon environmentally-determined conditions. He also holds a range of what one would now consider racist and sexist views as to why morality is the potential destiny of white male Europeans alone. Autonomy, and more broadly reason, is merely a natural predisposition of all human beings insofar as they are all *potentially* reasoning beings *(Vernunftwesen)*. Whether or not this is actualized depends largely on the course of history; but it also depends, somewhat paradoxically, on the *exercise* of reason and autonomy. The outcome depends upon whether human beings can *make* their own history in some significant sense.

The paradox consists, then, of the peculiar fact that the goal of an autonomous subject in the kingdom of ends presupposes this agency (even if not as conscious knowledge to the subject). As opposed to Hegel, however, Kant is not convinced that history will lead humanity to such a kingdom. He thinks that one ought to make it our maxim to work toward it, but should one ever achieve it, the force that brings us there will be our own *nonconscious* exercise of freedom, rather than any empirically-verifiable-deliberative action on our part. The central point here, however, is that a plausible theory of autonomy must at once presuppose autonomy (and take account of this presupposition metaphysically) and, simultaneously, hold it out as a collective end by way of a teleological principle.

The concept of *sensus communis*, as articulated in the third *Critique*, suggests a move to an intersubjective or collective notion of rationality, where our agreement on what constitutes the beautiful would reveal the universality of morality and, therefore, of autonomy. But, without a notion of calling or destiny *(Bestimmung)* coupled with it, Kant recognizes, one can neither suppose nor project a plausible concept. Hence, the importance of *Vernunftglaube*. Autonomy, in Kant's sense, is about the ability to legislate to oneself *who*, as moral agents, one wishes to be; and in this sense, too, it is absolute: either one is capable of doing this at *every* level of determination or one is not, and must either do without it and bind ourselves to irrational or at best nonrational forces, or appeal (as Kant does) to providence, to nature, to the future possibility of a noumenal subject actualized in history.

Kant's notion of "moral personality" (which identifies the autonomous subject) presupposes both the skill of our "animality" and the *prudentia* or "prudence" that brings human beings together as "humanity." By the former, he is thinking of that capacity of self-preservation that we share with animals; the latter, that capacity to negotiate with others as instrumentally rational agents. Through this association with other human beings, Kant thinks, one is forced to act according to ethical principles—and hence, one must feign our morality. Somewhat optimistically, perhaps, he thinks that if one continues to feign our moral character long enough, one just may accidentally acquire an authentic one. For through the situation, he comments, "that men play this role, virtue, whose appearance for a long time has only been contrived, will little by little really awaken and pass over into conviction."[42] The notion of self-determination operative at this level of "humanity" is similar to Habermas' intersubjective reconstruction of autonomy. Habermas is essentially rearticulating what one might call the pragmatic-political dimension of freedom in Kant's thought, while necessarily presupposing an anterior one which would allow (if only negatively) for its possibility.

Kant rightly views this, however, as a weak sense of freedom. As a contingent concept, it can never account for the conditions that allow it to exist. On its own, it confers no more autonomy than that of a "turnspit," as the example runs in the second *Critique*, which, once wound up, also carries out actions on its own. One might attribute autonomy to oneself; we might act *as if* one is we are our own authors because others hold us responsible for our claims, but this hardly provides assurance that this "self-positing" is not illusory. It does not provide the assurance, that is, that the positing is not as Kant would view it: as merely the outcome of the play of nature at various levels of determination, discursive practice being merely one. For the Jena Idealists, of course, such a self-positing derives its truth-content from the view that the objective world originates entirely within subjectivity. And if one were willing to grant this fantastic metaphysical claim, then a theory of mutual recognition among such world-creating subjects would have far more explanatory power for individual autonomy.

Habermas' reconstruction of autonomy as an appendage of social-linguistic individuation, then, is "postmetaphysical" in the sense that, like Mead's reconstruction of individuation, it suspends rather than overcomes the metaphysical problem. The place that metaphysics occupies in the Kantian version—as the positive freedom determining an empirically recognizable negative form and as the constitutive element that one must always presuppose in the pragmatic-political notion of freedom—is in Habermas' account an empty space.

But if intersubjective autonomy must presuppose an inextinguishable rational belief, so too must even its most vociferous critics: for a *truly* consistent denial of the metaphysical space for such *Vernunfglaube* would lead to irredeemable doubt, as Friedrich Jacobi long ago pointed out. Given the historical accidents that have allowed us to choose between superstition and rational belief, it may well be that the task at hand is to move beyond a purely moral theory of autonomy. Such a reconstruction, however, would still need to take account of the unfathomably full range of the world that stands against our autonomous selves.

Notes

1. Martin Gueroult is perhaps the first to have suggested this. See his "Canon de la Raison pure et critique de la Raison pratique," *Revue internationale de Philosophie* 8.30 (1954): 357; see also Bernard Carnois, *The Coherence of Kant's Doctrine of Freedom*, trans. David Booth (Chicago: University of Chicago Press, 1987), 79.
2. Eckhardt Förster, ed., *Opus Postumum* (Cambridge: Cambridge University Press, 1993), 244.
3. Peter Dews, *The Limits of Disenchantment* (New York: Verso, 1995), 169.
4. Immanuel Kant, "Was heisst: sich im Denken orientieren?", vol. 5 of *Werke*, *Sonderausgabe*, ed. Wilhelm Weischedel (1755; Darmstadt: Wissenschaftliche Buchgesellschaft, 1983), 277.
5. Immanuel Kant, *Kritik der reinen Vernunft*, ed. Raymund Schmidt, 2nd ed. (1781; Leipzig: Felix Meiner, 1930), 6.
6. Axel Honneth, *The Fragmented World of the Social*, ed. Charles W. Wright (Albany: State University of New York Press, 1995), 261.
7. Honneth, *The Fragmented World of the Social*, 261.
8. Albrecht Wellmer, *Zur Dialektik von Moderne und Postmoderne* (Frankfurt am Main: Suhrkamp Verlag, 1985), 71.
9. Wellmer, *Zur Dialektik von Moderne und Postmoderne*, 71.
10. Wellmer, *Zur Dialektik von Moderne und Postmoderne*, 77.
11. Wellmer, *Zur Dialektik von Moderne und Postmoderne*, 75.
12. Honneth, *The Fragmented World of the Social*, 261.
13. Wellmer, *Zur Dialektik von Moderne und Postmoderne*, 77.
14. Wellmer, *Zur Dialektik von Moderne und Postmoderne*, 78.
15. Wittgenstein cited in Wellmer, *Zur Dialektik von Moderne und Postmoderne*, 78.
16. Wellmer, *Zur Dialektik von Moderne und Postmoderne*, 78.
17. Honneth, *The Fragmented World of the Social*, 262.
9. Habermas, *The Philosophical Discourse of Modernity* (Cambridge: MIT Press, 1987), 297.
10. Habermas, *Postmetaphysical Thinking* (Cambridge: MIT Press, 1992), 153.
11. Habermas, *Postmetaphysical Thinking*, 170.
12. Habermas, *Postmetaphysical Thinking*, 170.
13. Habermas, *Postmetaphysical Thinking*, 187.
14. Habermas, *Postmetaphysical Thinking*, 172.
15. Habermas, *Postmetaphysical Thinking*, 177.
16. George Herbert Mead, *Mind, Self, and Society* (Chicago: University of Chicago Press, 1934), 173.
17. Habermas, *Postmetaphysical Thinking*, 152.
18. Habermas, *Moral Consciousness and Communicative Action*, 162.
19. Jürgen Habermas, *Justification and Application: Remarks on Discourse Ethics*, trans. Ciaran Cronin (Cambridge: MIT Press, 1993) 34.
20. Habermas, *Moral Consciousness and Communicative Action*, 207.
21. Kant, *Kritik der reinen Vernunft*, b578/9/a550/1, emphasis mine.
22. Immanuel Kant, *Grundlegung zur Metaphysik der Sitten*, ed. Karl Vorlaender (Leipzig: Felix Meiner, 1906), 459.
23. Kant, *Grundlegung zur Metaphysik der Sitten*, 445.

24. Kant, *Grundlegung zur Metaphysik der Sitten,* 458.
25. Kant, *Grundlegung zur Metaphysik der Sitten,* 461.
26. Immanuel Kant, *Critique of Judgment,* trans. Werner Pluhar (1790; Indianapolis: Hackett, 1987), 185.
27. Kant, *Grundlegung zur Metaphysik der Sitten* , 457.
28. Immanuel Kant, *Allgemeine Naturgeschichte und Theorie des Himmels,* vol. 1 of *Werke,* 394.
29. Kant, *Grundlegung zur Metaphysik der Sitten* , 77.
30. Immanuel Kant, *Anthropologie in pragmatischer Hinsicht,* vol. 10 of *Werke,* 418.
31. Kant, *Anthropologie,* 417.
32. Habermas, *Moral Consciousness and Communicative Action,* 207.
33. Kant, *Anthropologie in pragmatischer Hinsicht,* 442-43.

Chapter 8

CIVIL SOCIETY IN THE INFORMATION AGE

Beyond the Public Sphere[1]

Jodi Dean

Three Salons

Recently, I visited Borders Books' online magazine, *Salon*. During the first week of the Monica Lewinsky scandal I had enjoyed some of their commentary, so I thought it might be interesting to hear discussions on the website. From among hundreds of options, I could choose to chat with other mothers about the challenges of mothering, debate current events, or analyze television shows. I decided to join the group on current political and cultural events. Again, the site offered a smorgasbord of choices: gay parents, gays in the military, gay school teachers—the very range of options on queer matters opened a window onto contemporary cultural anxieties around perceived threats to straight sex. After ascertaining that most of these "discussions" were voyeuristic excuses to gay bash or painstakingly detail a variety of sexual practices and positions, I went to a group considering the pros and cons of establishing English as the official language of the United States. I found it difficult to follow—or find—the logic of the discussion: few of the comments seemed relevant; they weren't exactly reasons offered to justify a position or convince another participant. One thread concerned why Germans like to watch American blockbuster movies and whether *Titanic* would be a hit in Europe. Other remarks offered were "Hi," "Jimbo's remark was lame," and "Later."

This brief foray into *Salon*'s discussion list is not an exhaustive account of talk on the Internet or life in cyberspace. Rather, it provides a snapshot of the salon as a predominant form of computer-mediated discussion, of communication among persons linked not by proximity, tradition, or ethnicity, but by an ability to use, and interest, in networked interaction. Such a cybersalon, moreover, provides a window onto the broader complexities of communication, interaction, and information exchange in late-capitalist technoculture.

I want to contrast this salon with two other snapshots of salons, those offered by Jürgen Habermas and Seyla Benhabib. In his *The Structural Transformation of the Public Sphere*, Habermas presents the salons of eighteenth-century France as instances of the newly emerging bourgeois public sphere. There, bourgeoisie, nobles, and intellectuals only recently removed from their plebeian origins met on equal footing. As Habermas writes, "In the *salon* the mind was no longer in the service of a patron; 'opinion' became emancipated from the bonds of economic dependence."[2] People could exchange ideas and voice criticism of matters of shared interest or concern. The vitality of the exchanges was such that new works and ambitious minds first sought legitimacy in the salons.

Habermas links the salons with the *Tischgesellschaften* and coffee houses of Germany and England to abstract the various characteristics of this new form of interaction, which was for him the newly constituted sphere of private persons come together as a public. First, the salon disregarded social status; it offered a fundamental parity among all participants such that the authority of the better argument could win out over social hierarchy. Second, new areas of questioning and critique were opened up as culture itself was produced as a commodity to be consumed. Third, the newly emerging public was established as open and inclusive in principle. That is to say, anyone could have access to that which was discussed in the public sphere. Fourth, these abstractions lead Habermas to conceptualize the public sphere in terms of the public use of reason.

Benhabib's depiction of the salon comes from a rather different, and largely feminist, position. In her essay on Hannah Arendt's biography of Rahel Varnhagen, "The Pariah and Her Shadow," Benhabib views the salon as "a space of sociability in which the individual desire for difference and distinctiveness could assume an intersubjective reality and in which unusual individuals, and primarily certain highly talented Jewish women, could find a 'space' of visibility and self-expression."[3] Contrasting Arendt's conception of the public sphere in *The Human Condition* with her account of the salon in the biography of Varnhagen, Benhabib brings to light the feminine, ludic, and erotic components of the salon. She highlights the world-disclosing aspects of the language used in the salon, the joy and magic of shared speech. She stresses the play of identities at work in the salons, the ways in which self-revelation and self-concealment disrupt the ideal of the transparency part of the public sphere.

With this reading of Arendt, Benhabib counters Habermas's vision of the salon as a rational public sphere to envision it in terms of a sphere of civic friendship. She thus presents the ideals of the modern salon as the joy of conversation, the search for friendship, and the cultivation of intimacy. Finally, even as she foregrounds the difference, desire, and dissonance of salon interactions, Benhabib finds embedded in Arendt's vision of the salon one key element of overlap with Habermas. Both find in the salon a disregard for status and fundamental equality based on shared humanity.

I have introduced three salons: the cyber, the rational, and the friendly. All three are empirically drawn and historically informed. As Peter Hohendahl points out, Habermas's salon has been supplanted by a less situated, more abstract vision of the public sphere.[4] Benhabib's account functions as a supplement to some of the criticisms leveled at the rational public sphere model—one that she has accepted in the past—and provides a different, albeit similarly abstract, vision of the ideals of modernity.[5] My argument is that the cybersalon underscores the inadequacies of the concept of the public sphere for any critical democratic theory attuned to the complexities of the information age.

Hubertus Buchstein has recently brought the rational and friendly salons—that is, the abstracted ideals of the public sphere important to second and third generation Critical Theory—to bear on the cybersalon. Buchstein challenges advocates of computer-mediated democracy to defend their claims that the Internet can serve as a new critical public or counterpublic sphere.[6] He notes that, according to those "optimists" with high hopes for computer democracy, "the new technology seems to match all basic requirements of Habermas's normative theory of the democratic public sphere: it is a universal, antihierarchical, complex, and demanding mode of interaction. Because it offers universal access, uncoerced communication, freedom of expression, an unrestricted agenda, participation outside of traditional political institutions and generates public opinion through processes of discussion, the Internet looks like the most ideal speech situation."[7] Despite the similarity of the metaphors used by net-enthusiasts and critical theorists, Buchstein concludes that the Internet is not a new public sphere, that it fails to live up to these norms, and that computer-mediated interaction in fact may well distort citizenship.

While I agree with Buchstein's conclusion that networked interactions fail to live up to the norms of the public sphere, I would claim that this tells us more about the limitations of the notion of the public sphere as one grapples with the complexities of transnational technoculture in the information age than it does about the political and democratic potential of cyberia. As I've argued elsewhere, to territorialize cyberia as the public sphere is to determine in advance what sort of engagements and identities are proper to the political, and to use this determination to homogenize political engagement, neutralize social space, and sanitize popular cultures. Such a territorialization, moreover, configures those excesses of the Internet that resist compilation into a normative vision of the public sphere as pathologies and exceptions that do not apply to, that are outside of, that bind this public sphere, and so continue to reassure the public sphere's claims to freedom and democracy.[8] Just as Adorno's negative vision of mass culture inflected Habermas's valuation of the bourgeois public sphere, and his subsequent story of the fall into merely commercial and instrumental interaction, so does the normalizing discourse of the public sphere occlude potential freedoms and dangers in the information age. In light of the new possibilities and dangers that new forms of computer-mediated interaction pose, I suggest that critical and democratic theorists jettison the idea of the public sphere and adopt a more complex model of civil society. Such a model, I argue, is not only more appropriate to the networked interactions of cybersalons, but also better accords, more generally, with the complexities of power, knowledge, and communication in and among contemporary late-capitalist societies.

I would like to address a potential criticism in advance. One might agree that my criticism of the inapplicability of public-sphere norms to cyberspace may apply to early theorizations of the public sphere, the historically informed one of *Structural Transformation* as well as the more abstract versions influenced by discourse ethics; but one might argue that it does not apply to the differentiated, porous, and multiple spheres concept more recently developed by Habermas, Benhabib, and Nancy Fraser. Not only has Habermas concluded that his discussion of the move from a "culture-debating to a culture-consuming public" was too simplistic, but he has also rejected his earlier pessimism "about the resisting power and above all the critical potential of a pluralistic, internally much differentiated mass public whose cultural usages have begun to shake off the constraints of class."[9] Instead of a unitary public sphere, he now talks about "the informal networks of the public sphere" and "widely expanded and differentiated public spheres."[10] Benhabib similarly appeals to "a non-unitary and dispersed network of publics," to a "public sphere of mutually interlocking and overlapping networks and associations of deliberation, contestation, and argumentation."[11] She draws from Nancy Fraser's model of multiple, competing publics, of hegemonic and subaltern counterpublics.[12]

I am not convinced that adding an "s" to "public sphere" solves the problem. Indeed, the "s" confuses the theorization of democratic politics and gives a sameness and equality to different networks and spaces. It creates the illusion of options in a marketplace of ideas and opportunities. The multiple spheres approach suggests the old pluralist conception of democracy, in which various groups compete and compromise as equal players in the game of politics. Furthermore, despite its best intentions, the multiple spheres approach reinforces the priority of a bourgeois or official public sphere as a normative telos, as an ideal, as the fundamental arbiter of inclusion. Indeed, it tends to remain part of a theory that conceives democracy in terms of a general process of collective will formation rather than as a variety of multiple, conflicting processes of production, intervention, configuration, expansion, and exclusion.

Benhabib, for example, stresses that a moral ideal of impartiality should govern our deliberations in public.[13] How this stress can be reconciled with a notion of multiple spheres, however, is not clear: to what, exactly, does this ideal apply? If the ideal of impartiality should guide specific associations and discussions in civil society, then few discussions can be said to be aspects of a public sphere since few discussions have this ideal as their aim. From the specialized discourses of the academy to the commercialized discourse of some media; to the exclusivity of groups organized around interest, ethnicity, and sexuality; to the deliberately exclusionary think tanks and private clubs, the discussions institutionalized in civil society remain partial. For many who have voiced demands under the rubric of identity politics, the partiality of their discussions and interactions is crucial to their capacity to understand and present themselves as a group. If the ideal of impartiality applies to civil society as a whole, to the variety of discussions as they compete and overlap, then one set of norms is hypostatized over others, subverting the very heterogeneity that the notion of multiple spheres is supposed to provide. Finally, if the ideal of impartiality is understood strictly as a constitutional proviso—as a guarantee of the freedoms of association, opinion, and the press—then the public sphere remains tied to and dependent on the state, a demand only reinforcing a state-centered conception of democracy.[14] Indeed, with such a constitutionalist conception of impartiality, one overlooks the independence and creativity of interventions such as those of the new social movements, interventions that target not the state, but civil society itself.[15]

Not Just Another Public Sphere

Reliance on a top-down or unitary understanding of democratic deliberation hinders conceptualization of new terrains of contestation and debate. Judith Butler correctly points out: "To set the 'norms' of political life in advance is to prefigure the kinds of practices which will qualify as the political and it is to seek to negotiate politics outside of a history which is always to a certain extent opaque to us in the moment of action."[16] Using an ideal of impartiality to determine the boundaries of the public sphere misdirects critical democratic theory into a focus on closure, answers, and a preset categorization of discourses. Contrary to such a tendency, an emphasis on civil society can present a move toward openness, questioning, and the acknowledgment of the diversity of political styles and engagements.

The move to the public sphere shifts agents to the sites of political change. Whereas a current of Critical Theory from Marx to Marcuse found the potential for widespread political emancipation in the margins of society—in the revolutionary classes of the workers and then the students, racial minorities, and others excluded from the benefits of the capitalist state—the focus on the public sphere finds within society and the state, within the norms of the bourgeoisie, the potential for, if not universal emancipation, then at least the democratic legitimation of the late-capitalist state. Critical Theory has replaced revolutionary energy with democratic procedure. The "all" of the revolutionary class has become the "all" of democratic will formation.

The move to a concept of procedural democracy may well be a theoretical or even practical advance. Theoretically, procedural democracy suggests a more nuanced approach to political action, an awareness of differences among those who may occupy economic or racially similar subject positions. It may also offer a way of understanding how political conflict can be institutionalized within a constitutional state. Practically, it may posit political and social changes that do not require the violence of revolution. Nonetheless, the totalizing tendencies of the revolutionary impulse remain embedded in the concept of the public sphere. From a unified political or class consciousness, such theories shift the unity of public political reason to the unity of the procedures, as well as the outcomes of democratic deliberation, to a unity of the subjectivities capable of entering the terrain of the political. Their move back into society, moreover, downgrades the critical potential of the concept of the public sphere: now all are already equal, included, rational.

The concept of civil society I want to defend acknowledges the ubiquitous inequalities, constant exclusions, and competing rationalities characteristic of late-capitalist societies in an age of globalization. It does so by beginning not with a unified account of the political spaces, discussions, actions, and agents, but by stressing the multiple forms and forums of politics. Following Jean Cohen and Andrew Arato, I understand civil society as a space of social, cultural, and political interaction distinct from—although interconnected with—the state and the economy. The space demarcated by civil society includes a variety of institutions such as families, schools, media, churches, and activist groups. These various institutions have their own particular—and potentially conflicting—action norms. The differing forms of media connect with different and diverse audiences. Actors may be connected by proximity, interest, computers, DNA, or by a variety of economic and informational networks that transgress particular states and economies. For Cohen and Arato, what distinguishes civil society from the state and the economy is its primary mode of integration: whereas the state is organized around administrative power and the economy around money, civil society is integrated communicatively; it relies on communicative action.

To be sure, the distinction among these three domains does not mean that they don't influence or interpenetrate one another or deny their multiple intersections and overlaps. Instead, it indicates that civil society, the state, and the economy can be thought of as analytically separate terrains and attempts to provide a useful way for doing so. The utility of such an analytical distinction is that it permits the theorization of political actions not centered on the state or the economy. One can understand actions that target society, actions such as marches, parades, or kiss-ins, to be political because they try to change people's lives and perceptions. Symbolic practices constitute identities and define the norms of everyday life. At a time when ever fewer people are participating in electoral politics, reading the mainstream newspapers or watching the evening news on the major networks, the concept of civil society enables theory to avoid denigrating people as apolitical and instead consider how they directly experience and affect politics.

The analytical utility of the distinction between state, economy, and civil society should not, however, lead to the mistaken assumption that civil society is a domain free from power. So, instead of reading communicative action in terms of ideal Habermasian discourse, in which communication is opposed to power, I view it as always imbricated with power. Indeed, Cohen and Arato, even as they rely on Habermas, don't deny the role of power in civil society, that families are structured by power, for example, or that subjectivities are produced from within relations of power. Nonetheless, and especially with regard to the possibility of bureaucratic and economic encroachment on (or colonization of) civil society, they sometimes underestimate the violence, inequity, and domination in—or the impact of hegemonic power formations such as racism and homophobia on—civil society.

Foregrounding the inextricability of power from civil society signals a primary difference between it and the concept of the public sphere: namely, that the normativity of civil society does not rest on an opposition between consent and coercion, or between a terrain of idealized interactions and one of instrumentalized and/or hierarchicized interactions. Instead, the normativity of civil society rests in its capacity to secure plurality and difference, to allow for the variety of networks of power within which freedom is produced, and to remain open to the possibilities that might arise through conflict and contestation. Within such a conception of civil society, politics does not refer to the rational choices of rational actors or the rational agreements of citizens oriented toward reaching a unified understanding. Rather, the terrain of politics is understood as a site of struggles and contestations carried out by unequal partners under unequal conditions. This notion of civil society, moreover, works in theories that not only stress a decentered state, but also transgress the state to thematize global migrations, transnationalism, and the growth of global capital.

I would like to defend this view of civil society by returning to the site/nonsite of the salons, or more precisely, by considering the challenges that cyberia presents to the concept of the public sphere. Using four categories—interactivity, subjectivity, media, and site—I would like to contrast Habermas and Benhabib's public spheres with the cyberian conception of civil society I advocate. Again, I would like to suggest not simply that current conditions fail to realize the ideals of the public sphere. Rather the ideals of the public sphere are inadequate to the political potentials and problems of the contemporary world. They compel a misdiagnosis of the present.

Rational and Friendly Salons

Conceived as rational (Habermas) or friendly (Benhabib), the salons that inform the theory of the public sphere bring with them a set of basic assumptions regarding interactivity, subjectivity, media, and the site of the public sphere. Embodied subjects meet face to face, encountering one another directly in an unmediated space of interaction. Such encounters allow the subjects' orientations to the abstract norms of the developing constitutional nation-state, even as this state comes to be understood as securing the rights that enable the encounters themselves.

Interactivity

For Habermas and Benhabib the model of interactivity in the salon, a model that informs their conceptions of interaction in the public sphere, is in the first place based on face-to-face encounters: communicative exchanges between people who meet in person. They see each other—and indeed, both Habermas and Benhabib draw attention to the stylized and ceremonial dimensions of self-presentation in the public sphere. The underpinning assumption of face-to-face interactions enables Benhabib in particular to acknowledge both the already exclusive dimensions of the salon as well as the possibilities for intimacy: salon members could move into smaller groupings of twos and threes even as they remained participants in the larger gathering.

In the second place, the interactions among those meeting face-to-face are governed by norms. Public utterances should be authentic. For Habermas, this means that what one says in public is connected with a larger conception of reason, with an appeal to a common reason that transcends particular desires, machinations, or goals. For Benhabib, authenticity is more nuanced. She does not presume that interactions in the salon are transparent or that one's presentation in public is necessarily a presentation of who one is. At the same time, however, her account of intimacy in the salon still relies on a link between speech and authenticity. This reliance appears in her depiction of the salon as a place where the soul is "discovered" and in her appeal to civic friendship:

> The joy of speech culminates in friendship, in that meeting of hearts, minds, and tastes between two individuals. Particularly in the case of the German salons, the search for a "Seelensfreund," a friend of one's soul, one who understands oneself perhaps better than oneself, is predominant. With friends one shares one's soul; to share the soul though—an entity that itself comes to be discovered in this new process of individuation—one has to project a certain depth of the self; one has to view the self as a being whose public presence does not reveal all.[17]

Although Benhabib does not say so explicitly, it seems as if the presumption of a soul, of a deep authentic self, is a prerequisite for civic friendship. It provides the locus for trust and accountability, precisely those attributes necessary for the solidary bonds of citizenship, reciprocity, and respect.

Mentioned previously, in addition to the norm of authenticity, norms of equality and inclusivity govern interactions in rational and friendly salons. For Habermas and Benhabib, equality is an equality of persons based on shared humanity. Inclusivity refers to the possibility of access. Although specific salons are limited, in principle, anyone could discuss the same matters as those debated within them. For Habermas, the ideal of inclusion extends more explicitly to the possibility that any person could be part of "the" discussion. Benhabib refrains from such a strong claim even as she depicts the salons of Berlin as providing "spaces of visibility and self-expression" for excluded and secluded Jewish women.[18]

Subjectivity

In Habermas and Benhabib's accounts of the public sphere, the premise of shared humanity is buttressed by the sense that the meaning of humanity can be found in a deep, core interiority; in an interior having no connection with extrinsic purposes; in a subjectivity existing for itself.[19] This singular, unified, and embodied subjectivity was produced in the conjugal, patriarchal family. It was oriented toward an audience. The sense of self-presentation corresponded, moreover, to the sense of autonomy arising out of exchanges in the market.[20] Precisely because it functioned as the locus of love, self-cultivation, and autonomy, this conception of subjectivity is crucial to Habermas's argument in *Structural Transformation of the Public Sphere*: it makes possible the connection of the "role of property owners with the role of human beings pure and simple."[21] Benhabib extends Habermas's account of the intimacy of the family (or the intimacy aspect of the ideology of the bourgeois family) into the more playful and erotic intimacies of the salon. This enables her to hold onto a unitary conception of subjectivity even as she alleviates some of the tensions arising from its patriarchal origins.

Media

Although Benhabib's account of the salon in Hannah Arendt's biography of Rahel Varnhagen relies on a vision of unmediated face-to-face interactions, Habermas supplements his account with reference to two specific kinds of media, media that are particularly important to the newly emerging bourgeois public sphere. The first is the letter: "through letter writing the individual unfolded himself in his subjectivity."[22] As news-oriented letters evolved into "newspapers," the personal letter turned inward, coming to represent the deepest thoughts of the soul, its outpourings, sympathies, and longings. As such, the personal letter evoked and confirmed the subjectivity of the sender as well as the trust of the receiver.[23] Growing out of and extending from the letter is the second type of media—the domestic, psychological novel. The novel gave rise to new forms of association, to public libraries, reading circles, and book clubs. It gave people something to talk about, something to be held in common. It was a vehicle for their interactions with each other as a public. While the novel portrayed that cultivated subjectivity arising in the bourgeois family and sought to represent the deep emotions and intimacies of what was now understood to be human, it also led to a fictionalization of the human that challenged the boundaries of the real. As Habermas explains, "The reality as illusion that the new genre created received its proper name in English, 'fiction': it shed the character of the *merely* fictitious. The psychological novel fashioned for the first time the kind of realism that allowed anyone to enter into the literary action as a substitute for his own, to use the relationships between the figures, between the author, the characters, and the reader as substitute relationships for reality."[24] Needless to say, for Habermas the disruption of reality presented by the novel is not considered to be a problem; it is not understood as a challenge to the authentic interactions of embodied subjects meeting face to face. This challenge does not arise until the emergence of mass media, a public relations industry, and a culture-consuming public in the last decades of the nineteenth century.

Site

Finally, the salon, as the public sphere, is located within the nation-state. The nation-state is what gives unity and boundedness to Habermas's public sphere. Although he does not thematize the place of the public sphere in securing particular national identities, Habermas appeals to these identities as he highlights the German *Tischgesellschaften*, the English coffee houses, and the French salons. Furthermore, the political public sphere always targets the state: discussions are to impact upon the actions of specific governments within specific nations. Habermas writes: "The public of 'human beings' engaged in rational-critical debate was constituted into one of 'citizens' wherever there was communication concerning the affairs of the 'commonwealth.'"[25] Although, in his appeals to Kant, such citizenship is cosmopolitan—part of the greater world of reason—with each account of the connection between discussion and law, discussion and the constitution, discussion and fundamental rights, Habermas relies implicitly on the setting of the public sphere within the nation-state.

In her reading of Arendt, however, Benhabib, stresses an anti-statist vision of the public sphere. The world of the salon challenges the ethnic assumptions of the nation as it provides spaces for Jews; it challenges the patriarchal pretensions of the state as it allows women at least a momentary reprieve from their established roles. Consequently, Benhabib concludes her account of Arendt's call for a recovery of the public with a question: "If such a revitalization of public life does not mean the strengthening of the state but the growth of a political sphere independent of the state, where must this sphere be located, if not in civic and associational society?"[26] It is to the possibility of such a nonstate-centered, indeed transnational, civil society I now turn.

Cybersalons

Although it has chat and discussion, Borders Books' *Salon* is not just a chat room. The site includes ads, bookreviews, editorials, links to other sites in cyberia—be they on the World Wide Web or elsewhere in the contemporary politico-technocultural mediascape. It provides a model of interactivity, subjectivity, media, and political space significantly different from the rational and friendly salons of Habermas and Benhabib. It provides a model of political connection and contestation in civil society.

Interactivity

There are multiple modes of interactivity in cyberia. Folks posting to the discussion groups at *Salon* can communicate in real time, or they can read and respond on their own time: they can read without responding and respond without reading; they can jump to different sites; they can ignore what bores or frustrates them. Many of the interactions are interactive in name only—folks want feedback and response, not recognition. They don't presume full knowledge of, or full connection with, anyone or anything. People can consume the words of others, play with and satirize the words of others, or use the words of others for their own manipulative or erotic pleasures. Words may be used for pain or profit. They may attempt to get attention, to garner mindshare.[27] One can't predict how one's words will be used, encountered, extended. So considered, these multiple modes of interaction don't seem so very cyberian; they seem more like everyday communication, like table talk in coffee houses, like multilayered discussions among friends.

Contrary to the myth feared by some and celebrated by others, while participating in computer-mediated interactions, people do not leave their bodies. They feel them—certainly the titillations of net-porn and cybersex require as much. Nonetheless, even as they remain embodied, people's self-presentation to others on the net, in the cybersalon, is not necessarily dictated or determined by their embodiment. Since interactors do not have to meet face to face— although they may choose to and, indeed, accounts of the successes of the virtual community The Well emphasize the significance of members' occasional face-to-face meetings—their choices regarding how to represent their bodies extend beyond those easily available to people meeting in person.

This disconnection between bodies and words, although seemingly evoked by references to the rational exchanges of rational agents in public spheres, has in fact been thought of as one of the most disruptive and threatening dimensions of computer-mediated interactions. Seen from the standpoint of the public sphere where trust is linked to unified, embodied subjectivity, play with differing identities and personae is threatening. It is configured as a symptom of larger problems usually associated with fragmentation, postmodernism, or deconstruction. The projection and fabrication of personae independent of a specific embodiment are deemed particularly dangerous and usually a cause for psychiatric or juridical intervention. It is this multiple personality disorder, fraud, or cyberplay? Indeed, the failure to reproduce the solid link between citizen and body, presumed in the notion of the public sphere and enforced by the contemporary state, is generally taken to be a breach of trust, a violation, or a deception.

Rather than marking the pathology of cyberia, however, the disconnection between bodies and words points to the inapplicability of the concept the public sphere to contemporary technoculture. Furthermore, it suggests the critical potential of a normative conception of civil society. First, the disconnection reiterates the critique of transparency associated with face-to-face interactions. Second, it creates a space for analyses of the ways in which words become attached to specific bodies, ways that enhance as well as demean. Third, and consequently, it opens up the possibility of differing connections between words and bodies in different networks or communicative fields. Rather than presuming an already idealized consistency among performances targeted at different audiences, one can assess credibility and responsibility site-specifically. Who I am and what I say in *Salon's* lists may not have much to do with the person who speaks to a classroom or writes for an academic publication.

The model of interactivity in cyberia, and for civil society, offers a rich plurality including disembodied as well as embodied interactions. It thematizes flux, flexibility, and uncertainty: people may not be able to determine exactly what kind of interaction in which they are involved. It underscores mediation: whereas I've emphasized computer mediation, when extended into civil society, this model suggests that all interactions are profoundly mediated, at the level of language and representation, as well as at the very physical level of the tools and provisions that enable some people to be in certain locations at certain times.

Finally, concerning the norms of inclusion and equality that structure normative accounts of the public sphere: for the most part they do not apply in cyberia.[28] Although some wide-eyed cyberenthusiasts celebrate the Net for its inclusiveness, this kind of naivete has dwindled in the last few years as enthusiasts and critics alike have dealt with the issues like encryption, surveillance, modem speeds, incompatible protocols, the difficulty of finding useful information amidst all the Net clutter, the problematic dominance of English, the comparatively smaller numbers of women and ethnic minorities on line, and the basic economic inability of large numbers of people to take advantage of networked resources because they can afford neither a computer nor basic training. Consequently, the claim of inclusion has been replaced by an awareness of the variability of individuals and groups to use the Internet to connect with each other and to acquire information beyond that provided by traditional print and televisual media. As in civil society, there is no ultimate locus of inclusion: there are instead various sites open and closed to various persons in various ways. The claim to have, or be, the decisive, universal "we" is refused. Questions of access, then, have to be posed anew in specific situations. This variability might explain the simultaneous fascination and derision heaped upon hackers.[29]

Equality in cyberia is, at best, the equality of the snappy remark, the print equivalent of the audience comments that get whoops and applause on *Jerry Springer*. The witty rejoinder is the commodity form of cyberia. In cyberia, the blurring of reality that Habermas identifies with the rise of the novel becomes the leveling of distinctions among forms and producers of knowledge, the dissolution of a boundary between truth and falsity. Voices and photographs can be easily altered and inserted into sites that claim to represent actual events. The real and the virtual are equated to such an extent that they morph into one another: one really has virtual experiences after all. Ultimately, in cyberia, the leveling of status distinctions emphasized by some conceptions of equality morphs into a more general flattening out of distinctions per se: big and little, important and trivial, well-funded and spendthrift, authorized and underground—all interlink, coexist, and similarly vie for the fetishized hits. Corporations with large advertising budgets and expensive animation may be able to establish their Internet presence more easily, but rings, search engines, prizes, cool sites of the day, and multiple links give other folks a chance.

Subjectivity

This model of diverse forms of mediated interaction corresponds to a conception of subjectivity that is itself multiple, in flux, disembodied, and cyborgean. In civil society as well as online, people have more opportunities for identity play, for presenting themselves in different ways before different audiences. Given the rise of global media and transnational migration, ever greater numbers of different ways of being human, of different forms of subjectivity, come into contact with each other, disrupting the expectation of a single subjectivity among members of a population or even "single" community. Consequently, public sphere theories premised on a single notion of subjectivity forfeit from the outset the opportunity to theorize the synergies and confrontations as well as opportunities and threats that arise when different kinds of subjectivity come into contact.

For the relatively privileged, the body less and less determines opportunities. From cosmetic surgery to experimentation with visual media to networked communication, those with access to technology can present themselves in ways that have little to do with a single, localized embodiment. Technological possibilities produce societal pressures, putting a premium on mobility, adaptability, and often, conformity. For poor as well as rich, technological intervention invests bodies with ever more cyborgean meanings. Some become "food" for others as their organs, wombs, and corpses are commodified. Some are more likely to be seen, kept under surveillance by their employers, by pollsters and advertisers, their consumption and habits noted and charted and tied to benefits. Rather than a common humanity, there is the uncommonality of cyborgean experience that threatens to increase the gap between rich and poor and between those with information and those without it (gaps that are, importantly, not the same thing).[30]

This uncommonality points simultaneously toward increased opportunities of freedom for some as well as toward increasingly curtailed options for others. Those same technologies that enable previously infertile women to conceive and bear children later in life may compound normative expectations for women to have children. Those same advances in prenatal care that decrease the likelihood of birth defects or crib death may police women's behavior, may entail a new disciplining, control, and supervision of minute components of everyday behavior. They also may intersect with the already complex rhetorics of fetal life and maternal responsibility, producing situations in which the mother is blamed either for aborting a fetus on the basis of information gathered from genetic testing or for bringing a disabled or "defective" child into the world. On a larger level, networks of transnational capital open up new markets, enabling businesses that would have previously remained local to expand. Yet, such businesses face ever greater competitive pressures, finding themselves compelled to upgrade, invest, and digitize in ways they may not be able to manage. Amidst increasing competition, they no longer have the realistic option of remaining local and small, a phenomenon some have linked to rapid global homogenization.

Now, my remarks about subjectivity may well be controversial, one-sided, or even wrong. Even if one finds Habermas's contention convincing that there is a connection among the subjectivity of the bourgeois household, of the novel and the letter, the public sphere, then one has to grant that the age of networked interactions and global technoculture is already accompanied by a variety of different forms of subjectivity. Not only was Habermas's account of the bourgeois family already too narrow, but now, in late-capitalist democracies, there are, at least, multiple family structures, including, at the minimum, traditionalistic families, single-parent households, shared childrearing arrangements among adults working outside the home. For some, networked computing collapses the boundaries between home and work as well as between work and leisure. For others, these boundaries were never there. Whether the subjectivities I've evoked are empirically accurate or descriptively compelling is not the issue. The issue is simply whether the conception of a single, unified, deep subjectivity upon which the public sphere relies can still be convincing.

Media and Site

Since most of what I said already deals with cyberia's vision of media and space of interaction, I'll only mention them briefly. The vision of media involves multiple forms of permanent media. No political relation, encounter, or event is not already mediatized, produced and filtered through a variety of different media. Moreover, various media often give conflicting accounts of the same events. From the conspiracy theories regarding the crash of TWA flight 800 circulating on the Internet, to the differing assessments of mad cow disease in governmental, agricultural, and scientific circles, the mediatized discourses of civil society have no center. They need not converge or agree.

Consequently, the space of interaction presupposed by cyberia as well as by civil society extends through and beyond the nation-state. Both stress the variety of spaces in which people may interact. Both are part of economic globalization even as they cannot be reduced to it. With global media, activists can look beyond their own states in their efforts to affect political and social change. Previously isolated, marginalized, or extremist groups can find others of like mind beyond the borders of their town or country. And consumers can avail themselves of all sorts of hard to find items, of items that might not be legal on their home territory, of items like kiddie porn, anthrax, or plutonium.

Like the rational and friendly salons, then, the cybersalon provides political theory with structural and empirical information important for thinking about the democratic possibilities of certain kinds of social and political spaces. Like Habermas and Benhabib, I draw normative implications from the salon, although I want to resist the urge to recast it in terms of abstract and general norms. Instead, I use cyberia to point to the openness and diversity of civil society, to highlight the fact of political engagement in spaces marked by inequality and exclusion. I use cyberia to invoke the inescapable mediations governing political conversations and representations, and to see these sites as locuses of democracy.

Civil Society in the Information Age

A move from the concept of the public sphere to a normative and analytical category of civil society brings with it new political questions as well as new limitations. If it is the case that civil society makes no strong claim to equality, inclusion, or mutual respect, it may seem as if critical democratic theory can no longer address certain sorts of political inequities, exclusions, and violations. If the claim for a site from which the people can interrogate the state is forfeited, it may seem as if democracy itself is compromised as an ideal. Finally, if civil society as mediatized cyberia is implicated in the spread of transnational corporate technoculture, it may seem as if opportunities for critiques of the market, as well as new forms of colonial expansion, are lost.

These may well be some of the risks of replacing the notion of the public sphere with a concept of civil society. Acknowledging that myriad sites and discussions are exclusive, however, does not mean that no sites should aim for inclusion or that inclusion should not be sought in some locations. It simply means that no single site in civil society can claim to be the public sphere in the sense of serving as the locus for the political communications necessary for the democratic legitimation of the state or even of certain policies or principles. Furthermore, critique of the state does not need to come from—and in fact never has come from—a single social location. William Connolly, for example, offers a version of democratic pluralism that evokes the possibility of multiplying "lines of connection through which governing assemblages can be constructed from a variety of intersecting constituencies."[31] Finally, the interconnection between the bourgeois public sphere and the capitalist mode of production did not prevent the former from criticizing the latter. Similarly, the dependence of networked interconnections on global capitalism does not mean that such interconnections cannot serve as a vehicle for critical conversations about and struggles against market inequities. Indeed, precisely because new political threats appear with the movement of transnationalist capital throughout the globe, a model of civil society that stresses from the outset nonstatist or superstatist forms of political assemblage is crucial for theorizing the various meanings and effects of this movement.

Unlike a view of the public sphere that limits the political to rational conversation among people who respect each other as equals, the concept of civil society is part of a political theory that acknowledges that politics is about unequal exchanges among people who have fundamentally different ways of reasoning, who have differing conceptions of what is normal and what is appropriate. Unlike theories based on the public sphere, those employing a concept of civil society can interrogate processes of normalization and fundamentalization that seek to bound and limit what can be understood as politics.[32] Such theories may even be able to conceive of everyday actions and interactions as essential contributions to a vital democracy.

Notes

1. I am grateful for the responses from the conference participants, in particular Leslie Adelson, Eva Grossman, Peter Hohendahl, Martin Jay, and Christoph Menke. I am also indebted to Hubertus Buchstein, Claudette Columbus, Paul Passavant, and Lee Quinby for suggestions on earlier drafts of this paper.
2. Jürgen Habermas, *The Structural Transformation of the Public Sphere*, trans. Thomas Burger (Cambridge: MIT Press, 1989), 33-34.
3. Seyla Benhabib, "The Pariah and Her Shadow: Hannah Arendt's Biography of Rahel Varnhagen," *Political Theory* 23. 4 (February 1995): 17.
4. Peter Uwe Hohendahl, "The Public Sphere: Models and Boundaries," in *Habermas and the Public Sphere*, ed. Craig Calhoun (Cambridge: MIT Press, 1992), 100-01.
5. In a note, Benhabib stresses that she is not claiming that the salon can serve as a normative model today, but rather that it is a precursor of some of the potential of civic and associational society. Benhabib, 23-24.
6. Hubertus Buchstein, "Bytes that Bite: The Internet and Deliberative Democracy," *Constellations* 4.2 (October 1997): 250. This is a shorter, English-language version of the same essay that appeared earlier in German.
7. Buchstein, 251.
8. Jodi Dean, "Virtually Citizens," *Constellations* 4.2 (October 1997): 265-66.
9. Jürgen Habermas, "Further Reflections on the Public Sphere," *Habermas and the Public Sphere*, 438.
10. Jürgen Habermas, "Three Models of Democracy," *Constellations* 1.1 (April 1994): 8.
11. Seyla Benhabib, "Deliberative Rationality and Models of Democratic Legitimacy," *Constellations* 1.1 (April 1994): 41, 35.
12. See Nancy Fraser, "Rethinking the Public Sphere: A Contribution to the Critique of Actually Existing Democracy," *Habermas and the Public Sphere*, 109-42.
13. Benhabib, "Deliberative Rationality," 30-35.

14. For a longer version of this argument, see Jodi Dean, "Civil Society: Beyond the Public Sphere," in *The Handbook of Critical Theory*, ed. David Rasmussen (Oxford: Blackwell Publishers, 1996), 220-42.

15. See Jean Cohen and Andrew Arato, *Civil Society and Political Theory* (Cambridge: MIT Press, 1992).

16. Judith Butler, "For a Careful Reading," in *Feminist Contentions: A Philosophical Exchange*, eds. Seyla Benhabib, Judith Butler, Drucilla Cornell, and Nancy Fraser (New York: Routledge, 1994), 129.

17. Benhabib, "The Pariah and Her Shadow," 18.

18. Benhabib, "The Pariah and Her Shadow," 17.

19. Habermas, *Structural Transformation*, 47.

20. Habermas, *Structural Transformation*, 46.

21. Habermas, *Structural Transformation*, 56.

22. Habermas, *Structural Transformation*, 48.

23. For a discussion of "warranting" as the process through which discursive elements become articulated to physical bodies see Allucquere Rosanne Stone, *The War of Desire and Technology at the Close of the Mechanical Age* (Cambridge: MIT Press, 1996), 39-44, 88-93.

24. Habermas, *Structural Transformation*, 50.

25. Habermas, *Structural Transformation*, 106-07.

26. Benhabib, "The Pariah and Her Shadow," 20.

27. See humdog, "pandora's vox: on community in cyberspace," in *High Noon on the Electronic Frontier*, ed. Peter Ludlow (Cambridge: MIT Press, 1996), 437-44.

28. I would have liked to be able to claim that cyberian interactivity is unnormed, that there are no norms in cyberspace. But this is absurd. *Salon*, for example, posts rules for those who would like to participate in its discussion groups: "In the interests of open and honest discussion," participants are encouraged to register under their "real names." *Salon* recognizes that this may not be a norm in all of cyberia and that participants have other options. It simply instructs participants to identify themselves by their real names in *Salon* discussions. Interestingly, this instruction is at the level of "encouragement"; it is not a rule in the sense that a violation of it will get a member expelled. Expulsion-worthy violations include posting personal attacks on other members, posting advertising, and deliberately disrupting the conversation. Participants are warned three times before they are put on probation. If they persist in violating the rules, they will be expelled. These minimal rules are designed to encourage stimulating discussions: Since only those remarks designed to damage persons or cut off debate are disallowed, the rules in effect aim for ongoing disagreement, not final consensus.

29. See Douglas Thomas's fascinating research on hackers, "Hacking Culture," unpublished manuscript.

30. See the contributions to *The Cyborg Handbook*, ed. Chris Hables Gray (New York: Routledge, 1995).

31. William Connolly, *The Ethos of Pluralization* (Minneapolis: University of Minnesota Press, 1995), xx.

32. Connolly analyzes a variety of forms of fundamentalism and forces of fundamentalization in his *The Ethos of Pluralization*.

Chapter 9

BETWEEN RIGHTS AND HOSPITALITY

Cosmopolitan Democracy, Nation, and Cultural Identity[1]

Max Pensky

No nation indulges more freely in feasting and entertaining than the
German. It is accounted a sin to turn any man away from your door.
The host welcomes his guest with the best meal that his means allow.
When he has finished entertaining him, the host undertakes a fresh rôle:
he accompanies the guest to the nearest house where further hospitality
can be had. It makes no difference that they come uninvited; they are
welcomed just as warmly. No distinction is ever made between acquaintance and stranger as far as the *right to hospitality* is concerned.

— Tacitus, *Germania*

Shortly before his death, Theodor Adorno had described, in a typ-
ically elliptical way, the forms that the category of "progress"
might plausibly take in the strange historical constellation of the
cold war. In the absence of any morally acceptable doctrine of universal historical progress, and with an awareness of the internal connection between the category of totality and the will to eradicate
difference, progress had become a concept marshaling an array of
local resistances to the "relapse" of moral catastrophe, a resistance
to anachronies and decadences that, taken together, constituted
something closer to a moral-aesthetic fantasy of a proximate future

free of catastrophes than a moral-political ideology. "Progress," Adorno wrote, "is not a conclusive category. It wants to cut short the triumph of radical evil, not to triumph as such itself." Adorno understood that the bankrupt vision of uniform moral-historical progress, the "exhaustion of utopian energies," had driven the morally necessary notion of progress underground. And yet any coherent concept of progress still depended utterly on a totality that also unmasked its rootedness in a naked will to violence: resistance as a moral category depends, dialectically, on a concept of *another* universalism—to be mobilized against a false totality. The unmasking of humanism as terror calls not for the abandonment of the category of humanity, but for a concept of progress that would adequately express the task of first *creating* the very concept of the human:

> If humanity remains entrapped by the totality it itself fashions, then, as Kafka said, no progress has taken place at all, while mere totality nevertheless allows progress to be entertained in thought. This can be elucidated most simply by the definition of humanity as that which excludes absolutely nothing. If humanity were a totality that no longer held within it any limiting principle, then it would also be free of the coercion that subjects all its members to such a principle and thereby would no longer be a totality: no forced unity.[2]

"No forced unity": after thirty years and enormous political changes, this deceptively simple formula still retains its power to irritate. It remains an admirably compact expression of the conceptual challenges to thinking about the possibility of moral and political progress at the beginning of the millennium. For just as one is guided by an intuitively powerful idea of a cosmopolitan democracy based on the global institutionalization of basic rights, one can also still recognize the internal contradiction between institutionalized political accord, perpetual peace, and the survival of authentic cultural difference. An unforced unity appears to require the reconciliation of principles of unlimited solidarity and inviolable alterity; totality and resistance to that totality; universalism and, if not the particular, then whatever it is that lies outside of universalizing institutions and practices, for whose sake universalism extends moral claims and legal protections. In this sense, unforced unity encompasses the very demand and the paradox of constitutional democracy itself—collapsing the distinction, that is, between, on the one hand, the *rights* of subjects whom one encounters as equals insofar as one conceives the reasonable foundations of law to constitute subjects in the same way, and, on the other hand, the *hospitality* that one owes the stranger *as* stranger.

"Unforced global unity under the rule of law" describes the horizon of expectation still encoded in the contemporary theoretical and practical commitments to cosmopolitan democracy. Cosmopolitanism, in its current usage, captures the ambiguity at the heart of the idea of progress. It is, in fact, an enormously ambiguous term, capturing a wide range of historical experiences and interpretations, traditions of expectation and hope, gestures of guilt and renunciation, and intuitions about justice and equality. The notion of cosmopolitan democracy is a form in which moral-political progress is still thinkable *beyond* or *after* the end of the philosophy of history, but cosmopolitanism nevertheless still bears a powerfully utopian element. Cosmopolitanism retains the utopian content of moral and political universalism: no one lies outside of the community of moral agents. No contingently constituted political community can exert ties of loyalty and identification strong enough to undermine the recognition of the basic rights of each individual member; incontrovertible principles can be found that determine procedures guaranteeing respect and fair treatment for all.

As an ethical-political mode of reflection, cosmopolitanism's ambiguity is just as palpable in the problematic *reference* or subjects of cosmopolitan democracy. Here the ambiguity is built in, so to speak, to the *Wirkungsgeschichte* (history of the reception) of the term itself. Cosmopolitanism as "world citizenship" was recovered from the Stoics by a high Enlightenment Europe eager to find in the classical archive a reference to the claims of reason beyond the arbitrary limits of tradition and parochialism. As such, it was from its beginning as much a reference to an aesthetic of subjective self-creation as a political creed, for it expressed a mode of personal cultivation and comportment, a "worldliness" that was internally linked with economic and social privilege.[3]

For all its millennial humility, and notwithstanding its efforts to divest itself of any normative account of globalization processes, contemporary cosmopolitanism still retains this orientation toward an idealized image of the enlightened citizen of the eighteenth century. That model thematized, from a universal point of view, the specific historical experiences of the cultured bourgeoisie of western Europe. This bourgeoisie was successfully educating itself *out* of its own cultural particularisms and acquiring its distinctive virtues—

tolerance, breadth of outlook and experience, education of the senses and refinement of taste, an inveterate dislike of the parochial and the provincial—by turning the experience of colonial expansion and cultural modernization itself into an object of aesthetic contemplation. The cosmopolitanism of the enlightened citizen was thus a sort of refined statelessness, an ability to be comfortable, at home, anywhere in the world precisely insofar as the "world" became the idea of the all-encompassing nature of cultural difference: an object of knowledge and consumption. In historical fact, such a fantasy of stateless culture could easily be turned into an intellectual exercise by which a distinctive national culture could first be generated. For example, the German appropriation of the ideal of classical antiquity shows clearly enough: some of the deepest roots of German nationalism and particularism at the close of the eighteenth century consist of an initial attempt to forge "Germanness" out of the political fragmentation of the Holy Roman Empire, via the cultural vehicle of the "grand tour" of Italian and Greek antiquities.[4]

The cosmopolitan fantasy of the enlightened eighteenth century had at heart something to do with the power to cast away cultural identities, the cultivated capacity to relativize one's own ethical-political context—one could invoke, instead, the model of full, symmetrical membership in an abstract moral community. The echo of this initial, substantive notion of cosmopolitanism still resonates in today's theoretical anxiety, registered by political theorists from across the political spectrum, that cosmopolitan democracy is premised on the eradication of substantive cultural identities: such cultural identities, many argue, merit special political consideration or legal protections of various kinds in order to remain safe from the inherently predatory character of the dynamic of global democratization. This has served to polarize the terms of contemporary political discourse according to familiar lines: on one side, fearing that global democracy implies the eradication of concrete ties and commitments, the communitarians warn once again that communal membership and cultural identity is the point of, and not an obstacle to, democratic life. On the other side, contending that all group memberships and substantive commitments are reflectively available to, and revisable by, rational agents, the liberals assert that global democracy under cosmopolitan law would constitute something like the natural consequence of the internal logic of practical reasoning. In the more interesting mediating position, critical theorists (among other "compatibilists") strive to interpret cultural identity and moral-political universalism as mutually dependent—with varying degrees of success.[5] Jürgen Habermas's work stands as the most significant example of this latter, compatibilist alternative.

The relation among cosmopolitanism and national and cultural identity is the theme of my remarks here—in brief, I shall argue that Habermas's conception of cosmopolitan democracy, while remaining fairly narrowly juridical in character, is nevertheless premised upon a powerfully normative critique of the nation and of national identity. I shall then attempt to show that it is precisely the implications of cosmopolitanism—namely, the undermining of traditional understanding of state sovereignty—that renders the distinction between national identity and cultural identity deeply problematic. My closing remarks will suggest that the cosmopolitan project, rather than trying to find a way around this problem, should confront it squarely, and acknowledge that it is precisely the *loss* of cultural identities in the face of globalization processes that can serve as the basis for a substantive cosmopolitan global ethics.

Cosmopolitanism, as cultural conoisseurship, has never had an easy time dealing with the implicit asymmetry that it presupposes: from the cosmopolitan point of view, "unenlightened" forms of cultural identity have to be constituted both in terms of an object of knowledge (and of taste) as well as from a specific intersubjective viewpoint; from the perspective of one section of a totalizing concept of humanity that experiences its own culture as a merely contingent, de facto impediment to full participation in the global moral community. But if cosmopolitanism is understood as the political call for the global extension of basic rights, this asymmetry internal to the *addressees* of cosmopolitan claims becomes more apparent, since the availability of "culture" as refinement, as worldliness, stands in a directly inverse relation to the *need* for protection under globally secured rights. The poor are, statistically speaking, likely to be those whose particular states are unwilling or unable to offer them constitutionally established and protected basic rights. And at the extreme of poverty a certain strange symmetry between worldliness and wordlessness emerges: between the refined statelessness of the cosmopolitan point of view and the destitute and desperate statelessness of the extremely poor. Destitution is, in a strong sense, incompatible with national or cultural membership, a fact worth bearing in mind as we turn to the problem of cosmopolitanism and national identity in Habermas's work.

Perhaps as an indirect response to the ambiguities I have described so far, Habermas's account of cosmopolitan remains, for the most part, determinedly limited in its scope and application. It is, at heart, a *legal* cosmopolitanism that serves to advance a *moral* argument against the specific *ethical* substance of the modern nation-state; specifically, Habermasian cosmopolitanism is the claim that the inherent contradiction between the particularism of national identity and the universalism of subjective rights can only effectively be compensated for if the legal institutions and processes that recognize and enforce basic rights are removed from the level of the sovereign nation-state to an as yet unrealized institutional-ization of coercive cosmopolitan law.[6] In such a stance, Habermas effectively radicalizes Kant's own later view of the relation between cosmopolitan law and the sovereignty of the nation-state in Kant's essay "Perpetual Peace."

Kant's essay had proceeded from the assumption that interna-tional law could only serve to regulate a normally bellicose relation among sovereign states and subsequently introduced the notion of a cosmopolitan law that would bind constitutional republics together in a loose confederation of peaceful cooperation. Unlike his earlier work, "Perpetual Peace" insisted that a peaceful federation of states would recognize and maintain—indeed even strengthen—the inter-nal and external sovereignty of existing republican nation-states. Kant's view was that the republican nation-state could, under suit-able conditions, "enlighten" itself concerning its own sphere of autonomous activity much like a moral agent: according to this sce-nario, the older *raison d'etat* could be presented with various inducements—including the dynamics of global trade, for example, or the pressures of a global public, or even the cunning hand of providential nature—to abandon warfare as a means of foreign pol-icy. Hence cosmopolitan law obtained between republican states as a nonsupercedable level of legal blocks toward external aggression, but never seriously challenged the notion that the sovereign state should continue to serve as the only proper medium for its citizens' basic rights. Moreover, Kant's essay did not offer any coherent account of what supranational agency would be responsible for the maintenance of the "league of peace" binding republican states together, or for the enforcement of the legal prohibitions against external aggression. At the end of the eighteenth century, Kant's worry was that the prospects for global peace under the rule of law were threatened not by nationalism—of which he had only a vague premonition—but rather statism, construed in Hobbesian terms as the continuing war between sovereign, rationally calculating agents. While earlier essays had argued for a global republican government in which states would merge, "Perpetual Peace" relented, significantly, on just this point: it argued instead that only the continued—indeed, even strengthened—sovereignty of states could provide the institutional context for the global realization of articles of peace. On the subjective level, the basic allotment of rights, and the articles of peace meant to secure the continued cooperation of sovereign states, would need to be supplemented only by the quaint-sounding article of "cosmopolitan right" that protected "conditions of universal hospitality" or "the right of an alien not to be treated as an enemy upon his arrival in anothers' country."[7] Kant's simple insight was that natural right commanded the lifting of arbitrary restrictions on the free intercourse between strangers—that the only chances for an "unforced unity" rested in a more or less natural process of acquaintance, whereby persons discovered that they were not as strange to one another as they had supposed.

Despite this very genial sense of law and morality's conspiring to form a weak, compromised, but nevertheless definite tendency toward a cosmopolitan world republic, Kant took no account of national identities. He did not foresee that national identity was already transforming the principle of state sovereignty from a form of modified popular sovereignty via a contractual constitution into a constitutional expression of a prepolitical collective identity—in short, that nationalism could arise as a justification for statism. Habermas's own continuation of the Kantian cosmopolitan project takes just these problems—of nationalism and of the antinomy of national and popular sovereignty—as its normative point of departure. Hence Habermasian cosmopolitanism is in essence an expansion and intensification of his far older critique of nationalism and national identity.

It is difficult to underestimate the importance—or the force—of Habermas's critique of the nation as a political-ethical category; probing the various theoretical and personal commitments that underlie this decades-old critical project would be a very large undertaking in itself. Initially, it is therefore important not to over-simplify the relation between Habermasian antinationalism and that of other participants in the discourse of nationalism and national identity. On the one hand, Habermas shares a consensus view of modern political theory that nations are, to use Benedict Anderson's often-quoted phrase, "imagined communities": they are "cultural artifacts" whose claims to such substantial forms of collective identity like racial or ethnic homogeneity, a shared language, history and destiny, or even a "common sense of the good," are invariably the artificial constructs of a population that needs to adapt to changing political and cultural conditions and to generate better and stronger forms of social solidarity.[8] Anderson was careful to insist that the imagined character of *all* national communities did not itself imply that nations or nationalism were inherently deceptive and manipulative; he insisted on the (rough) normative neutrality of the processes of collective fictionalizing in which nations "arose." Another strain in this discourse, typified by Ernest Gellner, collapses the distinction between "artificial" and "deceptive" and describes the normative deficit of nations—typified here by nationalist movements—as intrinsically mendacious, in the sense that national identity normally constitutes an attempt at the strategic manipulation—the tricking—of a political mass in order to manufacture a form of mass loyalty otherwise impossible.[9]

Habermas, it appears, tends powerfully toward the Gellnerian side of this question of the artificial character of the nation. Since Habermas is not, and has never pretended to be, an empirically-minded political scientist, however, this critique of the strategic or ideological character of national identity has tended to be more moralistic than functionalistic—it has been largely driven by Habermas's role as an engaged public intellectual in the public sphere of the Federal Republic of Germany. Hence any broader critique of national identity in Habermas's work has, until relatively recently, only emerged by extending his bitter criticisms of the distinctive problems of German national identity. Habermas's role as a participant in an ethical-political discourse—with historical, ethical, and traditional problems and understandings specific to that ethical sphere—has often served as a shorthand for his position on national identity generally. On the other, contrastive hand, his views on the role of *cultural* identity have been much better developed in stricter theoretical terms.[10]

That unbalanced situation has now largely changed; the essays collected under the title *Zur Einbeziehung des Anderen (Accommodating the Other)* provide a much broader, decontextualized, and historically sweeping analysis of the function and limitations of national identity.[11] And while this analysis finally breaks free of Habermas's own self-imposed restriction on the specific ethical-political questions facing German collective identity, it nevertheless remains a powerfully normative analysis.

This normative analysis proceeds according to a rather thin historical reconstruction. In the case of modern Europe, Habermas argues, nationality—the concept of a national identity or "spirit of a people" that could serve as the ideological justification for a claim to collective self-determination—developed only subsequent to the emergence of modern states after the Peace of Westphalia. The "delayed nations" of Italy and Germany serve as exceptions that prove the rule. Modern states could no longer turn to traditional, metaphysical, or ecclesiastic sources for encouraging newly formed citizen-subjects to integrate themselves into the political and legal institutions and practices required for social stabilization. In this way, Habermas reconstructs the rise of national identity following the revolutions at the close of the eighteenth century as something like a prosthesis that temporarily provided levels of social integration and social solidarity necessary to bridge the conceptual and temporal gap separating the fragmented, particularistic present from the universalist, republican future of the modern state.

While always rooted in a particular form of ethical life, republican principles governing the formal requirements for political procedures, particularly democratic procedures, are almost always highly abstract. They are context-transcendent in the precise sense that they require individual citizens to regard themselves and their fellow citizens, in the final analysis, as political agents sufficiently unfettered by purely local contingencies so as to be capable of reasoned judgment on matters of general concern. The abstract procedural requirements of the constitutional state thus impose a heavy existential burden on individuals. "Nation" consists of an imaginary solidarity among strangers that cements the otherwise fragile bonds of reasonable cooperation. The myth of a common people with a common past and destiny thus provides "a cultural background for the transformation of subjects into citizens."[12] This transformation proceeds via the path of the juridification of political action: from subjects who can be defined only by their relation to self-legitimating state authority, citizens are constructed as persons bearing legal rights.

> But such a legal transformation would have lacked driving force, and formally established republics would have lacked staying power, if a nation of more or less conscious citizens had not emerged from a people identified by its subjection to state power. This political mobilization called for an idea which was vivid and powerful enough to shape people's convictions and appealed more strongly to their hearts and minds than the dry ideas of popular sovereignty and human rights. This gap was filled by the modern idea of the nation, which first inspired in the inhabitants of state territories an awareness of the new, legally and politically mediated form of community. Only a national consciousness, crystallized around the notions of a common ancestry, language and history, only the consciousness of belonging to 'the same' people, makes subjects into citizens of a single political community—into members who can feel responsible for *one another*. The nation or the *Volksgeist*, the unique spirit of the people,—the first truly *modern* form of collective identity—provided the cultural basis for the constitutional state.[13]

Those familiar with the previous decades of Habermas's denunciations of national consciousness in any form other than the approved commitment to "constitutional patriotism" will be justifiably startled by the underlying conciliatory tone of this genealogical reconstruction. Nevertheless, the functionalist account of the nation as a strategic compensation for premodern sources of social integration in the modern state remains more provocative than descriptive—it notably begs the question of whether this transition from premodern to modern forms of social solidarity should be regarded as an instance of a developmental logic or whether it is better seen as a particularly violent victory of one strategy of social organization over another.

The explanatory power of this functionalist reconstruction lies in its ability to criticize the concept of nation all the more powerfully by revealing both its internal contradictions and its anachronistic character. The universalistic value orientations required by the constitutional state invariably conflicts with the particularistic, substantive form of identity required by adherence to a specific nation and national tradition. Hence the nation-state becomes double-coded or indeed Janus-faced. The logic of moral and political universalism entails a normative demand to question the legitimacy of all particular allegiances insofar as they would take priority over egalitarian forms of moral and political recognition. Conversely, national solidarity invariably defines itself against the foreign and reacts to the foreign with isolation or aggression. The freedom grounded in universalistic categories that the state provides to its citizens internally— the codified system of legal rights freeing individuals negatively within a circumscribed sphere of civil society—is matched by the externally-directed freedom of assertive action of the nation as a whole, conceived as a superindividual with its own identifiable needs, ambitions, and "destiny." But conceiving the freedom of the nation naturalistically in this fashion—according to the prepolitical categories of place, history, ethnicity, language, and common destiny— can only come into conflict with constitutional principles.

The tension between the universalism of an egalitarian legal community and the particularism of a community united by historical destiny is built into the very concept of the nation-state. This ambivalence remains harmless as long as a cosmopolitan understanding of the nation of citizens is accorded priority over an ethnocentric interpretation that suggests the nation is in a permanent state of war. The nation owes its:

> historical success to the fact that it substituted relations of solidarity among citizens for the disintegrating corporative ties of early modern society. But this republican achievement is endangered when, conversely, the integrative force of the nation of citizens is traced back to the prepolitical fact of a quasi-natural people, that is, to something independent of and prior to the political opinion—and will-formation of the citizens themselves.[14]

Hence Habermas's critique of nationalism proceeds on three interrelated conceptual fronts: first is the functionalist argument that forms of national identity fill the "solidarity gap" for states, as they emerge from premodern political arrangements and acquire new forms of sovereignty based on the moral abstractions required to produce free and equal citizens. Concomitant with this argument is the weaker (that is, empirically undersupported) claim that as such, national identity is always "constructed" or fictionalized; the supposed "prepolitical values" of place, language, ethnic homogeneity, and historical lineage emerge as a discursive construction of an entity that never existed. Second is the conceptual claim that this function comes into open tension with the universalistic dynamic of republican principles. This conceptual claim entails the normative claim that the particularistic forms of solidarity, made possible by national identity, cannot be justified from the moral point of view as well as that, as a political and legal corollary, the system of basic rights that is legitimately extended to all individuals (the cosmopolitan claim) ought to effectively trump any form of national particularity that is incompatible with that system. The logic of democratic procedure requires the steady abandonment of a naturalistically construed population. And third, an essentially pragmatic entailment, is that, in the context of globalization, national differences are in any event becoming increasingly irrelevant in the face of current patterns of economic influence, global and regional migration, technological development, the rise of international institutions and arrangements, and the globalization of ecological and economic risk.

In the final analysis, these various moral, legal, and pragmatic objections point toward a political one, namely, that of sovereignty. I will return to the question of sovereignty, but at this point it is worth observing that nations and national identity effectively served as a medium for a series of historical compromises in a transition from premodern forms of sovereignty—with their various ecclesiastical, metaphysical, and power-political guarantees—to a modern conception of popular sovereignty grounded in principles. The heart of Habermas's *political* objection is that the discourse of nation misconstrues popular sovereignty as the power (and right) of national self-determination in contrast to the freedom and equality of citizens. Indeed this constitutes something like the basic formula of nationalism itself—the "Schmittization," one could say, of the principles of democratic procedure. And as such it is, for Habermas, the premier *disabling* condition for the growth and strength of global democratic institutions.

At the same time as Habermas continues his vigorous criticisms of national identity, however, he has come to give a simultaneous (if not as energetic) *defense* of cultural identity. He argues, in essence, a modified Taylorian position: namely, that culture, broadly construed, provides individuals with the specific sorts of background knowledges, vocabularies, shared historical experiences, and interpretive commitments—all ethical substances—that together constitute something like an *enabling* condition for the adoption of the abstract principles and procedures of the democratic constitutional state. Here, the need for access to an ethical substance on the part of individual citizens, in order to accommodate themselves to the requirements of the constitutional state, is met halfway, so to speak, by the "permeation" of the abstract principles of a democratic constitution by ethical substance. In both cases, the co-implication of ethical substance and moral form is an inference drawn from the more general, philosophical "individuation-through-socialization" thesis. Accordingly: "[a] correctly understood theory of rights requires a politics of recognition that protects the integrity of the individual in the life contexts in which his or her identity is formed," with the further implication that such protection succeeds best when it acts consistently according to its own purely formal principles, rather than tailoring forms of recognition and allocation of rights on a context-sensitive basis.[15]

In a sense, of course, the individuation-through-socialization thesis itself requires a degree of abstraction so high as to make the thesis not especially helpful in distinguishing between, on the one hand, the general sorts of requirements that persons might plausibly have to fulfill in order to live in a procedural democracy and, on the other, the specific challenges facing members of oppressed and marginalized minorities. The capacity for reasonableness and role-taking, for example, or for rational reflection, or for a decentered relation to one's own values, traditions, needs, and situation interpretations, can be thought of as basic existential requirements that anyone must fulfill, to some degree, in order to accommodate oneself to a modern political culture. The individuation-through-socialization thesis flatly attributes "a" substantive ethical context to each and every individual by arguing that all individuality arises only via a progressively deeper entwinement in a set of communicative relationships that are constitutive for the concrete ethical life of any society. It further assumes (though often implicitly) that such substantive contexts can be analytically distinguished *as* ethical, that is, as forming the basis of and providing the material for individuation—the ethical contrasted here with the specifically *moral* realm in which individuals are thought of as at least in principle capable of abstracting themselves from these contexts.

Such a perspective risks losing any critical insight into the asymmetries of power and other systemic problems according to which multicultural democracies form around the opposition between a dominant culture and minority groups. Trust in the reasonable outcomes of halfway-intact democratic procedures covers this need in terms of political theory. And, according to Habermas's own famously rigorous division of intellectual labor, both critical sociology and intellectual interventions in the specifically German public sphere are intended to cover the critical shortfall of political theory generally. What, then, is the most promising way to describe the distinction between national and cultural identity in the vocabulary of political theory?

Here again the various levels of analysis are not always easy to distinguish. "Nation," for Habermas, stands in an indeterminate, wholly politically contingent relation to the sovereign state; this contingent relation is due in large measure to the concrete historical genealogy of the modern nation-state, which finds itself (as outlined above) obliged to generate two incompatible forms of social solidarity at the same time. Habermas effectively solved that dilemma in advance, by insisting on the fictional or invented character of nation and national identity, which allowed him to conclude that the paradox of solidarity for the institution of the nation-state could be "solved" only insofar as national, conventional identity dropped out of the picture entirely.

As one moves from the category of "national" to "cultural identity," however, this assumption of artificiality is a good deal more difficult to defend. If cultural identity turns out to be just as constructed, just as artificial, and just as contingent upon the shifting political currents tending toward a globalization of politics as national identity proved to be, then Habermasian cosmopolitanism will be obliged to criticize the particularism and the arbitrary limitations on democratic solidarity of cultural specificity in *the same way* as he does national identity. If, on the other hand, cultural identity proves to be a qualitatively different, "authentic" form of *specific* ethical substance, then Habermas's universalism would run into trouble. If cultural identity requires a different analysis and different conceptual foundations than the general attribution of ethical substance to all individuals via the individuation-through-socialization thesis, then the heart of Habermas's argument—the uncompromisable universalism inherent in the very idea of constitutional democracy—would indeed appear to be in some difficulty.

One way to approach this question is to look briefly at the chief competitors to Habermas's approach here. The neoliberalism of Rawls and Kymlicka, in a certain *rapprochement* with Taylor, has tended to annex much of the available conceptual terrain in the discourse about the relation between the fact of cultural difference and the value of political accommodation within large constitutional democracies. We now find ourselves comfortably referring to the contestational, agonistic aspect of large democratic societies in a way that is not significantly different from the old liberal model of a civil society composed of more or less genially competing agents. Now "cultural groups" form a patchwork quilt of different, perhaps incommensurable interpretive communities, with their own self-sustaining and self-legitimating sets of identity-granting values and practices; they only need to reconcile these values and practices to a broader political culture in order to cohabit peacefully as fellow citizens. And in this sense, the notion of cultural groups has tended to adopt an emphatically hermeneutic conception of cultures as interpretive communities. Kymlicka's definition of "culture," specifically of what he refers to as a "societal culture," is an extreme, but not atypical example. He defines a culture as "an intergenerational community, more or less institutionally complete, occupying a given territory or homeland, sharing a distinct language and history." [16] Hence a cultural group "provides its members with meaningful ways of life across the full range of human activities, including social, educational, religious, recreational, and economic life, encompassing both public and private spheres." [17]

This emphatically hermeneutic conception of cultural identity is the foundation for Kymlicka's defense of group-differentiated rights, which represents a significant modification of the traditional liberal creed that the state should, above all, remain neutral concerning the varying substantive ethical commitments of its citizens. Yet this "substantialized" version of the individuation-through-socialization thesis has a direct bearing on the question at hand, for on this basis Kymlicka will also insist on the *indifference* between "societal culture" and "nation." Indeed Kymlicka's stipulative definitions of "nation" and "culture" are themselves virtually impossible to tell apart, since he defines "nation" as "a historical community, more or less institutionally complete, occupying a given territory or homeland, sharing a distinct language and culture." [18]

Much of Kymlicka's book is concerned with whittling down the range of problems that could fall under the rubric of "multicultural democratic politics": racial minorities, immigrant groups, the economically disadvantaged, gays and lesbians—thus all count only as "groups" in another sense than a "cultural" group. Now, Kymlicka clearly wishes to concentrate on the "hard cases" of distinct national minorities within multinational democracies, because he believes that doing so will draw out promising conclusions that can then be argumentatively extended to cover ethnic minorities and oppressed social groups as well. Nevertheless, the emphatic conception of "societal culture" that Kymlicka uses dramatically changes the entire argument, for the point of procedural democracy now becomes the *accommodation* of cultural identities, which is the same as the accommodation of nations. National identity, in turn, is read in a strong sense as the necessary *enabling* condition for the accommodation to democratic values—the precise opposite of the disabling condition that Habermas diagnoses. Hence Kymlicka's analysis of the entitlements for group-differentiated rights, within a multinational state, leads directly to a broader argument in favor of a "liberal nationalism." Kymlicka is convinced that "national cultures and polities provide the best context for promoting Enlightenment values of freedom, equality, and democracy."[19] In fact, Kymlicka argues, the historical record shows that—precisely where Habermas saw an inevitable collision between universalistic value orientations and particular national identities—national minorities often were powerful *advocates* of political universalism insofar as they sought to emancipate themselves from the broader *illiberal* political culture of a given state. The particularism and naturalism offered in support of a national culture often was employed as a way of resisting assimilation, and this resistance often implicitly claimed allegiance to a form of Enlightenment universalism (tolerance, for example) that was meant to trump the imperfect and implicitly dominating effects of the "broad" values and agendas of the host state. In so arguing Kymlicka returns to the older critique of Enlightenment cosmopolitanism: in its implicit hostility to cultural differences, cosmopolitanism aims to flatten out precisely the sorts of existential resources that individuals could rely on as the enabling condition for a healthy democracy. Liberal nationalism thus entails the claim that the Habermasian antinomy, "democracy versus national identity," is a false one.

Now, as plausible (indeed as intuitively attractive) as this position is, it is important to realize how utterly it depends upon the emphatic conception of national-cultural identity that Kymlicka presupposes—essentially drawn from the North American models of Native American tribal communities, Amish and Hutterite religious communities, or the French-speaking Quebecois. Kymlicka and other defenders of liberal nationalism have significantly decreased the justificatory burden for themselves by figuring "cultures" as more or less discrete interpretive communities, whose members appear to have relatively unambiguous and apparently dependent relations on the cultural group for the transmission of a "shared sense of the good," even if they retain an abstract capacity to reflect upon and revise the terms of their group membership. Indeed, it is only according to this overidealized, ideal-typical reconstruction that the liberal-communitarian dilemma of the priority of the right or the good remains conceptually coherent. It is less clear whether this model does the conceptual work that liberal nationalists believe it does in analyzing the full range of cultural identities and differences. Nor, as we shall see, is it even clear whether this emphatic concept is itself entirely coherent.

I introduced Kymlicka's argument as a contrast to that of Habermas: the emphatic concept of cultural identity argues for the indifference between nation and cultural group, based upon a naturalistic understanding of the sources of identity. It is just this understanding that Habermas will dispute, although one has to look a bit farther afield to find this argument.

First, Habermas will concur with Kymlicka and the liberal nationalists up to a point: multicultural societies entail a common political culture that is meant to integrate citizens with a variety of cultural identities, but these same identities provide the resources needed for integration. Hence "integration" needs to be differentiated into, on the one hand, a desirable political form (accommodation of and to cultural difference within a pluralistic political culture) and, on the other, an undesirable cultural form (assimilation and the end of culturally distinctive identities). Individuals can all expect to undergo a process of *political* integration into a constitutional democratic state insofar as they must "assent to the principles of the constitution within the scope of interpretation determined by the ethical-political understanding of the citizens and the political culture of the country." But no individual should be compelled to undergo a *cultural* integration that would demand "a willingness to become acculturated, that is, not only to conform externally but to become habituated to the way of life, the practices, and the customs of the local culture."[20] Habermas refuses to follow Kymlicka's insistence that this distinction requires that cultural identity be protected via group-differentiated rights, and this refusal leads him into the reconstruction of the relation between basic rights and democratic practice in *Between Facts and Norms*, which I will not pursue here. For the present context, the question is whether this distinction between political and cultural integration holds up on Habermas's own terms.

Like Kymlicka, Habermas assumes that *cultural groups,* as the object of analysis here, exist insofar as they are *already* coexistent with other groups as well as within a dominant culture and within a constitutional state. The problem that stands in need of analysis is the politics of multiculturalism within the democratic state; that is, precisely how cultural groups, with their own forms of concrete cultural identity, can survive within a broader democratic political culture. All cultural groups can be expected to undergo a political accommodation to the prevailing principles of democracy—on this point there is near unanimity between Habermas, Kymlicka, Taylor, and even the most sulphurous communitarians. Tough cases, for example, that construct a direct conflict between, on the one hand, practices that are constitutive for a culture's distinctive collective identity, and, on the other, the basic rights of one or some of its members, clearly have to be settled in favor of the latter.[21] This stance resonates against the perennial problem of intolerant (or "fundamentalist," in Habermas's terms) minority cultures.[22]

But this raises a central problem: do the specific requirements of such a political accommodation allow one to speak of the "distinctive" identity of cultural groups in the emphatic form? In the context of multicultural democratic states, is it even possible to distinguish between cultural groups *accommodating* to a common political culture, as opposed to a cultural group being *generated* by that culture?

The tidy distinction between political and cultural accommodation is rendered much messier by the specific requirements that even political accommodation imposes on individuals. Habermas's *Theory of Communicative Action* was at heart a theoretical elaboration of the basic insights of the sociological theory of modernity: *no* forms of cultural specificity can, in the final analysis, resist the process of modernization; *all* cultural traditions are devalued to the extent that they require some form of extramural justification on the part of their own participants; *all* life worlds, as they modernize, lose progressively their capacity to provide prediscursive justificatory strategies and situation definitions. No legal arrangements or political goodwill can protect life worlds from the dynamic of modernization, even under the proviso that robust, "authentic" traditions are a *sine qua non* for a nonpathological process of political integration. It is just this reading of societal and cultural modernization, as relentless and exceptionless, that seems often to fall out of Habermas's specifically democratic-theoretical analyses. Indeed the political accommodation that Habermas (not unreasonably) would require of all cultural groups can only be achieved insofar as those groups are capable of adopting a "decentered," reflective attitude toward their own beliefs and practices—no matter how foundational those beliefs and practices may be (or may once have been).

The subsequently decentered relation to one's own traditions, beliefs and practices has several entailments: it means that one is capable of regarding one's own beliefs *as beliefs*, that is, as possible interpretations of the world that can and do compete with others. It means that one has been obliged to cease regarding one's cultural identity as anything other than a cultural identity; that one regards the foundations of identity as validity claims that appear convincing. It means that one can intuitively reconstruct reasons why one's own traditions would be persuasive, to one's self or indeed to any rational agent. It means that one is capable (even if only a little bit) of engaging in a process of rational reflection on the bases of one's own traditionally-secured interpretation of the world. And it means that one is capable of a critical relation to tradition—a critical relation that allows some traditions to be carried on, others to be rejected, according to their ability to meet the requirements of public reason and their capacity to continue to convince social actors.

For Habermas, these pluralistic requirements constitute grounds for the rejection of Kymlicka's call for group-differentiated rights: "In the last analysis," Habermas writes,

> the protection of forms of life and traditions in which identities are formed is supposed to serve the recognition of their members; it does not represent a kind of preservation of species by administrative means... Cultural heritages and the forms of life articulated in them normally reproduce themselves by convincing those whose personality structures they shape, that is, by motivating them to appropriate productively and continue the traditions. The constitutional state can make this hermeneutic achievement of the cultural reproduction of the life world possible, but it cannot guarantee it. For to guarantee survival would necessarily rob the members of the very freedom to say yes or no that is nec-

essary if they are to appropriate and preserve their cultural heritage. When a culture has become reflexive, the only traditions and forms of life that can sustain themselves are those that bind their members while at the same time subjecting themselves to critical examination and leaving later generations the option of learning from other traditions or converting and setting out for other shores.[23]

True enough: but reflexivity also entails that the "critical examination" of traditions will follow justificatory criteria that derive from the public use of reason and not from the traditions themselves. Political accommodation, in other words, provides individuals with context-transcendent criteria for the evaluation of traditional contexts that themselves make a claim to holism. It is not clear how *any* holistic set of cultural traditions, of the sort that could provide a consistent and coherent cultural *identity*, can be expected to survive this form of analysis, for on the formal level the claim to holism is the first thing that has to go. Political accommodation *entails* cultural accommodation. Habermas depicts the devaluation and decay of cultural traditions as a learning process—which it surely is. But it is not entirely consistent to expect members of cultural groups to retain, except in fragmentary, self-conscious form, a set of beliefs whose claim to completeness and consistency is rendered operationally defunct. This fact explains the self-contradiction inherent even in cultural group's members' own self-descriptions *as* members of cultural groups requiring special legal protections and political recognitions. For in order to recognize *one's self* as a member of a given cultural group requiring protections and recognition, one must have *already* carried out the process of decentering and self-criticism, which is, in turn, not compatible with the emphatic, holistic notion of culture.

Just that notion of culture, I would argue, is needed to make the plausible claim that cultural groups impart a distinct and unique identity to their members. In a decentered, self-reflexive context, the values constitutive of a cultural group have no more foundational a status for identity formation for individuals than any other sort of validity claims. They may have a temporal priority—one may grow up with them—but that may indeed often make them even more likely targets for rejection. In the postmetaphysical context, a validity claim is a validity claim: procedurally one has no grounds for adducing any heightened prospects for justification to any of them according to whether or not they constitute the cherished beliefs of a given culture. Cultural survival, on these terms, is conducted in just the same way as the survival of any other kind of socially current norm. On Habermas's own terms, cultural groups survive, or perish, according to the reflective choices of members who vote with their feet and who are obliged to adopt the very attitude toward their culture that Sandel described as the "unencumbered self": one may not be "antecedently individuated," but our individuation through socialization makes any cultural claim up for grabs.[24]

If this is true (and I think it is) then we shall have to make do without the notion that "cultural identity" constitutes a privileged source of semantic resources within a multicultural state. This is not to say that cultural identities and cultural groups are irrelevant—far from it. It is just that the emphatic reading of them that I questioned above—that is, "distinctive" identity of cultural forms in the emphatic form—is implausible on its face. Indeed, it may be much more reasonable to regard cultural group identities as in many cases *arising from* the historical efforts to affect just the kind of political accommodation that Habermas (not unreasonably) requires. In multicultural states, cultural groups often form identities precisely as an incorporation of, and reflection upon, the historical experiences that a delimited group of people have undergone in their efforts to adapt successfully to the very heavy demands of modern life—both political and economic. A collective self-consciousness of groups, their literal construction *as* groups, often emerges only via the experience of seeking legal and political redress for specific oppressions. As an example, it is difficult to see the emergence of the specific group of "native Americans" in any other way. This constructed character of cultural groups leaves unanswered the naturalistic questions as to whether such groups establish a general social recognition, *as* groups, on the basis of prepolitical features such as ethnicity, language, an attachment to a particular geographical territory, and so on. But the shared collective experience of political "accommodation" (probably too gentle a word to cover the empirical facts) seems to provide as good a criterion as any for establishing group identity.

This means that, in a way that is almost the direct obverse of Kymlicka's liberal nationalism, Habermas effectively argues—though he may not want to read the implications of his own argument in this way—that cultural identity is just as "constructed" and hence just as "artificial" as national identity, if by "constructed" and "artificial" we mean "the discursive accomplishment of an empirically contingently constituted group of persons." Just as Kymlicka's emphatic notion of culture renders him unable to distinguish between national identity and cultural identity, so Habermas's reading of modernity effectively undercuts any meaningful distinction between nation and culture—introducing the specter of universalistic hostility to difference normally attributed to the cosmopolitan fantasy. "Nation" now appears as only one brief episode in the larger and longer historical adventure of the decline of cultures in the plural.

How, then, can one reconstruct the *normative* critique of nationalism and national identity, without also including cultural identity? It appears that the normative distinction between national and cultural identity—such that the one is deceptive, the other merely constructed—is not the hermeneutic concept of "identity" at all, but rather the political concept of *sovereignty*. As I argued earlier, Habermas sees the folly of nationalism consisting in the "Schmittization" of sovereignty, as I somewhat awkwardly put it: namely, the construal of the basic concept of popular sovereignty as a claim to *collective* or *national* self-determination, where the national collective is understood as a homogenous *Volk* united by prepolitical categories of shared descent, language, place, and destiny. Returning to this distinction, one can observe the only effective difference between national and cultural identity: *national* identity implies a claim for sovereignty in terms of collective self-determination; *cultural* identity is conceived as already forming a constituent part of a multicultural state whose sovereignty is understood in terms of popular sovereignty via constitutionally assured democratic processes.

Old-style nation-state sovereignty—the kind that Kant, grudgingly, affirmed as an intrinsic part of the cosmopolitan program in "Perpetual Peace"—consists, in the Weberian sense, in the capacity to maintain the rule of law, internally, via coercion and stable borders, externally, via an army; as such it constitutes something like the de facto claim that a specific territory distinguishes between foreign and domestic affairs and that the latter is off-limits for other sovereign states. Hence the Schmitt-style conception of popular sovereignty entails (in part) the idea that the internally homogenous construction of a *Volk* (people) corresponds to the capacity for the assertion of a collective will directed externally. But it is just this kind of sovereignty, as David Held has argued, that has grown increasingly irrelevant as a result of the dynamic of globalization.

Held argues instead for a porous understanding of state sovereignty as an overlapping, cross-cutting, and multiple set of spheres of inter-action entailing international, transnational, regional, and local forms of institutionalized interaction. For Held, Kant's apparently quaint and mild call for a "universal right to hospitality" in fact entailed a powerful critique of traditional state sovereignty, even as he defended it:

> Universal hospitality must involve, at the minimum, both enjoyment of a certain autonomy and respect for the necessary constraints on auton-omy. That is to say, it must comprise mutual acknowledgment of, and respect for, the equal and legitimate rights of others to pursue their own projects and life plans. Moreover, in a highly interconnected world, "others" includes not just those found in the immediate community, but all those whose fates are interlocked in networks of economic, political, and environmental interaction. Universal hospitality is not achieved if, for economic, cultural, or other reasons, the quality of the lives of oth-ers is shaped and determined in near or far-off lands without their par-ticipation, agreement, or consent. The conditions of universal hospitality (or, as I would rather put it, of a cosmopolitan orientation) is not cosmopolitan law narrowly conceived,—following Kant—but rather a cosmopolitan democratic public law in which power is, in prin-ciple, accountable wherever it is located and however far removed its sources are from those whom it significantly affects.[25]

However utopian such a formulation may strike us—we inher-itors of Foucault who are inclined to skepticism at the idea of the full accountability of power—the principle of a practical *and* a nor-mative argument against the continuation of the older model of state sovereignty strikes a chord. For Habermas, the Enlightenment conception of popular sovereignty, consistently realized, would already satisfy most, if not all, of Held's hopes. Popular sovereignty, consistently conceived, is in the final analysis incompatible with the arbitrary allocation of sovereign power to a given temporal state, since the principles that sovereignty is meant to realize—the full complement of subjective rights allocated to all members of an unbounded moral community—cannot support the limitation of full and equal rights on inherently contingent grounds. Democratic polities realize the basic moral intuitions of modern universalism via modern, i.e., positive constitutional law. Hence constitutions express abstract principles according to specific and ongoing inter-pretive practices and traditions. But this permeation of the ethical meets its limit, normatively, in situations where a given state's sovereignty makes it impossible to extend full rights to persons who *have good reason* to expect their recognition.[26]

Thus, the dynamic of cosmopolitan *democracy* holds that state sovereignty, like national identity, ought to be regarded as a pragmatic arrangement for the full global realization of human rights—as an institution it has no independent legitimacy, for there is no internal connection between popular sovereignty and the *raison d'etat* of specific states. This fact underlies the fundamental *legal* claim of Habermas's cosmopolitanism: that subjective rights ought to be recognized by coercive positive cosmopolitan law, thus effectively bypassing the category of the sovereign state altogether—a state of affairs that would directly conflict with the principles of international law as encoded in the United Nations charter.

Hence the final political differentiation between national and cultural identity—sovereignty conceived as the will to collective self-determination—is itself finally undermined by the core political ambition of cosmopolitanism, the emergence of a popular sovereignty beyond national borders. Neither national nor cultural identities of course simply disappear or become irrelevant: but in the contemporary scene, cultural identity does not retain the capacity to endow individuals with a sense of collective identity that is so qualitatively different from other sorts of social collectivities that any special arrangements are justified in protecting them. Moreover, even the thesis that cultural identity constitutes a *special* semantic resource for the accommodation to procedural democracy is rendered dubious, since it is, in the final analysis, an entirely empirical question of whether given persons will or will not find their own (often multiple, overlapping, or conflicting) group memberships particularly formative for their identities. In the general field of the ethical, in the agonistic space of democratic procedures, cultural identity is but one source of identity—or one source of trouble, or confusion, or creation, or bureaucratic construction, or delusion, or manipulation, or oppression, or insight, self-discovery or self-dramatization, political emancipation or political trickery—among countless others. The loss of such a privileged site of ethical substance is the *condition* of contemporary democratic practice, not the fear that democratic practice must overcome. Culture, in the emphatic sense I have used above, is *gone*. Its absence, in fact, composes something like the only distinctively *ethical* commonality that links a postnational world together into one ethical discourse.

Adorno had pointed out that, after Auschwitz, "progress" was only thinkable by holding the concept of a human totality in a tension with itself: only the thought of a human totality "that included absolutely everything" could help the vision of collective moral-political progress make a last stand against the force of the factual. Without a limiting principle the concept of a human totality would both fulfill and undo itself, for the overcoming of the internal contradiction of the concept of the human would, at the same time, render the concept itself incapable of *application,* hence negatively utopian. Adorno saw the maintenance of this tension (one could now call it the tension between the concepts of solidarity and alterity) as requiring a move from philosophy and political theory, as traditionally understood, to a range of melancholy sciences: a strange sort of ethical micrology, for example; or political theory that hid in aesthetic or musical criticism; or the oblique kinds of intervention in the postwar German political public sphere, at once deeply skeptical and childishly hopeful that stood in such sharp contrast with the final theoretical works. Any hope for "progress" that remained, Adorno felt, resided more powerfully in a certain memorialism than in any flaccid utopian fantasy. Moral progress, to count as progress, would have to consist of an expansion of the limitation of the human that consistently held in memory the precise image of what was irretrievably *lost* in historical time, at the moment of its disappearance.

At virtually the same moment that Adorno wrote of the hope that only such a strangely deployed notion of humanity could allow us to continue to figure the "unforced unity" of moral progress, Habermas, in the *Postscript* to *Knowledge and Human Interests,* wrote that

> only in an emancipated society, whose members' autonomy and responsibility had been realized, would communication have developed into the non-authoritarian and universally practiced dialogue from which both our model of reciprocally constituted ego identity and our idea of true consensus are always implicitly derived. To this extent the truth of statements is based on anticipating the realization of the good life... Only when philosophy discovers in the dialectical course of history the traces of violence that deform repeated attempts at dialogue and recurrently close off the path to unconstrained communication does it further the process whose suspension it otherwise legitimates: mankind's evolution toward autonomy and responsibility.[27]

Cosmopolitanism, to be worthy as a progressive doctrine in the face of the world as it is, would need to establish itself as a form of

critical historiography, just as much as a part of a speculative political and legal theory—as a normatively inspired, unquenchable
curiosity about the forms of cultural identity that have been lost in
the process of forming the very possibility of an "unforced unity" of
global democracy and rights.

I have argued, perhaps implicitly, that Habermas's more or less
juridical conception of cosmopolitan democracy—the bypassing of
nation-state sovereignty in the recognition and enforcement of global
human rights—is not, in the end, the relevant focus of a discourse-
theoretical model of cosmopolitan democracy, because this legal call
is coherent only as a consequence of a powerful, normative critique
of national identity. I then argued that, if Habermas's own theory of
modernity is to be taken seriously, then the only differentiation
between national and cultural identity is the political concept of sovereignty; but sovereignty, from the cosmopolitan point of view, is
precisely popular sovereignty, which cannot be restricted to the normatively arbitrary limitation of the particular sovereignty of nation-
states, implying instead a global, popular sovereignty under the rule
of law. Cultural identity *in the emphatic sense* is not a price paid by
the call for a cosmopolitan democracy—it is not cosmopolitanism,
but the fact of modernization itself, that has rendered cultural identity only one of many competing, agonistic, conflicted, politicized,
indeterminate, and partial sources of ascriptive identity in large
democratic societies. Cultural identity, in my view, is insufficiently
differentiated from other forms of social identification to justifiably
require any special legal protection under the rubric of Kymlicka's
group-differentiated rights. Furthermore, it makes little sense to
speak of *protecting* cultural identities from modernization processes
that so often turn out to have been crucial in the process of *creating*
just those identities. Ultimately, the "unforced unity" that cosmopolitan democracy calls for means neither uncritically affirming,
nor simply erasing, the fact of cultural identities. It rather calls for
understanding them as "limitations" to the totalizing concept of the
human—limitations that both constitute and, at the same time, mark
the limit of the thought of moral-political progress. Such an understanding may contribute to the realization that the *real* subjects of
cosmopolitan democracy are members of the growing global plurality of the destitute, whose destitution deprives them of membership—cultural, national, and otherwise—more surely and more
completely than any political theory could.

In the final analysis, cosmopolitanism does not call merely for a juridical redress of violated rights, nor for a *merely* moral embrace of abstract principles of the right, casting about for transnational institutional support. Cosmopolitan is at heart an ethical claim, in the specifically Habermasian sense of that word: it is the claim that the concrete ethical substance of a given community—the discussion of "who we are and who we want to be"—ought no longer to confine itself to any spatially bound polity but, in questions that directly affect the interests and needs of all, ought to be extended to include all human beings. The moral principle of inclusion in discourse, in other words, is met and matched by the ethical call to revise who we are and who we want to be.

If there is a global consciousness on which a cosmopolitan democracy could find some substantial support, it is not in a Taylorian "republican consciousness" in which each temporal nation would realize a moment of unity between love of the universal and of the particular state; nor is it in Kymlicka's liberal nationalism, where individuals, bereft of other resources, depend on ethical particularism as a translation tool for accommodating themselves to the unique challenges of modern society. Nor, I think, would a global ethical substance be adequately described as a nationally unbounded Habermasian constitutional patriotism, in which each nation would critically rework its *own* ethical substance and national history to put some flesh on the bare bones of moral universalism. Cosmopolitanism as a global ethics would intend something a bit different: an ethics of collective remembrance in which "who we are and who we want to be" could be addressed only indirectly via a discourse about "who we were and what happened to us." Such a discourse—call it a global ethical *Vergangenheitsbewältigung* (mastery of the past)—would no doubt be as difficult, jagged, ambiguous, angry, and potentially endless as one could imagine. Who "we" are and what "we" lost are terms that invite ethical gymnastics over victimhood and collective history and would certainly lead to all manner of repugnant "rereadings" of history. Such things can neither be ruled out nor are they even to be avoided—as opening positions to ethical discourses, expository claims over identity and of victim status set the terms for ongoing processes in criticism, even when they do so negatively. The image of loss does not imply a flattening out of our ethical sensibilities; loss is not an equalizing force. But collective loss can also be read as a source of solidarity and identity and need not efface the political differences between marginalized and oppressed groups and members of a privileged culture. Indeed, it is possible that only through a dramatically greater feeling for loss and the effects of loss can members of a global community come to any better understanding of the history, sources, and nature of the oppression that they experience. The ethical discourse of modernity is a discourse of loss—of the loss of cultural difference, the loss of opportunities for the reasonable adoption of scientific and technological discovery, the loss of life, the loss (to put it in discourse-theoretical terms) of "repeated attempts at dialogue." A global ethical discourse that would discover, and register, the "traces of violence that deform" such repeated attempts at dialogue would be a discourse that took as its subject the historical processes in which oppressed groups have been constituted, how they responded to that oppression, and how they vanished. To keep alive the history of this process is not just to engage in a form of historical antiquarianism, but to respond to an intuition that can, one last time, be registered in a transformed formula of Adorno: *"Eingedenken der Kultur(en) im Subjekt."*

Notes

1. A shorter version of this essay appeared in *Constellations* 7.1: 64-79 as "Cosmopolitanism and the Solidarity Problem: Habermas on National and Cultural Identities."

2. Theodor W. Adorno, "Progress," in *Critical Models*, ed. and trans. Henry Pickford (New York: Columbia University Press, 1998), 145. Emphasis added— M.P.

3. See Martha Nussbaum, "Kant and Cosmopolitanism," in *Perpetual Peace: Essays on Kant's Cosmopolitan Ideal*, eds. James Bohman and Matthias Lutz-Bachmann (Cambridge: MIT Press, 1997).

4. I am grateful to Steven DeCaroli for this reference. See Steven DeCaroli, "Matters of Taste, Matters of Fact: The Emergence and Integration of Aesthetics and History within the Philosophical Discourse of Eighteenth Century Europe," (Ph.D. Dissertation, Binghamton University).

5. For an illuminating summary of the spectrum of current positions on the question of cosmopolitanism, see the editors' introduction to *Perpetual Peace: Essays on Kant's Cosmpolitan Ideal.*

6. "The point of cosmopolitan law is ... that it goes over the heads of the collective subjects of international law to give legal status to the individual subjects and justifies their unmediated membership in the association of free and equal world citizens." "Kant's Idea of Perpetual Peace, with the Benefit of Two Hundred Years' Hindsight," in Bohman and Lutz-Bachmann, 128.

7. Immanuel Kant, "To Perpetual Peace: A Philosophical Sketch," in *Perpetual Peace and Other Essays*, trans. Ted Humphrey (Indianapolis: Hackett, 1983), 118.

8. Benedict Anderson, *Imagined Communities* (London: Verso, 1983).

9. See Ernest Gellner, *Nationalism* (London: Weidenfeld & Nicolson, 1997).

10. For more on Habermas's critiques of German national identity see my essays, "Universalism and the Situated Critic," in *The Cambridge Companion to Habermas*, ed. Stephen K. White (Cambridge University Press, 1995), and "Habermas and the Antinomies of the Intellectual," in *Habermas: A Critical Reader*, ed. Peter Dews (London: Basil Blackwell, 1999).

11. Jürgen Habermas, *Accommodating the Other*, eds. Ciaran Cronin and Pablo De Greiff (Cambridge: MIT Press, 1998).

12. Habermas, *Accommodating the Other*, 109.

13. Habermas, *Accommodating the Other*, 112-13.

14. Habermas, *Accommodating the Other*, 115.

15. Jürgen Habermas, "Struggles for Recognition in the Democratic Constitutional State," in *Multiculturalism: Examining the Politics of Recognition*, ed. Amy Gutmann (Princeton: Princeton University Press, 1994), 113.

16. Will Kymlicka, *Multicultural Citizenship. A Liberal Theory of Minority Rights* (Oxford: Oxford University Press, 1995), 76.

17. Kymlicka, *Multicultural Citizenship*, p 18.

18. Kymlicka, *Multicultural Citizenship*, 11.

19. Will Kymlicka, "From Enlightenment Cosmopolitanism to Liberal Nationalism" (unpublished manuscript, 1997), 2.

20. Habermas, "Struggles for Recognition," 138.

21. For an interesting analysis of this see Kymlicka, chapter 8, "Toleration and its Limits," in *Multicultural Citizenship*.

22. "In multicultural societies the national constitution can tolerate only forms of life articulated within the medium of such non-fundamentalist traditions, because coexistence with equal rights for these forms of life requires the mutual recognition of the different cultural memberships: all persons must also be recognized as members of ethical communities integrated around different conceptions of the good." Habermas, "Struggles for Recognition," 133.

23. Habermas, "Struggles for Recognition," 130.

24. Another way of making this point is a legal one: even the case that Habermas adduces as evidence for the normative demands for the right to leave cultures, *Wisconsin v. Yoder*, illustrates the double-edged aspect of cultural identity within the constitutional state. By suing the state for forbidding them the right to remove their teenage sons from state educational requirements, the Yoder family claimed, substantively, that their Amish cultural and religious community could only hope to survive if its children were protected from the influences of the prevailing secular culture, whose basic principles were incompatible with the Amish religion. In order to do this, however, the Yoders are obliged to translate just this problem into the terms of that same prevailing culture, by

insisting that the Wisconsin requirements violated their own constitutionally protected rights to freedom of religious belief and practice. It was as citizens, in other words, and not as members of a particular cultural group, that the Yoders were able to prosecute (successfully) their claim. See *Wisconsin v. Yoder*, 406 U.S. 205 (1972).

25. David Held, "Cosmopolitan Democracy and the Global Order: A New Agenda," in *Perpetual Peace: Essays on Kant's Cosmopolitan Ideal*, eds. James Bohman and Matthias Lutz-Bachmann (Cambridge: MIT Press, 1997), 244.

26. We get an intuitive sense of this limit whenever we encounter cases where noncitizens of particular democratic constitutional states claim protection under the rights that state constitutions guarantee to its own citizens according to universalistic moral and legal reasoning. From country to country, it is a matter largely of high-court precedent whether, and how far, noncitizens will be protected by constitutionally secured legal rights, even though the moral rights on which they are based cannot coherently be articulated as applying to one demarcated group of state citizens.

27. Habermas, "Postscript," in *Knowledge and Human Interests* (Boston: Beacon, 1974), 314-15.

Chapter 10

A QUESTION OF GROUNDING

Reconstruction and Strict Reflexion in Habermas and Apel

Peter Dews

I

Faciticity and Validity—the literal translation of the title of Habermas's 1992 book on the philosophy of law—faintly but distinctly echoes, in its basic conceptual contrast, the title of a dissertation on Schelling that was submitted to the Philosophy Faculty in Bonn by a young doctoral student in 1954 . This dissertation, "The Absolute and History," was also authored by Jürgen Habermas. The resonance between these titles across the years is surely significant—indeed, it could be said to indicate one of the central, abiding concerns of Habermas's thought. For despite his many borrowings from analytical philosophy, Habermas remains—in the deepest sense—a thinker of the continental European tradition. And one sign of this is that Habermas has always been convinced that philosophy changed irrevocably after Hegel. For Habermas, as for so many European thinkers of his and earlier generations, including ostensible antagonists such as Derrida, Hegel is the turning point. Hegel is at once the culmination of the tradition of Western metaphysics, as well as the point at which that tradition is pushed to the very limit of its capacity to accommodate what is apparently external to it, including the field of historical contingency. Hegel is the last thinker for whom human reason is merely one expression of a rationality that runs like a thread through the labyrinth of being as a whole. Accordingly, the immediate Hegelian aftermath, when facticity and validity began to fall apart, is a defining philosophical and historical moment for Habermas.

One is reminded of this when, in *The Philosophical Discourse of Modernity*, Habermas asserts that, philosophically speaking, we are still the contemporaries of the young Hegelians. By this he means that our task is still what he terms the "desublimation of a spirit." Such a desublimation "draws the contradictions irrupting in the present into the wake of its absolute self-positing only in order to de-realize them and transpose them into a remembered past—where they are deprived of all seriousness."[1] Habermas believes this is still our task because bringing Spirit, or reason, down to earth requires a distinctive balancing act. On his account, although the young Hegelians wanted to protect the present and its openness towards the future from the *diktats* of a superior reason, they had no wish to dissolve the intrinsic relation of history to reason *("der Vernunftbezug der Geschichte")*. And preserving this connection involves navigating a delicate course between the dogmatism of the philosophy of history, on the one hand, and the defensive mechanisms of historicism, on the other.

The centrality of this historical and intellectual moment for Habermas's work is suggested by the fact that it already stands at the heart of his doctoral dissertation on Schelling. Depite its ostensible topic, and despite its reputation as a Heideggerian text, the dissertation begins with an extended discussion of the Hegelian aftermath that runs over a hundred pages. What excited the young Habermas's interest were the various strategies adopted by thinkers after Hegel in order to accommodate the openness of human freedom and the irreducible contingency of history, without lapsing into the metaphysical dualisms whose untenability Hegel had definitively exposed. Thus, Habermas reviews the thought of Bruno Bauer, Max Stirner, and Ludwig Feuerbach, the late idealists Weisse and Immanuel Hermann Fichte as well as—most crucially—Marx and Kierkegaard. It is these various efforts to think beyond Hegel that provide the backdrop, painted in considerable detail, for his discussion of the later thought of Schelling. But, one might ask, if Habermas's central interest—even at this early stage of his thought—was specifically in the desublimation of reason, why should he pay so much attention to a thinker of the great Idealist generation like Schelling?

It is now increasingly recognized that Schelling's later thought elaborated many of the motifs that were to become crucial in the later critiques of Hegel—indeed, in the general development of post-Hegelian European philosophy. In particular Schelling's insistence on the gulf between the "*Was*" ("What") and the "*Daß*" ("That"), or between the "ground" of existence and existence itself, can be seen as a driving force behind both Marx's deflation of the demiurgic powers of the Hegelian concept through the disclosure of the material basis of thought, as well as behind Kierkegaard's insistence on the ungraspable singularity of the individual's existence (not to mention Heidegger's "ontological difference"). But, even if this historical influence is conceded, does it not seem likely that these motifs, which express the resistance of being to absorption by philosophical reason, must be more adequately elaborated in Marx, Kierkegaard, and later thinkers, than in Schelling's cumbersome and seemingly antiquated speculations on god and the origin of the world?

In his dissertation, however, Habermas does not draw this conclusion. For he is dissatisfied with the solutions that both Marx and Kierkegaard propose to the difficulty of thinking, after Hegel: "What Marx and Kierkegaard have in common is that they sublate (*aufheben*) Hegel's mediations, but substitute for them a new, real mediation, whose result is the communist society or religious existence."[2] As Habermas goes on to suggest, however, these new forms of mediation ultimately entail an abandonment of philosophical thought as such: "The critique of Hegel is directed towards the central problems of existence and freedom ... Hegel's presentation of the history of spirit, for all its brilliance, short-circuits the very focus of history, the freely acting human being in engagement with factically encountered reality and does justice neither to human freedom nor to the facticity of the real. At the same time, these two conditions of possibility of history are the toughest antagonists of a form of thought that—like speculative thought—raises the claim of the concept. For this reason, Marx set a limit to thought in the form of praxis, and Kierkegaard in the form of faith."[3] It is clear, however, that for Habermas neither of these moves is satisfactory: one can neither rely on the historical advent of communism nor commit ourselves uncritically to religious faith in order to solve these specifically conceptual problems. And the interest in Schelling, one can deduce, lies in the fact that he gives the conceptual apparatus of idealism an *internal* twist that reveals its limit, rather than appealing to some dimension of reality that is supposed to elude the grasp of the concept and therefore become exempt from critical reflection. The outcome of Schellings's enterprise in this regard is Habermas's main concern in his doctoral dissertation. He explores how Schelling ultimately retreats from the notions of a "thrown" god who is forced to free her- or himself from a compulsive entrapment in nature, to the notion of a god who, in a supertemporal creative decision, is restored once more to the status of "lord of being."

As I suggested at the outset, many of the preoccupations that lie at the heart of "The Absolute and History" remain central for Habermas throughout the later phases of his writing. On the one hand, he wants to sustain the possibility of a *systematic* understanding of history and society that is based on something other than a perspective or a set of value postulates—a systematic understanding that can detect an immanent, but unfulfilled, rationality of the historical process and thereby provide an objective basis for critique. On the other hand, he wants to do full justice to what he calls in his dissertation "the freely acting human being in his engagement with factically encountered reality." The *Vernunftbezug der Geschichte* (intrinsic relation of history to reason) that Habermas invokes in *The Philosophical Discourse of Modernity*, far from being something which he has succeeded in characterizing, remains a conundrum at the heart of his work. In fact, one might go so far as to say that there is an unresolved "dichotomy" in Habermas's thinking, comparable to that which, as a young man, he analyzed in the thought of Schelling.

It is important to emphasize the tension of this dichotomy because, in much recent critical commentary—not only that coming from poststructuralism—there has been a tendency to portray Habermas as a more or less straightforward neo-Kantian, to portray him as someone primarily concerned with a transcendental justification of moral and critical norms, in abstraction from issues of social and historical context. But as the constant motif of the "desublimation of reason" makes clear, this has never been Habermas's own understanding of his project. Whether in the form of his earlier theory of cognitive interests, or in the form of a pragmatics of language, Habermas has repeatedly sought to mediate between nature and

Spirit—to employ the Idealist categories—rather than absorbing the former into the latter or screening it ultimately out of account.

It is this basic orientation that leads him, for example, to insist in *Between Facts and Norms* that the "sociological disenchantment of law" is an essential moment in the *philosophical* appraisal of law—and not just the extraphilosophical addendum to which some of his more conventionally Kantian critics would like to reduce it. Nevertheless, despite his best efforts, it is clear that Habermas has remained pulled in two directions, and—in what follows—I would like to try to reach a more firm understanding of this fundamental tension in his thought. I shall try to do this by examining the critique of Habermas's thought developed by his longtime friend and colleague, Karl-Otto Apel. For Apel challenges Habermas by suggesting that his thought has become so contextual and "desublimated" that is no longer able to sustain its rational and critical impulse. Habermas attempts to defend himself against this charge without falling into what he regards as Apel's dubious apriorism, outlining the difficult middle ground that he aspires to occupy, even if they are not entirely successful in doing so.

II

One point that may be worth making at the outset is that Apel—no less than Habermas—sees himself as an opponent of metaphysics. For Habermas, the claim of philosophical reason to capture the eternal structure of being has to be abandoned in the light of the critique of the young Hegelians. Apel, on the other, metaphysical hand, frequently appeals to two twentieth-century thinkers who have, in a sense, continued this protest by exposing the relentless abstraction of philosophical thought from our primordial practical engagement with the world: one of the most influential of Apel's early essays was a comparison of Wittgenstein and Heidegger.[4]

In this essay, Apel thoroughly endorses the notion that metaphysics overlooks fundamental aspects of itself—including the language games within which expressions acquire their meanings and the "pre-ontological understanding of Being" that is at work in every grasping of something in the world *as* something—and that these shortcomings cannot be captured within the discourse of metaphysics, which in fact presupposes such language games or forms of disclosure. The "suspicion of meaningless" that Wittgenstein raises against philosophical discourse is entirely justified, insofar as philosophy seeks to leap over this background awareness in its description of the ultimate structure of the world. Yet, at the same time, Apel believes there is a point at which such contextualizing strategies must come to a halt, namely, when they begin to bring into question the validity-basis of philosophical argumentation as such. For example, as soon as the boundaries of language games come to be regarded as defining the limits of what can and cannot be regarded as meaningful, then, according to Apel, a new "monadological metaphysics" emerges, which is no less suspect, no less a form of hypostatization than the traditional metaphysics that it replaces.[5] Similarly, Heidegger's *Seinsgeschichte* ("history of Being"), understood as the story of a series of incommensurable world disclosures, cannot be articulated without violating its own account of the conditions of meaningfulness. To avoid such difficulties, Apel argues, one must assume a series of reflexive stages built into natural language: "The philosophical logos ... which, in turning back toward the hermeneutic logos, makes possible the 'formal indication' of such concepts as 'individuality,' 'historicity,' and so on, comprehends the 'hermeneutic *logos*' in principle, just as the latter comprehends the objectifying theoretical *logos* of 'object languages' (for example, that of the natural sciences)."[6] The characteristic of this philosophical logos is that it points beyond the boundaries of individual language games, or the boundaries of the history of Being, toward an ultimate consensus achieved by argumentation within what Apel terms an "unlimited community of communication" *(Kommunikationsgemeinschaft)*.

It is important to note that for Apel this conception of an unlimited *Kommunikationsgemeinschaft* in no sense represents a "return" to metaphysics. On the contrary, any axiom or principle concerning the nature of being is dissolved within what Apel refers to as the "infinite dialogue of the indefinite community of interpretation." Despite its open-endedness, however, this dialogue is not entirely indeterminate in its structure. For Apel believes that the very fact of entering into dialogue commits us to acknowledging the validity of certain normative conditions of communication that cannot be further relativized. Since these conditions cannot be accounted for, by regress to any further reflexive level of language, their validity must reveal itself in another manner than that of demonstration or justification. Apel writes: "To the fact ... that *philosophical reflection* can and must grasp the paradigmatic evidence of particular language games as revisable in principle, there ... corresponds the fact that the *philosophical language game* itself must have recourse to evident truths that cannot be equated with any of the empirically revisable language game paradigms."[7]

It is at precisely this point, however, that Habermas wants to resist Apel's line of argument. He is concerned, one might say, that Apel has not carried the desublimation of reason far enough. Apel apparently repudiates the presuppositions of the philosophy of consciousness along with those of objectifying metaphysics—in the name, I have observed, of Heidegger and Wittgenstein, among others. But he does not repudiate the distinctive kind of reflexive evidence that comes to light in the Cartesian *cogito*. Indeed, Apel writes that: "the certainty of the 'ego cogito, ergo sum' is a transcendental-pragmatic condition of the possibility of the language game of argumentation in our sense ... In other words, the propositional component contradicts the performative component of the speech act expressed by that self-referential sentence. The irrefutable certainty of the 'cogito, ergo sum' thus rests not on an axiomatically objectifiable deductive relation between sentences, but rather on a transcendental-pragmatic reflexive insight mediated by the actual self-reflexivity of the act of thinking or speaking."[8] Through similar acts of "strict reflexion," Apel believes it possible to identify a normative structure to which one is committed by virtue of our participation in the philosophical language game of argumentation. The unlimited communication community that we necessarily anticipate as the ultimate forum of validation of our truth claims presupposes an egalitarian, and reciprocal, system of relations among human beings. Accordingly, Apel suggests, our acknowledgement of the moral demand to foster such relations is by the mere fact of our entry into dialogue.

For Habermas, this still sounds much too fundamentalistic. It seems to him that Apel is still trying to set up a hierarchy of discourses in which empirical knowledge is trumped by a "transcendental language game" that rests on fundamental and indubitable insights. This program is incompatible with the project of a desublimation of reason since it seeks an ultimate escape from that *Geschichtsbezug der Vernunft* (intrinsic relation of reason to history), which, one could say, is the necessary complement of the *Ver-*

nunftbezug der Geschichte (intrinsic relation of history to reason). Furthermore, such a refusal of desublimation has potentially anti-democratic implications. Because Apel is still in search of a *prima philosophia*, a metaphysical foundation for cognitive and moral norms, Apel imagines himself in possession of insights that are immune to the fallibilistic reservations that apply even to philosophical claims in a postmetaphysical context.

III

This difference between Habermas and Apel comes, perhaps most clearly, to light in the contrast between the procedure which Apel calls "strict reflexion" and the philosophical activity which Habermas calls "reconstruction." For Habermas, the reconstructive sciences (for example, Lawrence Kohlberg's developmental psychology), which explore the nature of fundamental human competences, "explain the presumably universal bases of rational experience and judgement, as well as of action and linguistic communication." But he goes on to stress that "all they can fairly be expected to furnish ... is reconstructive hypotheses for use in empirical settings ... Fallibilistic in orientation, they reject the dubious faith in philosophy's ability to do things single-handedly, hoping instead that success might come from an auspicious matching of different philosophical fragments."[9]

The notion of reconstruction is one essential expression of Habermas's enduring commitment to a conception of critical social theory as a collaboration between philosophical and empirical investigation. In this respect, Habermas's position can be seen as both continuing, and reacting, to the legacy of the earlier Frankfurt School, in particular to that of Adorno. For, on the one hand, Habermas wishes to correct what he takes to be the *normative* deficit of earlier critical theory, by providing a foundation for the theory that can no longer fall under suspicion of partiality, or particularism. But, on the other hand, throughout his career, Habermas's thought has been deeply marked by Adorno's critique of the philosophy of origins, of the search for ultimate foundations. Habermas's way of accommodating these apparently conflicting impulses has been to seek a form of justification that is not bound up with claims to a priori insight. Thus in turn Habermas has sought to achieve by envisaging a complementary relation between, on the one hand, the rational reconstruction of pretheoretical knowledge or "know-how," and, on the other, procedures of empirical investigation on the other.

Habermas's most compelling presentation of this complementarity can be found in an essay entitled "Reconstruction and Interpretation in the Social Sciences." Here he first develops the proposal that "There is a sense in which any interpretation is a *rational* interpretation."[10] What he means is that, in seeking to interpret a text or cultural artifact, one is in search of *reasons* for its being the way it is, for example, for why a particular metaphor—obscure as it may be—is employed at a particular point in a poem. But in searching for reasons, Habermas suggests, one cannot remain content with those attributable to a creator or author, as if these were self-legitimating. For—so Habermas contends—one cannot even appreciate reasons *as* reasons without taking an evaluative stance towards them. Hence, the very activity of interpretation—contrary to the assumptions of certain extreme hermeneutic positions—presupposes an underlying shared rationality, whose core is the expectation (however deeply implicit) that the claims to truth, rightness, and truthfulness that speech conveys will meet with universal acceptance. In this way Habermas seeks to reconcile the "hermeneutic" dimension of reconstruction with its claim to objectivity.

It is this embedded rationality of communication that the process of reconstruction is intended to retrieve. This process can proceed on several levels. Domains such as "logic and metamathematics, epistemology and the philosophy of science, linguistics and the philosophy of language, ethics and action theory, aesthetics, argumentation theory, and so on" all share the goal of "providing an account of the pretheoretical knowledge and the intuitive command of rule systems that underlie the production and evaluation of such symbolic expressions and achievements as correct inferences; good arguments, accurate descriptions, explanations, and predictions, etc."[11] But such reconstructions might simply be an articulation of implicit cultural know-how, with no claim to universality. Because, at a more abstract level, rational reconstructions can inquire into conditions of validity, they provide a critical vantage on deviant or defective cases. Finally rational reconstructions, in analyzing very general conditions of validity, can sometimes "claim to be describing universals, and thus to represent a *theoretical* knowledge on a par with other such knowledge."[12] At this stage, Habermas admits what is involved may not simply be a matter of describing the essential structure of what *is* done, but of that which cannot *help* but be done, since there are no available, or even imaginable, alternatives: "At this level weak *transcendental* arguments make their appearance, arguments aimed at demonstrating that the presuppositions of relevant practices are inescapable, that is, they cannot be cast aside."[13]

Habermas, however, immediately goes on to stress that reconstructions of the last kind should not be burdened with "claims to ultimate justification": "*All* rational reconstructions," like other types of knowledge, have only hypothetical status. There is always the possibility that they rest on a false choice of examples, that they are obscuring or distorting correct intuitions, or, even more frequently, that they are overgeneralizing individual cases. Such theories therefore require further corroboration, an indirect verification. Kohlberg's theory of moral development provides an example of this. Sometimes Kohlberg speaks misleadingly, as if the theory of psychological development and the normative philosophical theory of moral stages were simply two aspects of one theory. But in fact— Habermas contends—it is better to see them as distinct but complementary, in a "relationship of mutual fit": "The empirical theory presupposes the validity of the normative theory it uses. Yet the validity of the normative theory is cast into doubt if the philosophical reconstructions prove to be unusable in the context of application within the empirical theory."[14] Thus, Habermas claims, the "hermeneutic circle is closed only on the metatheoretical level."

There are clear echoes here of the later Schelling's distinction between "positive" and "negative" philosophy. According to Schelling, negative philosophy can decribe a priori the underlying rational structure of reality; but only positive philosophy can reveal that this structure is being progressive instantiated, through an immersion in—and interpretation of—the actual course of history. In his doctoral dissertation Habermas claimed that Schelling never achieved a satisfactory integration of these two dimensions of philosophy. And unsympathetic commentators might well claim that there is something equally unsatisfactory about Haberms's hybrid notion of "reconstruction."

IV

Apel, for one, objects strongly to this conception of the philosopher's task, since its implication is that "a rational reconstruction of the quasi-transcendental type, specifying highly general conditions of validity could be empirically falsified." By contrast, Apel claims that there are certain conditions of argumentation that cannot be falsified in this way, since they are also preconditions of the very process of confirmation or disconfirmation. The most obvious example, to which Apel returns repeatedly, is the basic principle of fallibilism itself—of the potential revisability of all truth claims—which follows from the assumption that such claims could only be conclusively redeemed by an ideal, never-to-be-achieved consensus. In this domain Habermas seems to side with the critical rationalists, the German followers of Karl Popper such as Hans Albert, who insist that the principle of fallibilism must itself be regarded as a hypothesis that could in principle be falsified. This, Apel contends, is incoherent—for to insist that the principle of fallibilism may itself be falsifiable is to admit the possibility of apodictic, infallible truths, and thus to contradict its status as a principle. By contrast, what Apel calls the "*discourse principle*," which defines the structure of validity claims and their redemption under ideal conditions, is a condition of possibility of the principle of fallibilism itself.[15] In general, Apel contends, there are deep assumptions of argumentation whose status as a *fundamentum inconcussum* is secured not, as Habemas contends, by their apparent *unavoidability*—which may in fact be a culturally-conditioned illusion—but rather by the fact that contesting them generates a *pragmatic* or performative self-contradiction. Furthermore, Apel argues, for there to be a *genuinely* complementary relation between transcendental principles and empirical theories, there has to be a difference of kind between them—a gulf that, since his writings of the early 1960s, he has called the "transcendental difference." Otherwise, how could one form of inquiry supply a distinctive *additional* form of corroboration for the other?

What is Habermas's response to this apparently compelling line of argument? Habermas focuses on the question of fallibilism. In his reply to Apel, he denies the need to assume a hierarchy of discourses in which fundamental philosophical truths are secured by a distinctive form of reflexive insight. In his view, the justification of a the-

ory of argumentation rules is no less open to argumentative challenge than the justification of any other theory, or the reasons that
one proffers in grounding "harmless—for example—everyday
utterances." For the postmetaphysician "there is only ever one and
the same locus for justifications. There are no metadiscourses. And
the outcome of discourses cannot be predicted."[16]

In response to the obvious question of how he knows this,
Habermas's replies that this is simply intrinsic to the grammar (in a
Wittgensteinian sense) of the word "grounding." Thus he states: "I
understand fallibilism simply in the sense of a grammatical elucida-
tion, which must in turn be justified, and is therefore fundamentally
open for revision."[17] But this begs as many questions as it resolves.
Habermas's asserts that "The reservation of fallibilism simply relates
to the fact that that we cannot exclude the possibility of a falsification even in the case of convincingly grounded theories which are
accepted as valid. Otherwise we have not understood what 'being
grounded' means."[18] Yet—as Horst Gronke has pointed out—this
final contention seems to undermine Habermas's position.[19] For
Habermas does not say that anyone who excludes the possibility of
falsification must have a different conception of grounding, and that
the superiority of the conception would have to be decided by the
"play of argument." On the contrary, since the proponent of the
opposite view has failed to understand what grounding *means,* there
would be no point in entering into a discussion with them, just as
there would be no point in discussing whether a player was offside
with someone who did not know the rules of soccer. Thus it looks as
though, behind his apparently innocuous talk of grammar, Habermas is indeed laying claim to some incorrigible a priori insight, and,
thereby, entangling himself in precisely the performative contradiction of which Apel accuses him. He has failed to respect the "transcendental difference" between discourses raising truth claims that
could in principle be corrected and the insights into the conditions of
possibility of all discourse that are attained in strict reflexion. And,
to put Apel's worry as starkly as possible, if there were no such difference, there might really be some substance to "postmodern"
claims that the notion of resolving moral conflict by reaching consensus through discussion—one in which everyone's interests are
considered—is merely a Eurocentric prejudice.

V

Even allowing that Apel has the upper hand in this particular argument, however, what—concretely—is gained by his insistence? Apel tries to allow for "error" by stressing that although the ultimately grounded principles cannot be doubted as principles, our interpretations of them may be corrigible. But, having made this concession, Apel is convinced he can derive a remarkably strong set of normative assumptions from the thin basis of "strict reflexion." He believes that, by virtue of participation in argument, one has always already acknowledged the obligatory status of a complex set of arrangements that—under idealized conditions—would make possible a convergence on the ultimate "truth" of any matter through discussion. But Apel goes one stage further than Habermas in this regard—for he wants to claim that, by virtue of participating in discussion, not only is one committed to the idealizing assumption that such conditions of discussion apply now, he assumes that, if one is committed to attaining the truth when we "seriously engage in argument" (*"ernsthaft argumentieren,"* as he often puts it), then one must also be committed to bringing about, as far as possible, the conditions under which that truth could actually be achieved. Thus the search for truth involves any participant in an elaborate system of ethical commitments: in effect, a commitment to the practical realization of the ideal *Kommunikationsgemeinschaft.*

This equation of a commitment to truth with a commitment to bringing about the conditions under which truth could be achieved, is a fundamental point for Apel that Habermas contests. Habermas wants to draw a distinction between the "weak" normativity of the conditions of communication, and the stronger force of valid moral norms. As he puts it: "Communicative reason is not, like practical reason, a source for norms of right action *per se* ... Normativity and rationality *intersect* in the field of moral insights, which are won in a hypothetical attitude and ... only bring with them the weak force of rational motivation, and certainly not the burden of an existential understanding of self and world."[20] One could approach this conception from another angle by saying that, for Habermas, even the suspension of interest—the "hypothical attitude"—or moral discussion is driven by an interest in the *nonviolent* resolution of conflict. It is not the expression of an entirely disinterested quest for truth as such. But, if this is the case, then the future existence of a

Kommunikationsgemeinschaft that is better equipped to engage in a disinterested quest for truth can have no special relevance for the task of resolving a situation of practical conflict here and now.

The outcome of this dispute is a perplexing and ambiguous one. On the one hand, Apel seems right to insist on the ineliminability of the "transcendental difference," for its denial leads to self-contradiction. Yet, any attempt to spell out what the normative implications of this difference seems to overextend the basic reflexive insight. For once one moves beyond an immediate core of propositions whose contrary clearly implies a "performative contradiction"—such as the "cogito, ergo sum" of Descartes—it becomes increasingly implausible to suggest that such an inconsistency between the normative claim and the normative *presuppositions* of the claim is at issue. For example, in suggesting that reason requires a constitution in which different social "estates" have different rights of representation, is Hegel engaged in a performative contradiction? Is he violating democratic and egalitarian principles that his very engagement in philosophical discussion commits him to? If this were the case, then a great deal of the history of philosophy could be dismissed out of hand. Similarly, can it really be the case that a philosophical defense of religious revelation would involve its proponent in a performative contradiction?

VI

I began by describing some of the concerns of Habermas's doctoral dissertation, and by suggesting how some of these concerns have persisted throughout his career. But if it is possible to trace a Schellingian influence in Habermas's suspicion of a priori philosophising, it is equally plausible to suggest that Apel's work repeats, and has probably been directly influenced by, the strategies of Schelling's great contemporary and rival, Johann Gottlieb Fichte. Whereas Schelling, from an early point in his career, tried to balance the claims of ideality and materiality, self-consciousness and nature, insisting that transcendental philosophy must be complemented by a *Naturphilosophie*, Fichte sought to radicalize the Kantian procedure of the transcendental deduction. Fichte's aim was to show that the "transcendental history" of the self—one which begins from the bare, undeniable, spontaneous activity *(Tathandlung)* of the subject's self-positing—results in a structure that is identical with that of empirical experience. A full transcendental deduction—one which avoids presupposing any mental or conceptual apparatus that cannot be shown to be a necessary feature of self-conscousness—will thereby overcome the residual subjectivism (and hence skepticism) clinging to the Kantian notion of the "conditions of possibility" of experience.

Of course, despite Fichte's ambition of overcoming the gap between self-awareness and the world, his philosophy has acquired a popular reputation as the embodiment of an extravagant form of subjective idealism, as the *nec plus ultra* of what Habermas terms the "philosophy of consciousness" *(Bewußtseinsphilosophie)*. Ostensibly, Apel shares this hostility to the starting point of individual consciousness, as his central concept of the "communication community" suggests. But I would like to suggest, on closer inspection, Apel's position turns out to be not so remote from that of Fichte. For, notwithstanding his emphasis on intersubjectivity, ultimately, the locus of reflexive insight, even in Apel's work, can only be the self-consciousness of the individual thinking and experiencing subject.

One can see this, firstly, from the fact that individuals have to grasp *for themselves* the inconsistency between the content of their moral claim and what is normatively presupposed by the activity of arguing in defense of it. The moral philosopher who, from Apel's perspective, has strayed into skepticism in the course of the difficult transition between conventional and postconventional morality cannot be shown the error of her or his ways simply by pointing to the inconsistency between two determinate claims which she or he makes. The individual concerned has to achieve the attitude of "strict reflexion," grasping the contradiction between a tacitly or explicitly relativist claim and the anticipation of universal consensus implied by its "performance." In an interview, Apel has admitted the difficulty of this task:

> if I regard reflection as an act directed towards an act, as the attempt to objectify my own act of thought, so to speak, then it becomes clear that—to achieve this—an act is necessary which cannot itself be objectified. An infinite regress of self-objectifications arises. This is an argument which is often used against ultimate grounding through reflection. But there are counter-arguments which show that we do indeed know what we can never objectify. We also know that an infinite hierarchy of metalanguages arises. We know this though another reflexive insight which is harder to grasp.[21]

There is a striking parallel between this argument and that put forward by Fichte in the first chapter of his *Attempt at a New Presentation of the Wissenschaftslehre* (1797/98). Here Fichte seeks to show that all consciousness of objects presupposes self-consciousness: "I can be conscious of any object only on condition that I am also conscious of myself, that is, of the conscious subject ... It was, however, further claimed that, within my self-consciousness, I am an object for myself and that what holds true in the previous case also holds true of the subject that is conscious of this object: this subject too becomes an object, and thus a new subject is required, and so on *ad infinitum*. In every consciousness, therefore, the subject and the object were separated from each other and each was treated as distinct."[22] Fichte concludes from this that it is impossible to comprehend the possibility of *self*-consciousness on the basis of such a regress. Hence, threading through the series acts and holding them together, there must be "a type of consciousness in which what is subjective and what is objective cannot be separated from each other at all, but are absolutely one and the same."[23] Apel's claim that we must assume a nonobjectifiable form of knowledge, an underlying reflexive insight, in order to preclude an endless regress, points in the same direction.

Of course, Apel avoids employing terms such as "self-consciousness" or "intellectual intuition" to characterize this nonobjectifiable knowledge. But this cannot disguise the fact that the connections between his own position, and those of traditional transcendental philosophy, are far more intimate than his stress on the historical break achieved by his semiotic and communicative paradigm suggests. More specifically, the community of communication cannot always play the role of ultimate court of appeal that Apel is determined to allot to it. For although the *Kommunikationsgemeinschaft* is a condition of achieving truth, insight into its *status* as a transcendental structure can only be achieved through "strict reflexion," which is necessarily carried out by the individual thinker. Here, Apel's philosophical convictions pull him in two contrary directions.

To give one obvious example, Apel is keen to combat what he sees as the potential solipsism of the traditional Cartesian "*cogito, ego sum*," arguing that even this self-evident thought presupposes the empirical existence of a language community for its formulation. "Along with ego-consciousness," Apel affirms, "a language-game is presupposed as the *fundamentum inconcussum* ... In this language game the existence of a real lifeworld and the existence of a communication community are presupposed along with the actual evidence of thinking myself as existing in the sense of paradigmatic language-game evidence."[24] However, this notion of an empirical precondition of transcendental insight seems to be contradicted by Apel's claim, a little earlier in the same essay ("The Problem of Philosophical Foundations in Light of a Trancendental Pragmatics of Language"), that "the certainty of the 'ego cogito, ergo sum' is a transcendental-pragmatic condition of the possibility of the language game of argumentation in our sense."[25] For if the *cogito* is a condition of possibility for argumentation, how can it in turn be dependent on the prior existence of a communication community, in other words, a community in which argumentation occurs? In fact, Apel goes on to say that "it is of prime importance that the Cartesian insight (solitary as it actually is) must be capable of being reexamined and, in this case, also capable of being confirmed by a communication community that is in principle indefinite." But, if the *Kommunikationsgemeinschaft* is simply there to *confirm* what Apel calls a "certain insight," [26] what work is it doing? Why would an insight that is already certain already need confirmation? And, does not the fact that this confirmation cannot be doubted transform the communication community into a mere projection or externalization of reflexive insight?[27]

At this point it becomes clear that the notion of an unqualified "a priori of the commmunity of communication," as Apel terms it, is no less incoherent than the notion of the absolute priority of transcendental consciousness. Furthermore, not only is Apel's position closer to Fichte's than he would like to admit, from his middle period onward, Fichte can in fact be regarded as "one jump ahead" of Apel, at least so far as an appreciation of the problems generated by an unqualified transcendental standpoint are concerned. By 1800, when he wrote *The Vocation of Man*, Fichte had reached the conclusion that a radicalized transcendental deduction could not lead back from skepticism to everyday reality. Rather than making possible an ultimate convergence of the conditions of experience and the actual content of experience, of the subjective and the objective, the speculative point of view, which begins from the self-positing "I," *cannot help becoming* an outlook that locks us into a world of illusion: "What comes to be in and through knowledge is only knowledge. But all knowledge is only a depicting, and in it something is always demanded which would correspond to the image. The demand can be satisfied by no knowledge, and a system of knowledge is necessarily a system of mere images."[28] The only way one can escape from the hall of mirrors of a self-enclosed subjectivity is through a recognition—through the awareness of a moral claim—of the existence beyond the self of other self-conscious beings, a recognition that is deeper than anything one could call knowledge. Fichte terms this recognition "*Glaube*" (faith or belief): "I just said that I *think* of them [others outside me] as being like myself. But strictly speaking it is not thought by which they are first presented to me as such. It is the voice of conscience, the commandment, 'here limit your freedom, here suppose and respect other purposes,' which is first translated into the thought, here is certainly and truly a self-existent being like myself."[29]

Significantly, this concession to the role of "faith" is picked up by Schelling in his philosophical correspondence with Fichte, a correspondence which became increasingly polemical, and finally broke off in 1802. Schelling points out that Fichte is on shaky ground in accusing him of relying on an unprovable point of departure, an "absolute identity" of the subjective and the objective, which lies beyond the domain of experience. For Fichte himself has to appeal to faith in order to show that there is indeed a world which lies beyond subject-centered knowledge: "The necessity of beginning from seeing [from what can be directly experienced or intuited] keeps you and your philosophy within a thoroughly conditioned series, in which nothing of the absolute can be encountered. You must have had an awareness or feeling that this was so, which already obliged you, in *The Vocation of Man*, to transfer the speculative to the sphere of faith, because you cannot in fact find it in your account of knowledge. But in my view it should no more be a question of faith in philosophy than in geometry."[30] At this point in his career Schelling is arguing from the standpoint of his *Identitätsphilosophie*, a systematic theory of reality grounded on the principle of absolute identity. He is not opposed to philosophy straying beyond the bounds of experience, of what can be "seen," but merely to Fichte's claim that the result will be no more than an arbitrary, speculative construct. As he progressed, however, Schelling came to realize that absolute identity could no more be assumed as an ultimate grounding principle than Fichte's principle of self-consciousness. Schelling, too, developed a philosophy which hinges on an "ecstatic" leap beyond purely rational deduction *(Vernunftwissenschaft)* into the inexplicable contingency of being, a leap from "*Was*" to "*Daß*." As we have seen, it is this feature of Schelling's thought, the attempt to balance the claims of reason and contingent existence, which has profoundly influenced Habermas, from his doctoral dissertation onwards. Indeed, it does not take much effort to hear the debate between Apel and Habermas as an echo of those earlier Idealist debates, in which the limitations of the transcendental standpoint were at issue.

And as was also the case with earlier debates, the ultimate stakes in the confrontation between Habermas and Apel are moral and political, rather than purely theoretical. Habermas is not just concerned that Apel seeks to achieve something that philosophical reflection cannot achieve. He does indeed insist that: "Philosophy is overtaxed by what Apel terms 'the existential question concerning the meaning of being moral'"[31] on Habermas's account, moral theory is competent to clarify the moral point of view and justify its universality, but "the normative content of the general presuppositions of argumentation is appealed to ... solely in response to the *epistemic* question of how moral judgements are possible and not the *existential* question of what it means to be moral.'[32] This is partly a matter of a realistic appraisal of the sources of moral motivation. On Habermas's account, "We learn what moral, and in particular immoral, action involves, *prior* to all philosophizing; it impresses itself upon us no less insistently in feelings of sympathy with the violated integrity of others than in the experience of violation or fear of violation of our own integrity."[33] It would be absurd to think that a demonstration of the immanent rationality of communication could do this job, when such experiences are lacking. But more importantly, Apel's position encourages him to think that he can preempt the decisions of an ethical community. He is led to believe that the realization of social and political conditions under which moral action would no longer bring strategic disadvantage can be stipulated a priori as the highest good, one to which the mere status as communicating beings commits us. Habermas concludes that "Apel clearly allows himself to be misled by the hierarchical structure of his theory into immediately addressing questions of political ethics 'directly from an above' through a superprinciple ... Behind the solitary politician of Apel's imagination there lurks the philosopher king who want to put the world in order, not the citizen of a democratic state."[34]

In opposition to this autocratic tendency, Habermas suggests that "In a democratic state, political will formation—even reforms with far reaching political ramifications—is always pursued within the institutions of a legally constituted social and political order."[35] And yet, of course, a niggling doubt persists. For, what if the institutional framework encourages bad decisions? And what if these decisions, in turn, lead to the deterioration of the framework, thereby initiating a downward spiral? Such anxieties will always encourage philosophers of Apel's bent to seek for an Archimedean point, an ideal community of communication as "ultimate subject of validity-claims," beyond the unsatisfactory contingencies of actual moral and political communities. And in Apel's case, the experience of German history in the twentieth century gives him an additional powerful motive for doing so.[36]

Notes

1. Jürgen Habermas, *Der philosophische Diskurs der Moderne* (Frankfurt am Main: Suhrkamp Verlag, 1985), 68.
2. Jürgen Habermas, "Das Absolute und die Geschichte: Von der Zwiespältigkeit in Schellings Denken" (Ph.D. Dissertation, University of Bonn, 1954), 71.
3. Habermas, "Das Absolute und die Geschichte," 85-86.
4. See Karl-Otto Apel, "Wittgenstein und Heidegger: Die Frage nach dem Sinn von Sein und der Sinnlosigkeitsverdacht gegen alle Metaphysik," in *Transformation der Philosophie. Band 1: Sprachanalytik, Semiotik, Hermeneutik* (Frankfurt am Main: Suhrkamp Verlag, 1976), 225-75.
5. Karl-Otto Apel, "Heideggers philosophische Radikalisierung der 'Hermeneutik' und die Frage nach dem 'Sinnkriterium' der Sprache," in *Transformation der Philosophie. Band 1*, 334.
6. Apel, "Heideggers philosophische Radikalisierung," 247-48.
7. Karl-Otto Apel, "Das Problem der Letztbegründung im Lichte einer transzendentalen Sprachpragmatik: Versuch einer Metakritik des 'Kritischen Rationalismus'," in *Sprache und Erkenntnis*, ed. B. Kanitschneider (Innsbruck: Tama, 1976), 69-70.
8. Karl-Otto Apel, "The Problem of Philosophical Foundations in Light of a Transcendental Pragmatics of Language," in *After Philosophy: End or Transformation?*, eds. Kenneth Baynes, James Bohman, and Thomas McCarthy (Cambridge: MIT Press, 1987), 278. (This is an English translation of the article cited in the previous footnote, revised and amplified by the author.)

9. Jürgen Habermas, "Philosophy as Stand-In and Interpreter," in *After Philosophy: End or Transformation?*, 311.

10. Jürgen Habermas, "Reconstruction and Interpretation in the Social Sciences," in *Moral Consciousness and Communicative Action* (Cambridge: MIT Press, 1990), 31.

11. Habermas, "Reconstruction and Interpretation in the Social Sciences," 31.

12. Habermas, "Reconstruction and Interpretation in the Social Sciences," 32 (trans. altered).

13. Habermas, "Reconstruction and Interpretation in the Social Sciences," 32.

14. Habermas, "Reconstruction and Interpretation in the Social Sciences," 39.

15. Karl-Otto Apel, "Normatively Grounding Critical Theory through Recourse to the Life-World? A Transcendental-Pragmatic Attempt to Think with Habermas against Habermas," in *Philosophical Intervention in the Unfinished Project of Enlightenment*, eds. Axel Honneth, Thomas McCarthy, Claus Offe, and Albrecht Wellmer (Cambridge: MIT Press 1992), 142.

16. Jürgen Habermas, "Entgegnung," in *Kommuikatives Handeln*, eds. Axel Honneth and Hans Joas (Frankfurt am Main: Suhrkamp Verlag, 1988), 350. ("Fur Begründungen gibt es immer nur ein und den selben Ort. Es gibt keine Metadiskurse … Und der Ausgang von Diskursen lässt sich nicht voraussagen.").

17. Habermas, "Entgegnung," 352.

18. Habermas, "Entgegnung," 352.

19. See Horst Gronke, "Apel versus Habermas: Zur Architektonik der Diskursethik," in *Transzendentalpragmatik*, eds. Andreas Dorschel et al. (Frankfurt am Main: Suhrkamp Verlag, 1993), 273-96.

20. Jürgen Habermas, "Erläuterungen zur Diskursethik," in *Erläuterungen zur Diskursethik* (Frankfurt am Main: Suhrkamp Verlag, 1991), 191.

21. Karl-Otto Apel, cited in Alfred Berlich, "Elenktik des Diskurses: Karl-Otto Apels Ansatz einer transzendentalpragmatischen Letztbegründung," in *Kommunikation und Reflexion*, eds. Wolfgang Kuhlmann and Dietrich Böhler (Frankfurt am Main: Suhrkamp Verlag, 1982), 265.

22. Johann Gottlieb Fichte, *Introductions to the Wissenschaftslehre and Other Writings*, trans. and ed. Daniel Breazeale (Indianapolis: Hackett, 1994), 112.

23. Fichte, *Introduction to the Wissenschaftlehre*, 112.

24. Apel, "The Problem of Philosophical Foundations," 280.

25. Apel, "The Problem of Philosophical Foundations," 280.

26. Apel, "The Problem of Philosophical Foundations," 280.

27. It is worth noting that Apel often describes the insights achieved through strict reflexion as *"apriori konsensfähig"* (capable of consensus a priori), which again underlines the fact that reflexive insight is not dependent on intersubjective validation—and seems to confirm Habermas's worst fears.

28. J.G. Fichte, *The Vocation of Man* (Indianapolis: Hackett, 1987), 64-65.

29. Fichte, *The Vocation of Man*, 76.

30. Schelling to Fichte, 3 October 1801, *Fichtes und Schellings philosophischer Briefwechsel*, ed. I.H. Fichte and K Fr.A Schelling (Stuttgart and Augsburg: Cotta, 1856), 97.

31. Jürgen Habermas, "Remarks on Discourse Ethics," in *Justification and Application* (Cambridge: Polity Press, 1993), 75.

32. Habermas, "Remarks on Discourse Ethics," 77.

33. Habermas, "Remarks on Discourse Ethics," 75-76.

34. Habermas, "Remarks on Discourse Ethics," 86.
35. Habermas, "Remarks on Discourse Ethics," 86.
36. See K.-O. Apel, "Zurück zur Normalität —Oder könnten wir aus der nationalen Katastrophe etwas Besonderes gelernt haben?" in *Diskurs und Verantwortung* (Frankfurt am Main: Suhrkamp), 1992.

A CONTEMPORARY CHALLENGE TO CRITICAL THEORY

Systems Theory

Chapter 11

CRITICAL THEORY AND SYSTEMS THEORY[1]

Wolfram Malte Fues

In the summer of 1989, Francis Fukuyama saw the emerging collapse of real socialism in Eastern Europe as a sign that "liberal democracy might represent 'the end of the ideological evolution of humanity' and the 'ultimate form of human government.' It would thus be 'the end of history'," for "the *ideal* of liberal democracy is not in need of improvement."[2] Not ten years later, Niklas Luhmann has countered that the history of modernity has only really begun with the globalization of liberal democracy, and that a theory of society capable of grasping and analyzing this beginning is now necessary. According to Luhmann, philosophers from Aristotle to Habermas have understood and judged social life on the basis of normative ideas. In contrast, the old masters of sociology, since Max Weber, understood society through general categories, successfully using those categories to open specialized fields of research. In this light, social theory splits into a social philosophy based on moral maxims, and a social science based on abstract axioms, two perspectives with only one thing in common: from the perspective of an established and establishing subjectivity, they take society as their object, an object outside themselves. "However, the sense for problems has now shifted from ideas into reality itself; *and only now is sociology called for.*"[3]

Since the establishment of this theoretical apparatus, the limits of its object have shifted so far in the direction of this subjectivity that subjectivity has finally become part of its object. Hence, all conceptions of society must now assess and understand themselves as conceptions of what Luhmann calls the society of the society; in them, sociology must be "discovered ... as the self-description of society" (GdG 33). Social philosophy and social science come together in a sociologic, in which the social secures its structure, evolution, genesis, and history in a "self-referential, self-reflexive, and self-implicating"[4] manner.

If one assumes, however, that Fukuyama is right about ideological evolution, what then? When "the individual can contribute to the formation of laws, either in his or her own person, or via a representative,"[5] then the ideal of liberal democracy, now requiring no improvement at all, is reached and realized. The ideal of liberal democracy requires a social subjectivity for individuals that posits in reality that which is imposed upon it—everything objective is originally subjective, nothing but a moment of the subject itself that is dispensed, commissioned, and equally present. Because this ideal overtaxes the power of the individual in the social reality, certain political strategies—in this subject's name—have to be developed. With the help of these strategies, there should be representatives and institutions in which the subject can be symbolically duplicated, such that the representatives reproduce and achieve the will of the subject. "To sumbolon" means in Greek not least the recognition that married people have for one another in order to remain mutually recognizable to each other. The ideal of liberal democracy is therefore rooted in the ideal of a subject to which, in nature and history, nothing is foreign, but to which all is untrusted and unfamiliar, such that this subject can make it trustworthy and recognize it: "We have given to thee, Adam, no fixed seat, no form of thy very own, no gift peculiarly thine, that thou mayest feel as thine own, have as thine own, possess as thine own the seat, the form, the gifts which thou thyself shalt desire. A limited nature in other creatures is confined within the laws written down by Us. In conformity with thy free judgment, in whose hands I have placed thee, thou art confined by no bounds; and though wilt fix limits of nature by thyself."[6]

This humanizing subjectivity is, in a double sense, the subject of modernity: on the one hand, the persons and the institutions of modernity; on the other hand, the absolutely general imagination, the ideal, the category, the *sujet*, that understands itself, and then interprets itself in history and society. If this interpretation is completely achieved today, then not the ideological evolution of humanity, but rather that of its humanitarian modernization has reached its conclusion. Such a development must yield unavoidable consequences that realize this ideology for the science of the society.

When one methodically, theoretically describes society under the condition of such an end, one must handle the subject of a so purely liberalized society that everything that is considered an object becomes either a symbolic moment of the subject, or a symbolic subject itself. Such a discourse merely leads the searching subject back to nothing but itself and, therein, back to its origin and beginning. The society speaks about itself as society in a mode that socializes itself, reproducing itself and nothing but itself, varying the reproduction, if at all, through new metaphors. Because the absolute value of modernity, its humanizing and liberalizing subjectivity, is socially realized, every normative description that is based on the difference between philosophical ideality and the social reality—therein inevitably demanding the social reality's elimination—is worthless. Moreover, a value-free approach, as is fundamental in classical sociology since Max Weber, does not solve the problem, but merely avoids it. If Fukuyama's hypothesis arises from a misunderstanding in his particular philosophy of history, then the suspicion about the alleged end of modernity and its society, requires a scrutiny in which social science considers the historical prerequisites and the social conditions of its theoretical approach. Social philosophers from Rousseau to Rorty, on the basis of their subjectivity, have always interpretatively ended up back with modernity's own subjectivity. Perhaps today it all depends on analyzing them without identifying with them. Niklas Luhmann, in his major work, meets the fulfillment of this challenge.

I

The space and medium of all socialization can be found in what Luhmann calls "meaning": "Society is a system for constituting meaning" (GdG 50). The primary basis of meaning is the category of difference, which is revealed and defined in operations of differentiation. A subject differentiates itself from its object as follows: it

determines one way in which its object is determinable by relating
that mode of determination to a different mode of determination
and, then, by excluding all other such modes from their relationship.
Everything that includes this difference and its connecting operations forms a system; everything that this difference excludes forms
that system's environment. Hence, meaning arises from the internal
fixing of meaning-laden elements into a system and from that system's definition of itself against its external environment; it arises
from the simultaneous doubling operation of two differences: one
path-breaking, the other revolutionary. The relation in this unfolding of difference comes from its subject, which completes it by
observing it, and which can only observe it by completing it. "Social
systems shape their operations as operations of observation that
make it possible to differentiate the system itself from its environment ... To put it another way, they differentiate self-reference and
other-reference. For them, limits are thus not material artifacts, but
two-sided forms" (GdG 45).

The differentiation between system and environment establishes both the system's operative closure and its openness to what
it excludes, because, as difference, the system's limit is permanently
pendent, and pending in its differentiations. It can, at any time,
become the object of further differentiation. All operations of meaning aimed at systematic continuity are subject to this reservation: a
violation of the limit, repeating and renewing those operations in a
completely different manner otherwise previously unforeseen in the
system, is always possible. "The world provides an immeasurable
potential for surprises; it is virtual information that, however, needs
systems to generate information, or, more precisely, to give selected
irritations the meaning of information" (GdG 46). The system is
irritable, because there are no limits to how it can be determined; at
the boundary between self-reference and other-reference, this irrita-
tion hardens into determined information, which can be continually
redetermined. Finally, the problem of meaning, as a system of
socialization, is not the difference from an identity that always pre-
cedes that difference but, on the contrary, the production of identity
from a difference that always undermines that identity. Identity
derives primarily from recursive operations of repetition which,
through "selective condensation and confirming generalization,"
generate a structure of meaning that "in contrast to others, can be
called the Same" (GdG 47).

Is this theoretical construction self-referential, self-reflexive, and self-implicating? At first glance: no. As before, a sovereign subject makes the field of the social its object by defining it as a meaning. But this subject also differentiates the social from everything that is not meaningful, using the difference he has described as "system/environment" to further elaborate the system, and attending to the context of every differentiation he performs. Thus, this theory-building process, and the structure of the theory it produces, are mirror images of each other. What the theory describes is just as much a description of the theory, as of its object. Further, this theory's apparently sovereign subject recognizes itself as a moment added to the object that it thinks it controls. By virtue of its theory of society, sociology now shows itself to be the society in the theory, the society of the society.

Sociology does not owe this insight to its theory building. In constructing its theory, it is solely occupied with observing the difference between system and environment and the differentiations within the system. The unity, in the relation of the subject to its object, conditions both, and makes them possible; this unity is exempt from subjective observation because it completes that observation. All attempts to observe it would only make that unity the object of the differentiations whose basis it is. Knowledge of the self-implicating character of this theory of society, stems much more from another observer's observation, a second-order observation. In it, a subject makes its object the difference, between the theory-building process and the theory's structure, by understanding that difference as the starting point of a system, and thus maintaining its difference from all of the environment outside its fields of differentiation. Of course, this second-order observation can itself be observed: a third-order observation could make its object the difference between sociology and social theory as self-implication, as the society of the society, by understanding that difference as the starting point of a system, and thus maintaining its difference from all of the environment outside its fields of differentiation. This theory of society appears to be the form of socialization as such, "that theory of the surrounding social system that includes all other social systems in itself" (GdG 78), so its environment can only be made up of the nonsocial, as such.

In the meantime, however, the observation of observing has led to an important realization: the difference between system and environment is not material but just as functional as those differences developing the system; it can be seen as equivalent to them. This must lead the third-order observation, which observes the observation of the observation, to the following conclusion: the system/environment-reference, between the social on the one hand and the nonsocial, which is the foundation of the social on the other, can—at any time and from anywhere—be made into the starting point of another system and its environment by an observation which observes that reference. This process can correct such observation. "Society is ... the extreme of a system forced to observe itself without, in the process, seeming like an object about which there could only be one single correct opinion, so that all deviation would have to be treated as error" (GdG 88).

Against all definitions based on normative principles, the theory of this society depends on the principled openness of limits, even of that limit that guarantees the system's difference from its environment and thus also guarantees that the system has meaning and can be defined. "This may ... lead the descriptions to include *moments transcending the descriptions themselves*, or, to put it another way, it may lead a description's meaningfulness to be communicated along with it as selectivity" (GdG 1141). Social critique no longer seeks to condemn every deviation as error by judging the agreement of its object with principles applied from within the critique itself. Rather, it describes the social process society uses to judge itself. This critical description explains the conditions of judgment as an occasion for the sublimation of judgment. In other words: this critique keeps society from understanding itself as substantial and monumental, by understanding it as momentary and configurational—as the society of the society.

For social individuals, procedures for creating meaning take the form of communication. *Ego* differentiates itself from *alter*, "whereby *ego* is the one who understands a communication and *alter* the one to whom the communication is attributed" (GdG 1136f). By sharing information with each other, *ego* and *alter* complete an operation that repeats and varies what came before in their social system, prefiguring what will come. Otherwise, they would have nothing to share with one another and would not understand one another. However, the pieces of information that this communication contains only make sense if, as their form demands, they take the difference between the system and its environment into account.

That is, they must take the system/environment-reference as part of the communication to be understood. (Communication both preserves the system's closure and opens it up to its environment.) *Ego* can react to *alter's* offer of communication in three ways: first, by testing the character of the communication (serious/ironic, honest/dishonest, etc.); second, by accepting or doubting the communicated information (this system-internal operation redefines the border between system and environment); and third, by accepting or critiquing the chosen mode of communication. However, these three reactions are only alternating moments in *ego's* process of understanding *alter's* offer, by *ego* transforming itself into the *alter* of a new communication to a different *ego*. Acts of communication, in Luhmann's sense, are not integrating moments of what is ideally an agreement made by society as a whole. Rather, they are operations that risk such agreement by repeatedly renewing it, and conditioning it away through their social consequences. According to Habermas, "a speech act is successful only when someone accepts the offer it contains by ... saying yes or no to a fundamentally critiquable claim to validity."[7] A speech act succeeds, Luhmann would counter, when someone begins to negotiate the offer of understanding that the speech act makes. The goal of these negotiations is part of another offer into which the conditions of the initial exchange do not extend. (In any case, as Luhmann notes, social self-description tends to demand transcendence in order to secure the unity of society, not only operatively, but also ideologically.)

II

Luhmann sees his theory of society as a revision of that "project of modernity" that has until now been "incomplete, indeed, not even adequately sketched." Hegel thus becomes especially important: Luhmann sees him as the "single previous attempt at a full analysis. But one should not put something like Spirit at the end of history, nor see in it any final thought, any superior figure ... The observer of the observer is not a 'better' observer but merely another observer" (GdG 1142). *Ego* functions as the subject of a communicative operation by differentiating itself from *alter*, describing the relationship of this difference, and observing the processes thus begun. This figure cannot ever break through or transgress any *alter*

ego. "Observing simply means ... differentiating and describing...
Formulated in the terms of traditional logic, differentiation is, in
relationship to the sides it differentiates, the excluded third. And
thus observation, in the completion of its observation, is also the
excluded third" (GdG 69). This displaces what modernity understands as the absolute idea of its self-foundation and its complete
self-representation that Fukuyama, as we saw above, celebrates as
the end, the completion of its history: the subject of symbolic self-
determination, which is grounded in a subjectivity of pure, not-to-
be limited mediation.

What role does this excluded third play in the original concept
of modernity? Why and how has its meaning taken the form of
exclusion? "A mediating relationship is a relationship in which the
items related are not one and the same thing but an Other for each
other and only one in a Third."[8] For Hegel as for Luhmann, meaning is based on a difference in which differences are related to each
other in such a way that they work both with and against each
other. The differences remain different, but they are at the same
time united in their difference. For Hegel, however, in contrast to
Luhmann, the unity which is the basis of this oneness is not the
excluded, but the included Third of mediation, its center, its beginning and end, around which everything turns, and from which
everything comes: "The nature of speculative thought ... consists
solely in the comprehension of the opposed moments in their
unity."[9] The founding subject of speculative thought, which also
guarantees its own foundation, proves to be the unity made up of,
and including, all differences. Finally, this subject is absolutely
mediated in all its objects, determined by them as much as it determines them, and the perfectly completed process of mediation is
sublimated in absolute immediacy. The observing subject sees itself
more and more clearly in every operation of differentiation, description, and observation until, enlightened about itself to the point of
completely transparent self-observation, it is no longer different
from all its differentiations. As a result, society, as a system social-
izing through meaning, moves from the "peace of order ... , a distribution of equal and unequal things, giving each its place"[10] to the
dynamic of the "modern world," whose basis is "absolute substantiality, the unity of in-itself and self-awareness."[11] The program of
producing meaning is reversed: once, reason could only try to comprehend, as well as it could, the validity of what really is, a validity

transcending reason; now, for what really is valid, it must confront reason using rational terms and finally come out as reason itself.

III

The history of dialectic is the history of dialectic's mistrust of dialectic. "The mediation of ... concept and thing does not remain what it was, the moment of subjectivity in the object. What conveys facts is not so much the subjective mechanism performing and grasping them as an objectivity heteronomous to the subject, an objectivity behind what the subject can experience."[12] In the history of modernity, what really is has by no means escaped the claim of reason. On the contrary, it has fulfilled that claim to such an extent that it now confronts reason with its own heteronomous rationality, which has begun to displace rational subjectivity from its task, its consequence, and its result. Strained by its own inherent power of concretization, the dialectic tries to mediate itself with the middle between maintaining that middle and reaching still stand. It does so in order to think "absolute substantiality ... of the modern world" as the unity of the in itself *(an sich)* and simultaneously of self-consciousness as under the suspicion of its division. "Contradiction within reality, dialectic is contradiction against reality."[13] The observing subject sees itself more and more completely in every operation of differentiation, description, and observation, but, as time passes, it recognizes itself less and less in its differentiations. Further, it opposes itself to the middle it assumes itself to be, in order to preserve itself, in the middle, in the face of the middle's increasing estrangement.

In contrast, Luhmann's theory of socialization excludes the subject—on which the symbolic objectification of substantial Being is originally based—from the emergence of meaning. Instead, it grounds a theory of socialization entirely on an objectivity heteronomous to it, with its own laws and rules. Instead of realizing itself in a unity-creating way, the mediating subjectivity of modernity loses any reality, degenerating to a merely methodologically-necessary theoretical fiction. "As difference, the unity of form remains a prerequisite, but difference itself does not sustain the operations. It is neither substance nor subject; it replaces such classic figures in the history of theory" *(GdG* 63). Truth, the real power of difference, no longer lies in the unity generated in, and from, its differences, a unity coming out as principle and consequence of truth's unfolding. Rather, truth lies in how the determination of that unity's meaning excludes it from the mediation of its meaning. Unity is only still subject to this determination as a condition through its elimination as a condition. The objective interpretation of a differentiation, in itself concrete, originally started from a subjective middle; that middle is now reduced to the perfectly abstract possibility of difference, an abstraction losing all concretizing power of decision the moment it becomes real. A middle working, to secure how meaning is produced socially and historically, is replaced by a universal trade-center-organizing society as a market, and meaning is produced as the exchange of wares. In this society of the society, no result of any differentiation process can raise a claim of validity which a yes or no would decide. Rather, each individual offers a possible decision, about which a further differentiation process decides, itself taking the form of an offer. The determining power of modernity's speculative self-understanding is limited to mere exchange value; under the rule of this power, a society for all possible forms of sociability develops. The temporal and spatial globality of this society derives from how it never appears as such: "The ambition of a common foundation, a founding symbol, a conclusive thought, must be renounced ..." (GdG 1122).

This "structural revolution of value,"[14] which Luhmann's theory has as both its object and its method, actually does make it possible to understand today's world society as an end of history, although in a completely different sense than Fukuyama's. The original project of modernity, the proof of being as consciousness of being (*Bewusst-Sein*) through the self-realization of substance as subject, has collapsed and ended because the project was heteronomously overdetermined by the power of its own self-differentiation. It ends not with the ideal of liberal democracy established in principle everywhere, but with the ideal's replacement by the transcendental reality of capital, which identifies the social with its own accumulation, no matter what ideological, apparently normatively, transcendent maxims it lets itself be represented by in the process.[15] The project of modernity ends insofar as it turns itself into itself, and begins again as its own peculiar other, "incomplete, indeed, not even adequately sketched" (GdG 1142).

IV

Does this end of the original project of modernity, of the classical sense of meaning, also signify the end of the subject that mediated, steered, realized, and justified it? "Society is ... a complete system exclusively determined by itself. Everything determined as communication must be determined by communication. Everything experienced as reality arises from communication's resistance to communication and not from the imposition of an outside world somehow present in an ordered way" (GdG 95f.). Following Luhmann, society is a system completely determined by itself, as long as its self-determination is defined as excluding the basis of its determination from itself, and making its otherwise unlimited determinability dependent on an unordered outside world that disappears as soon as it is ordered as an outside world. The subjective middle between substance and its symbolic objectivity, in a manner appropriate to its meaning, shifts from the origin of modernity into its excess, its parasites: "Somebody is in relation to an other or to a thing. A third is added which has no relation to the beings or the things but only to their relationship. Superimposing itself on the channel, it disturbs the relationship."[16] Reduced to mere exchange value, the subject of mediation cannot even disturb the relationship it is related to, for it is only superimposed on it in order to transcendentally mark it with the sign of the relational. But therein, the subject of mediation always, and everywhere, accompanies the social production of meaning – it accompanies the determination of communication by communication, as the exclusive present of undetermined generality, whose positivity alone lies in its simply immediate overturning into negativity.

The heteronomy of social objectivity, in which difference holds sway over identity, originated in the history of modernity. In order to ground its authority, this heteronomy again makes itself dependent on identity's pre-original form. Being, the result of the process of consciousness, returns into that process: "*Being, pure being*— without any further determination. In its undetermined immediacy, being is only equal to itself and also not unequal to Other... the Being, that is, the undetermined immediate is indeed *nothing* and nothing more or less than nothing."[17] The mediating subjectivity of modernity must be able to be accompanied in Luhmann's society of the society, as a pure form of difference, by every act of differentiation, designation and observation, because the act, without subjectivity, would never come into being. This subjectivity has the form of totality, of unconditioned presence, of the absolute self-identity *(Sich-selbst-gleichheit)* and with it that of the pure being. While the subjectivity accompanies every act of distinction, designation, and observation, it is also, at the same time, excluded from the act, and, with it, from every determination that the act could lend the subjectivity—it therefore goes immediately from pure being to pure nothingness. This mediating subjectivity is a pure form of difference that holds unendingly the social process of exchange. At the origins of modernity, this mediating subjectivity is to be understood as pure being that is perfectly self-identical (through this subjectivity's complete abstraction all determinations are formed in this motion); it is also to be understood as pure nothingness, "also not nonidentical with anything else."

Luhmann's sociological theory obviously describes a historical experience that both produces the subject of modernity with its socialization, and at the same time teaches that the process of the subject's realization *(Verwircklichung)* is its derealization *(Entwirklichung)* – that is, the success of its project also excludes it in the last instance from its own project. In contrast, Fukuyama considers this exclusion a complete inclusion, because he confuses the absolute indifference of all symbolization of the modern subject with its absolute validity. Are there already signs in Adorno's negative dialectics, vis-à-vis Hegel's speculative dialectics, in the skepticism of modernity, in the face of its own confidence, are there already signs and traces of the experience that is theoretically and methodologically worked out by Luhmann?

Negative dialectics holds back from itself at the locus of its mediation, because it mistrusts its subjective middle as the basis of an observation that it makes on its own dynamic:

> In coming to America, all places look alike ... One thinks that qualitative differences would have really disappeared from life, just as progressing rationality is annihilating them in method. Once back in Europe, even places that seemed incomparable in childhood look suddenly similar to one another... whether it be because what used to be style already possessed something of that normative force that one ascribes guilelessly to the industry... However, the experience of happiness, of the nonexchangeable, can only be made at one particular place, even if in retrospect it will be proven that it was not singular.[18]

The subject of modernity now experiences, along with the most modern products of its reason, that it belongs to rationality heteronomous to itself—a heteronomy in which the abstract equality pushes aside, and replaces, concrete comparisons. This experience makes the subject distrustful of any originary reality, and, subsequently, of itself as its own origin. But in this restraint qua itself, it holds tightly on to itself because it understands itself as the only place, on the one hand, where it might tend to mistrust itself and, on the other, where it can prove the suspicion that it withdraws into itself against itself and does not remain what it is.

When the supposition that the rationality (so successfully achieved) sets itself finally against itself, when this supposition begins to become clear to the subject of modernity—then at what other place could the subject check this supposition, and raise the supposition to self-certainty, than at that place of reason out of which the subject threatens to expel the history of the same reason? Therefore the subject accompanies its self-realization, the social production of meaning (to invoke Luhmann), with the undetermined universal of alternating skepticism and confidence, a universal of the present that rebukes itself, and therein points itself in another direction. It is a present whose positivity only resides in its simple immediate overturning in negativity. "*Being, pure being*—without any further determination. In its undetermined immediacy, being is only equal to itself and also not unequal to Other... Being, the undetermined Immediate is indeed *nothing* and nothing more or less than nothing."[19] The subject of mediation, the absolute symbol-empowered middle, represents for the modern individual—the individual marked and determined by that subjectivity—the only guarantee of objective happiness. Such a symbolic determination of itself is inexchangeable, because this determination stands already in relation to every other possible determination of this self: "*Being, pure being*—without any further determination." In precisely this universal referentiality, the references of the inexchangeable become real for themselves *(werden für sich)*, and reflect their mediation as exchangeability, into the purely abstract form of their mere difference, of the universal exchange. The subject of mediation, the only guarantee of objective happiness, no longer guarantees, "nothing more or less than nothing." It also stays, however, and stays precisely in this nothingness, the being for each and every successful symbolic objectivity, "equal to itself and also not unequal to Other."

Critical Theory, originating in a contradiction against a contradictory reality, regains its original critical capacity, if the project of modernity (to which, despite mistrusting it, it remains committed) contradicts itself so purely that it excludes its contradiction from itself. The "society of the society" and "negative dialectics" give up both the negation of negation and the third, which includes the unity of the distinction in the differentiation of a rationally-determined world. Luhmann locates the principle of his analysis, and the maxims of its practice that is insinuated in society—in the methodological continuity of this giving up; Adorno understands it, at the same time, as the task to introduce this third in every moment in which it appears and to begin with it anew. Being and nothingness, to which meaning of modernity returns, is only equal to itself, and, at the same time nonidentical, with nothing that is different from itself. This undetermined universality of unity and difference lets itself be understood as the unity *(Einheitlichkeit)* of contingent differentiation, as a background of unending self-ordering and self-organizing decay, also as a differentiation of centrifugal unity, a field of identity that is unendingly self-situating and self-concretizing: "The parasite is a pathogen. Far from transforming a system in its nature, its form, or its elements, relations, and ways ... it leads the system to change its condition in small steps."[20]

If Critical Theory accepts the society of the society as its propaedeutic and its condition, its basis and point of departure, it can then make every exclusionary procedure, which meets and annuls the self-observation of the observer, into the approach of the question about the significance, the form and the necessity of this exclusion. With it, Critical Theory can win back that history of political valuation that the exclusion should frustrate. In the wake of the description of the society of the society, writes Luhmann, "the ambition for a founding symbol has be to given up or left to philosophers." Critical Theory, which thinks radically against the tradition of its meaning in order to renew such meaning even more radically, might be able to thematize the selectivity that is communicated with this result—in a meaning *(Sinnhaftigkeit)* transcendentally different than what it brings forth in the communication between *ego* and *alter*.

V

The project of modernity begins with the resolution of Rene Descartes, lonely in a snowed-in farm house near Ulm: "as far as the opinions which I had been receiving since my birth were concerned, I could not do better than to reject them completely for once in my lifetime, and to resume them afterwards, or perhaps accept better ones in their place, when I had determined how they fitted into a rational scheme."[21] It begins with an "I" that separates itself from all objectivity conscious to it in order to hold the objectivity more available—the I can take the objectivity in its older improved form when it will have measured its form with reason. It is a subjectivity so empty, so determination-impoverished that it means nothing other than the point of approach and point of departure for each separation—and at the same time so complete, so determination-rich, that it not only makes conscious every objectivity that can take the form of knowledge, but also compares and measures this consciousness with the necessary form of certainty. The I of this subjectivity becomes, in the operative trinity, a pure nothing, as well as a pure being, as well as, finally, the middle, the mediation of the mere overturning of the two, which maintains and arrests its immediacy, characterizing and moderating in order to solidify and generalize this subjectivity to discourse, to method, to system.

How does this I test the strength of its opinions and convictions against reason? The I relates a certain discursive structure of objective knowledge to another that differentiates itself from the first. It does this such that it contains unrealized opportunities of determinations, and such that it allows itself to be known in precisely that moment, in which comes the first completely determined, realized relation with it. The I of modernity makes itself the middle, makes itself the subject of mediation between a history of the already-become figure of reason (the paradigm of all objectivity of the known being that is possible through the subjectivity described above) and a history becoming: a determination that tries to be valid as much for the individual I as for its symbolic representative.

How does this subjective middle determine itself in the historical process that drives it forward and unfolds it? As mediation, in which the figure of reason that has *become* history and the figure of reason that is *becoming* history are so different from one another, that that-which-was and that-which-is-becoming appear as moments of a simple present contradiction, whose presence develops and elaborates its simplicity as a category. This category sublates the contradiction, in that it brings a common reality to that-which-was and that-which-is-becoming. Even then, however, when the success of this project reveals itself, the I of modernity threatens to lose its double objectivity, which achieved its capacity for symbolization and threatens to become a simply determined being (*Dasein*), itself to become an object. (Alienation is nothing that would be done to the I of modernity; rather the I of modernity is actually doing it to itself coercively in the process of its self-realization.) The I therefore puts seriously aside all of its opinions when they begin to become identical with themselves, "I could not do better than to reject them completely for once in my lifetime, and to resume them afterwards, or perhaps accept better ones in their place, when I had determined how they fitted into a rational scheme. " A reason that is a newly-determined, newly-configured figure of history-that-has-become tests its strength against a reason that is an equally newly determining, newly configuring figure of history-that-is-becoming—all due to the development of a differently mediating category in its middle. With this, modern reason proves itself to be in its history as its "temporal core *(Zeitkern),* which inhabits the recognized and recognizing simultaneously."[22] "Not only does the truth reveal itself in historical process," this truth as grounds for determination of absolute mediation "is nothing certain, rather subjected to the historical transformation."[23]

The project of modernity appears then to reach completion when it succeeds, due to its history, in discovering a category of its self-realization whose power of mediation includes a critique that could be practiced on the project itself and that would represent with it the absolute self-worth for the I of modernity. Even in the historical moment, however, when such a value as "the ideal of liberal democracy"[24] brings the contradictions between that-which-was and that-which-is-becoming to a common reality, this contradiction in the name, and under the form of the ideal, turns back with the corresponding generalness and absoluteness: absolutely-mediated positivity turns immediately into a negativity demanding mediation. The apparent fulfillment of modernity repeats only the origin of the modern, above all as the figure of reason that has become history, which still awaits its mediation with a history that is becoming. The exchange value reveals itself as the core of all values that in the era of modernity unfold and determine their history. Its project completes itself, for itself, precisely when for the I, whose mediating subjectivity drives it, it becomes opaque and decays into unrecognizability. This "logic of the decay" to which Critical Theory, in all its dialectics of mistrust against the dialectic, cannot push through, describes Luhmann's sociology as the contemporary process of the modern society with the society of the modern.[25] But this description also gets stuck halfway. The historical realization of a categorical value of mediation brings forth the contradiction between that-which-was and that-which-is-becoming to a common reality *and* therein simultaneously renews that contradiction. The dominance of exchange value does not conclude this simultaneity, this immediate overturning; rather, in direct contrast, it lets it come forth as the temporal core (*Zeitkern*) of the truth of modernity for really the first time in its history. But only according to its form, its simple middle, its immediacy. The project of modernity—in its supposed completion "incomplete, indeed, not even adequately sketched" (GdG 1142) yet showing in, the globalization of exchange value, the conditions of its completability—is now departing its prologue and entering its main act. It demands therein a depiction adequate to this transition. Critical Theory of society, engaging in a logic of destruction as much as a logic of construction, is challenged to take up this depiction in its nondeceivable unity of truth and historicity, positivity and negativity.

"Today, nobody is in a position to make himself the subject of power, knowledge, or history."[26] We have known a subject by this name, its adventures, tricks, and escapes, since the 9th book of the *Odyssey*. Critical Theory, in the sense described above, must also find it under the thickest fleece.

Notes

1. The author would like to thank Andrew Shields and Jaimey Fisher for their translations.
2. Francis Fukuyama, *Das Ende der Geschichte. Wo stehen wir?* (Munich: Kindler, 1992), 11. All quotations, unless English editions are cited, are translated by A.S.
3. Niklas Luhmann, *Die Gesellschaft der Gesellschaft*, 2 vols. (Frankfurt am Main: Suhrkamp Verlag, 1997), 22. From now on appearing parenthetically as "GdG" in the text.
4. Niklas Luhmann, "Ich nehme mal Karl Marx. Interview mit Walter van Rossum," in *Archimedes und wir. Interviews mit Niklas Luhmann*, eds. Dirk Baecker and Georg Stanitzek (Berlin: Merve Verlag, 1987), 18f.
5. Immanuel Kant, *Über ein vermeintes recht aus menschenliebe zu lügen*, in *Werke* A 309.
6. Pico Della Mirandola, *On the Dignity of Man*, trans. Charles Glenn Wallis (Indianopolis: Library of Liberal America, 1965) 4-5.
7. Jürgen Habermas, *Theorie des kommunikativen Handelns*, vol. 1 (Frankfurt am Main: Suhrkamp Verlag, 1981), 387.
8. G.W.F. Hegel, *Phänomenologie des Geistes*, in *Gesammelte Werke in zwanzig Bände*, vol. 3, eds. Eva Moldenhauer and Karl Markus Michel (Frankfurt am Main: Suhrkamp Verlag, 1970), 482.
9. G.W.F. Hegel, *Wissenschaft der Logik*, in *Gesammelte Werke*, vol. 5,168.
10. Aurelius Augustinus, *De civitate dei*, Book XIX, Chap. 14.
11. G.W.F. Hegel, *Vorlesungen über die Geschichte der Philosophie*, in *Gesammelte Werke*, vol. 20, 270.
12. Theodor W. Adorno, *Negative Dialektik* (Frankfurt am Main: Suhrkamp Verlag, 1970), 170.
13. Adorno 146.
14. Jean Baudrillard, *Der symbolische Tausch und der Tod* (München: Matthes und Seitz, 1982), 8.
15. "The lesson that appears to be emerging is that only free market systems exhibit the flexibility and robustness to accommodate human nature ... Despite the ebb and flow of governments of differing persuasions, the face of the world economy continues to edge ever-more toward free-market-oriented societies." Alan Greenspan, "Market capitalism: The role of free markets," address to Annual Convention of the American Society of Newspaper Editors, Washington D.C., 2 April 1998, in *Vital Speeches of the Day* 64:14 (1 May 1998): 418-421.
16. Michel Serres, *Der Parasit* (Frankfurt am Main: Suhrkamp Verlag, 1987), 165.
17. G.W.F. Hegel, *Wissenschaft der Logik* in *Gesammelte Werke*, vol. 5, 82.
18. Theodor W. Adorno, *Ohne Leitbild. Parva Aesthetica* (Frankfurt am Main: Suhrkamp Verlag, 1967), 23.
19. G.W.F. Hegel, *Wissenschaft der Logik*, in *Gesammelte Werke*, vol. 5, 82.
20. Michel Serres, *Der Parasit*, 293
21. Rene Descartes, *Discourse on Method and Meditations*, trans. Laurence J. Lafleur (New York: The Liberal Arts Press, 1960), 12.
22. Walter Benjamin, *Das Pasagen Werk*, in *Gesammelte Schriften*, vol. V/1, 2nd ed. (Frankfurt am Main: Suhrkmap Verlag, 1982), 578.

23. Peter Bürger, *Prosa der Moderne* (Frankfurt am Main: Suhrkamp Verlag, 1988), 48.

24. Fukuyama, *Das Ende der Geschichte*, 11.

25. Adorno, *Negative Dialektik*, 407.

26. Jean Baudrillard, *Die fatalen Strategien* (Munich: Matthes und Seitz, 1985), 140.

Chapter 12

OBSERVATIONS ON OBSERVATIONS
Some Remarks on Adorno's Aesthetic Theory

Harro Müller

There are, without a doubt, many different ways to observe Critical Theory. I shall begin with a somewhat commonsensical conception of observation, with a not very sophisticated approach to the task of discussing the contemporary relevance and historicity of Critical Theory. First, one can ask if Critical Theory is a homogeneous theory, if the Frankfurt School—given its different generations—is really a school with a single coherent message. Second, one can ask how one should differentiate between Critical Theory and noncritical theory, especially when this distinction entails an asymmetrical relationship between the first and the second term. So if someone is using the distinction between Critical and noncritical theory, and is arguing in her or his self-description that she or he is a representative of Critical Theory, then one could, even should, question this very self-definition itself as critical or noncritical. Third, the somewhat innocent "and" between "contemporary relevance" and "historicity" causes considerable trouble. Is it conjunctive or disjunctive? In a strict sense it cannot be disjunctive, because contemporary relevance has its own historicity; so it is conjunctive; but, if it is conjunctive, can there be a precise difference between contemporary relevance and historicity?

It is difficult to answer this question, so it might be better to reformulate the problem and to ask for the truth content—truth contents or truth claims—of Critical Theory. If one directs the inquiry this way, the answer depends on the way one observes Critical Theory today. Because there is a variety of observation theories, there cannot be one single answer. In light of this wide field of Critical Theory and observation theories, I want to make some remarks on Adorno's aesthetic theory using some concepts of the observation theory of Niklas Luhmann's systems theory.[1] Systems theory always starts with assumptions of difference and can be described as an observation theory that stresses pluralism, relativism, and historicism. I will start with some admittedly sentimental historical self-observations, which will lead me to Adorno's own self-observations and back to his theories in light of the processes of observation.

In the 1960s I studied German literature, history, and philosophy at Kiel University. In retrospect it was rather a provincial environment, but I remember how in the fall of 1965, a seminar on German classical poetry invoked Adorno's essay "Rede über Lyrik und Gesellschaft." I began to read Adorno's work and soon ascertained that in 1947 Adorno and Horkheimer had published a book entitled *Dialectic of Enlightenment*. One could not buy the book then; in dogged pursuit at the university library, I was only frustrated further to discover there was no copy there, making it pretty difficult to get enlightenment on the dialectic of enlightenment. My department had its own library separate from the university library. This departmental library had a copy, but it was already borrowed and would be for sometime: a Ph.D. student had "borrowed" this book for his personal library more than three years before. Nobody during the entire "loan" period asked him to return the volume.

Left to read *Dialectic of Enlightenment* in this 1947 edition, I got the impression that I was the first reader to read the book from beginning to end because the book was in a pristinely unused condition. Pioneering as I was, I was deeply impressed by it. What a breathtakingly brilliant opening it offered in its mixture of analytical power, decisiveness, and rhetoric of the superlative: "In the most general sense of progressive thought, the Enlightenment has always aimed at liberating men from fear and establishing their sovereignty. Yet the fully enlightened earth radiates disaster triumphant."[2] At that time I had a deep affective attachment to this book's dark pathos, this preference for the color or noncolor black. Even at an international conference on *Dialectic of Enlightenment* in New York in February 1998, many participants confessed that they still loved this book, though they had to admit that, from a cognitive perspective, they could not really defend it very vigorously anymore.

What makes this book so attractive that teaching it is always more or less a great success, much like—to make an ironic connection—the teaching of Carl Schmitt's *The Concept of the Political*? It is not only the style of presentation, the sweeping gesture of enchantment and disenchantment, but also a specific mixture of complexity, simplicity, and vagueness. Adorno and Horkheimer are rewriting traditional Marxism in grand style, combining their grand narrative of a "history as/of catastrophe" *(Unheilsgeschichte)* with anthropology and psychoanalysis. Offering a very complex structure that combines narrative and nonnarrative together, they reduce the big question of history as/of catastrophe to a simple answer: the bad guy is always instrumental reason with his politics of identity and his cult of self-preservation, while the good guy seems to be the nonidentical and mimetic in its positive inflection, with his hints of happiness and "freedom from domination" *(Herrschaftsfreiheit)*.[3]

Their conception of mimesis is difficult to explain. I remember quite clearly that I was fascinated by precisely this ambivalent riddle of "*Angleichung*" (mimesis), and I tried at least to articulate it. My suggested explanation was: a concept that attempts to criticize the identical cannot be itself identical. Therefore the nonidentical and mimesis cannot be demonstrated in a strict sense because this form of argumentation always invokes presuppositions based on identity. To sum up my reading at the age of 23 : I got the impression that for modernity at least, there is, on the one hand, an "*Unheilsgeschichte*" (history as/of catastrophe) including: fascism, capitalism, culture industry, anti-Semitism, and sexual exploitation. On the other hand, there is art as ambivalent "*Heilsgeschichte*" (sacred-history) with its subversive, utopian power that, as broken "*promesse du bonheur*," is, at least to a certain degree, a reliable weapon against all forms of instrumental reason. As a student within the humanities, I was naturally a representative of art as a form of "*Heilsgeschichte*."

At the end of the eighties I was asked to write an article on "Autonomy and Function" for *Grundkurs Literaturwissenschaft* (*Introduction to Literary Studies*), published by Rowohlt. In this article I tried to sum up Adorno's aesthetic conception and formulated four critical points at the end, which I present here in a slightly revised form:

I. Adorno takes as a given, and then proceeds from, a universal delusional context of reification *(universaler Verblendungszusammenhang)*, but such a perspective is at most a plausible articulation of his own historical experiences (fascism, Stalinism, exploitation of cultural traditions in America); in no way does it yield a systematically identified category that is empirically supported in an adequate manner.

II. The critique of instrumental reason is not logically linked with genuinely Marxist categories. Along these lines Jürgen Habermas remarks laconically: "Adorno did not deal with political economy."

III. Adorno overestimates as well as underestimates the functional possibilities of the art system in modernity; his aesthetic conception is—despite his ban on images, and his ban on utopia—not free of the philosophy of history and its dreams of dedifferentiation.

IV. Adorno remains captive to a work aesthetic fundamentally oriented toward production aesthetic. Such an approach is most capable of theorizing literary modernity from Baudelaire to Beckett, but not postmodern art with its manifold codings, its merging of high art and entertainment, or its ironic play of quotations. Adorno's aesthetic assumes that the aesthetic handling of materials results in a progress culminating in authentic art. This presupposition of progress, which is perhaps not always adequately explicit in Adorno, is no longer shared by postmodernity.[4]

One way to continue my essay would be to explain and elaborate these four points. And it would be interesting to add a fifth point that would discuss the tacit dogmatism (according to Habermas) of Adorno's use of Freud. If one examines recent books on Adorno—including those of Joel Whitebook, Hauke Brunkhorst, Fredric Jameson, Albrecht Wellmer, David Roberts, the careful book of Peter Hohendahl, and the instructive introduction of Simon Jarvis[5]—it would not be very difficult to locate my points within the current discussion of scholarship on Adorno. But I would like to concentrate on the third point above, on Adorno's overestimation and underestimation of the art system, on his assumptions based on a certain philosophy of history and his dreams of dedifferentiation; I shall start these observations with some remarks on Adorno's own self-observations.

In 1967 Adorno published with Suhrkamp a paperback entitled *Ohne Leitbild. Parva Aesthetica* (*Without a Role Model. Parva Aesthetica*). In this book there is a short autobiographical section, called "Amorbach." The name Amorbach refers to a small village situated in the Odenwald, where Adorno frequently spent his holidays as a child. Amorbach becomes the base and basis of Adorno's later observations:

> In coming to America, all places look alike. The standardization, a result of technology and monopoly [capitalism], is frightening. One thinks that qualitative differences would have really disappeared from life, just as progressing rationality is annihilating them in method. Once back in Europe, even places that seemed incomparable in childhood look suddenly similar to another—whether it be because of the contrast to America that rolls over anything else, or whether it be because what used to be style already possessed something of that normative force that one ascribes guilelessly to the industry, particularly to the culture industry. Even Amorbach, Miltenberg, Wertheim are not excluded from this, whether it be only by virtue of the basic, common tone of the red sandstone or something else, the topography of the area communicates with the houses. However, the experience of happiness, of the nonexchangeable, can only be made at one particular place, even if in retrospect it will be proven that it was not singular. Unjustly or justly so, Amorbach remained for me the origin of all small towns—the others were nothing but its imitation.[6]

In this passage one can observe how Adorno observes his own past. He is always mixing the reconstruction of perceptions, the reconstructions of experiences, with concepts. On the one hand, it is the remembrance of bliss, of happiness, of *Glück*—for Adorno, a state of uniqueness beyond reification, beyond alienation, beyond the principle of equivalence. On the other hand, there is the "*Unheilsgeschichte*," the history as/of catastrophe, which is—culminating in the culture industry of America—also always part of his own past. So there is a remembrance of *Glück* (unique happiness)—but at the same time not only concepts, but even this *Glück* has its own ambivalences, at least in retrospect.

Adorno is deploying here a specific rhetorical strategy by which he constructs strong dichotomies like happiness/unhappiness, qualitative/quantitative, unique/repetitive, and *Heilsgeschichte/Unheils-*

geschichte; and then he recursively rewrites the dichotomy under the first term. So *Heilsgeschichte* becomes *Heilsgeschichte* and *Unheilsgeschichte*, happiness becomes happiness and unhappiness, and so on. In this way Adorno is always producing paradoxes: in both *Negative Dialectics* and *Aesthetic Theory*, paradox proves Adorno's main cognitive strategy, his main rhetorical device. In these examples it is symptomatic that the second term is not rewritten by Adorno—rather, the first term reveals its paradox in retrospective rewriting. This rhetorical strategy is often used by Adorno to produce the effect of strict negativity. Wherever one looks, whatever one observes, there is always the *"universaler Verblendungszusammenhang"* (the universal delusional context of reification) and *"die verwaltete Gesellschaft"* (the totally administered society).[7]

One can deparadoxize the paradoxes; but for Adorno there is no positive transcendental signified that could be used as the starting or ending point, the *"Ursprung"* (origin) and *"Ziel"* (goal/objective) of all paradoxes. There is no positive knowledge about the first or last, about the starting point or telos. The material philosophy of history, in its idealistic or materialistic versions, and negative dialectics, with its history as/of catastrophe, are mutually exclusive. Although there is no positive knowledge about a transcendental signified, there is repeatedly negative knowledge about history as/of catastrophe:

> Universal history must be construed and denied. After the catastrophes that have happened, and in view of the catastrophes to come, it would be cynical to say that a plan for the better world is manifested in history and unites it. Not to be denied for that reason, however, is the unity that cements the discontinuous, chaotically splintered moments and phases of history—the unity of the control of nature, progressing to rule over men, and finally to that over men's inner nature. No universal history leads from savagery to humanitarianism, but there is one leading from the slingshot to the megaton bomb. It ends in the total menace which organized mankind poses to organized men, in the epitome of discontinuity. It is the horror that verifies Hegel and stands him on his head. If he transfigured the totality of historic suffering into the positivity of the self-realizing absolute, the One and All that keeps rolling on to this day—with occasional breathing spells—would teleologically be the absolute of suffering.[8]

Or to quote an often quoted sentence from *Minima Moralia*: "Es gibt kein richtiges Leben im Falschen." But from what perspective, from what place does one observe, if one is asserting: "There is no true life within the false"? My answer—and this is often said within research on Adorno—is the following. One can formulate such an assumption, but only within negative dialectics that is not a form of negative metaphysics with its reliance on negative declarative sentences:

> The only philosophy which can be responsibly practiced in the face of despair is the attempt to contemplate all things as they would present themselves from the standpoint of redemption. Knowledge has no light but that shed on the world by redemption: all else is reconstruction, mere technique.[9]

> Yet the need in thinking is what makes us think. It asks to be negated by thinking; it must disappear in thought if it is to be really satisfied; and in this negation it survives. Represented in the inmost cell of thought is that which is unlike thought. The smallest intramundane traits would be of relevance to the absolute, for the micrological view cracks the shells of what, measured by the subsuming cover concept, is helplessly isolated and explodes its identity, the delusion that is but specimen. There is solidarity between such thinking and metaphysics at the time of its fall.[10]

To put it bluntly: there is no objective knowledge of redemption, for that would be a form of positive metaphysics; but there is also no objective knowledge of the nonexistence of redemption, for that would be a form of negative metaphysics or a form of dogmatic atheism. The solidarity between thinking and metaphysics at the time of its fall means that one has to contemplate all things as if they would present themselves from the standpoint of redemption. "Redemption" is, from this perspective, not an ontological fact or concept, but something like a regulative idea with which one must start unless one wants to support history as/of catastrophe. I am not sure if Adorno is using a form of transcendental argumentation here, but the political implications of this form of statement are clear: this is a radical politics of exclusion because all people who will not subscribe to this as-if-construction of redemption are supporting *Unheilsgeschichte* (history as/of catastrophe) and must be treated as adversaries. That explains to a certain degree why gentle Theodor W. Adorno often "embraces" extremely harsh, illiberal judgements. Redemption is taken by Adorno in an absolutely serious way—I cannot see any hints in his texts where he might be parodying or ironizing redemption. And likewise there is not history as "*Leidensgeschichte*," as history as/of suffering, or on his reflections on death. Contrary to his reflections on aesthetic terms like tragedy, comedy, parody, irony, poetry of nature, or on the beginning and possible end of art, Adorno does not historicize redemption, because it functions, at the least, as an unquestioned Archimedean point for the construction of his aesthetic theory.

Redemption remains a necessary idealization, a functional equivalent to Benjamin's "weak messianic power" in his "Theses on the Philosophy of History." This is where any postmodern reading of Adorno will find its limits in a strict sense. Observing history as if there were redemption, allows Adorno to formulate a utopian perspective, although Adorno is always stressing that there is *Bilderverbot* (a ban on images) and *Utopieverbot* (a ban on utopia). Adorno approaches the elusive, even forbidden concept of utopia in another passage from his autobiographical remarks in *Ohne Leitbild*:

> The border between Bavaria and Baden once ran between Ottorfszell and Ernsttal. It was marked on the street by guard houses that carried the states' seals and that were painted in spirals in the land's colors, the one white-blue, the other, if memory doesn't fail me, red-yellow. Sufficient space between the two. In that space I liked to remain under the pretext—in which I certainly did not believe—that this space did not belong to either of the states, was free, and that I could establish my own authority there according to my wishes. This authority was not serious, but that did not diminish my delights. It probably emerged from the state colors whose limitations I felt I had escaped ... the feeling for the international was by nature always dear to me ... This international was not a uniform state. Its peace promised itself through the colorful ensemble of multitudes, colorful like the flags and innocent border posts, which, as I discovered with amazement, did not all cause an observable change of the landscape. But the land that they surrounded and with which I was occupied while playing by myself, was a no man's land. Later, during the war, the word came up for the devastated area between the fronts. However, it is the faithful translation of the Greek—Aristophanes'—which back then I understood the better, the less familiar I was with it—utopia.[11]

This utopian perspective looks forward to "das festliche Ensemble von Verschiedenem," to the festive ensemble of the different, of the nonidentical. This feast is the marriage of the identical with the nonidentical, of construction with mimesis, without alienation, without reification; it is the end of history as/of catastrophe, it is the return of paradise, but this return takes place in "Niemandsland," in no man's land.

One can inquire from the external perspective of systems theory what code Adorno is using in his as-if-construction of history as redemption. Adorno, I would suggest, is using the religious code immanent/transcendent in a radically secularized way.[12] The program is redemption, but the representative of redemption in modernity is not the religion system, but rather the art system, especially the authentic artist or the authentic artwork:

> The artist who bears the work of art, is not only one who brings it forth, but rather, he becomes, by work and active passivity, a plenipotentiary of the societal collective subject. In that he subjugates himself to the necessity of the work of art, he eliminates from it everything that could be attributed purely to the happenstance of his individuation. In representing the collective subject of society, however, a condition is simultaneously considered, which effaces the fate of isolation, in which the collective subject finally realizes itself societally.[13]

> Art is not only the plenipotentiary of a better praxis than that which has to date predominated, but is equally the critique of praxis as the rule of brutal self-preservation at the heart of the status quo and in its service. It gives the lie to production for production's sake and opts for a form of praxis beyond the spell of labor. Art's promesse du bonheur means not only that hitherto praxis has blocked happiness but that happiness is beyond praxis. The measure of the chasm separating praxis from happiness is taken by the force of negativity in the artwork.[14]

So for Adorno's radically secularized conception of history and for his conception of modernity, there is one master code and one program: the artist, and, especially, the artwork, as the "plenipotentiary of a better praxis." Therefore Adorno can say: "Artworks are neutralized and thus qualitatively transformed epiphanies."[15] But the artwork is not the bible, because even the authentic artwork, with its quality of secularized epiphany and its monadic character, is part of the universal delusional context of reification. So the one and only perfect authentic artwork does not exist: "The ideological, affirmative aspect of the concept of the successful artwork has its corrective in the fact that there are no perfect works. If they did exist reconciliation would be possible in the midst of the unreconciled … "[16] Or to remark on the same contradiction from a different perspective: "Art is the ever broken promise of happiness."[17]

To bring the analysis back to the nexus of observation and art, one may now pose the question: how is Adorno observing the artwork? It seems to me that he follows the same procedure as mentioned above. He begins with a strict dichotomy, here authentic versus inauthentic. Inauthentic art is his litany of bêtes noirs: culture industry, jazz, "Abhub," mere positivism, affirmative art in the sense of Herbert Marcuse. The second term of his dichotomy authentic/inauthentic is only interesting for producing a gesture of strict negation. The first term is rewritten by Adorno in reintroducing the dichotomy authentic versus inauthentic into it. As I explained above, this form of re-entry produces a paradox. Authentic art is both authentic and inauthentic. Now if one reads Adorno's *Aesthetic Theory*, one can observe a long list of paradoxes—to mention but a few: art is autonomous and fait social, is mimesis and construction, is critical and affirmative, is finite and infinite, is true and false, is happiness and sadness, is voluntary and involuntary, is process and moment, is expression of the expressionless, is language without language, is communication without communication, is illusion of the nonillusory *(Schein des Scheinlosen)*, and so on.

For Adorno, then, artworks are nonconceptual and nondiscursive temporal deparadoxizations of these paradoxes, which even makes (e.g., in literary texts) reparadoxization possible, but there cannot be any form of strict synthesis. So artworks use temporalization as a form of deparadoxization, a form that negates the presuppositions of identity necessary for formulating paradoxes and opens up the field for a play between the identical and the nonidentical, between construction and mimesis. The product of this move of temporalization is what Adorno calls constellation. The artwork as constellation is always a risk, because every form of deparadoxization has to traffic in undecidabilities, is impure, has its blind spots. In this way one can explain that all authentic artworks are always, as Adorno puts it in French, tour de force. The constellative artwork is an enigma, "it cannot be solved, only its form can be deciphered, and precisely that is the requisite of the philosophy of art."[18] Now it would be easy to show that the philosophy of art is complementary to the art system and has to play the play between mimesis and construction, between mimesis and concept, between mimesis and discourse in quite a different way. In his late *Aesthetic Theory*, Adorno also produced constellations, and he wrote about it in a letter: "The book must, so to speak, be written in equally weighted, paratactical parts that are arranged about a midpoint that they express through their constellation."[19] So what might be the midpoint Adorno is highlighting? I think it is his concept/nonconcept of redemption, which is the Archimedean/non- Archimedean point of his aesthetic theory. Can this concept/nonconcept of redemption be saved for a possible rewriting of Adorno's *Aesthetic Theory* today?

My answer is: No. Why this negative answer? In backing my negative answer I want to present some key arguments of systems theory: Modern society is a functionally-differentiated society with no general code. Rather, each partial system has its own code, and the partial systems are not functionally equivalent, so no partial system can represent the whole. There is no place for a general utopian perspective, so art cannot be the plenipotentiary of a better praxis. But the art system can irritate other systems, which have to deal with these irritations in their own way. The code immanent/ transcendent is the code of the religion system. Within the religion system, religion can claim that its code is universal, but it is the code of the religion system and it is therefore still particular. Systems are in need of conceptions of present future, in need of idealizations. But such idealizations must be strictly historicized, and one always has to think that the present future and future present are different.

So Adorno's concept/nonconcept of redemption does not seem to be complex enough. But in this way one can explain why he permanently overestimates and underestimates the art system. On the one hand, he absolutely overestimates the art system in ascribing to it a redemptive function. On the other hand, his normative aesthetics, with its preference for authentic art, underestimates the internal complexity of the art system. His gesture of strict negation is really only a gesture, because from a systematic point of view, the second term—i.e., inauthentic art—must be treated in the same way as the first term.

Is it possible to save the way in which Adorno treats paradoxes? My answer this time is: yes and no. Yes, because it is always fruitful to look for paradoxes and see how they are treated. The recursive way that Adorno is using paradox is an elegant solution. So he is extremely versatile in switching from first-order-observations to second-order-observations to third-order-observations and vice versa. But, from the standpoint of the observation theory of Niklas Luhmann, there are no strict first or last observations with which one must start or end or with which one has to posit a "regulative idea" as a necessary idealization. This is also relevant for the art system. So for the art system, there is no general rule for stopping observations; and even the concept/nonconcept of redemption cannot function as a form of closure.

It is difficult to explain why Adorno constructs his *Aesthetic Theory* in the way he does. There are certainly many possible explanations. I want to mention at least one possibility that may be able to offer a certain amount of plausibility. Adorno has always stressed that, for thinking in modernity on modernity, radical secularization is absolutely necessary. I think this concept of radical secularization should be questioned and dedramatized because his overestimation and underestimation of the art system seems to be a consequence of this form of radical secularization. For Adorno art in modernity is the successor of religion, from his perspective the art system and the religious system are functionally equivalent in modernity. Systems theory strictly negates this form of functional equivalence. If one is observing modern society as a functionally differentiated society, one can easily see that in modernity there is a religion system, which is as good as it gets. One can be a member of this partial system, and then redemption may be a possible option, but one of the advantages of modern society is that one is not required to be a member of the religion system, just as one must not be required to be a member of the weak art system. This is an increase in liberty that I would like to defend.

Notes

1. Niklas Luhmann, *Die Gesellschaft der Gesellschaft*, 2 vols. (Frankfurt am Main: Suhrkamp Verlag, 1997). Compare my introduction to systems theory as observation theory: Harro Müller, "Systemtheorie/Literaturwissenschaft," in *Neue Literaturtheorien. Eine Einführung*, ed. Klaus-Michael Bogdal, 2nd ed. (Opladen: Westdeutscher Verlag, 1997), 208-24.
2. Max Horkheimer and Theodor W. Adorno, *Dialectic of Enlightenment* (New York: Continuum, 1996), 3.
3. Compare the concept of mimesis and its ambivalence in Simon Jarvis, *Adorno. A Critical Introduction* (New York: Routledge, 1998), 145-56.
4. Harro Müller, "Autonomie und Funktion," in *Literaturwissenschaft. Ein Grundkurs*, eds. Helmut Brackert and Jörn Stückrath (Reinbek: Rowohlt, 1992), 512.
5. Joel Whitebook, *Perversion and Utopia. A Study in Psychoanalysis and Critical Theory* (Cambridge: MIT Press, 1995). Hauke Brunkhorst, *Theodor W. Adorno. Dialektik der Moderne* (Munich: Piper, 1990). Fredric Jameson, *Late Marxism. Adorno and the Persistence of the Dialectic* (London: Verso, 1990). Albrecht Wellmer, *Endgames. The Irreconcilable Nature of Modernity. Essays and Lectures* (Cambridge: MIT Press, 1998). David Roberts, *Art and Enlightenment. Aesthetic Theory after Adorno* (Lincoln: University of Nebraska Press,

1991). Peter Uwe Hohendahl, *Prismatic Thought. Theodor W. Adorno* (Lincoln: University of Nebraska Press, 1995). Simon Jarvis, *Adorno. A Critical Introduction*. Compare also Max Pensky, ed., *The Actuality of Adorno. Critical Essays on Adorno and the Postmodern* (Albany: State University of New York, 1997); Tom Huhn and Lambert Zuidervaart, eds., *The Semblance of Subjectivity. Essays in Adorno's Aesthetic Theory* (Cambridge: MIT Press, 1997).

6. Theodor W. Adorno, *Ohne Leitbild. Parva Aesthetica* (Frankfurt am Main: Suhrkamp Verlag, 1967), 23.

7. Theodor W. Adorno, *Aesthetic Theory* (1970; Minneapolis: University of Minnesota Press, 1997), 168.

8. Theodor W. Adorno, *Negative Dialectics* (New York: Seabury Press, 1973), 320.

9. Theodor W. Adorno, *Minima Moralia* (London: Verso, 1974), 247.

10. Adorno, *Negative Dialectics*, 408.

11. Adorno, *Ohne Leitbild*, 23-24.

12. Gerhard Plumpe, *Ästhetische Kommunikation der Moderne*, vol. 2. of *Von Nietzsche bis zur Gegenwart* (Opladen: Westdeutscher Verlag, 1993), 217-31, esp. 229.

13. Theodor W. Adorno, *Notes to Literature I* (New York: Columbia University Press, 1992), 194.

14. Adorno, *Aesthetic Theory*, 12.

15. Adorno, *Aesthetic Theory*, 80.

16. Adorno, *Aesthetic Theory*, 189-90.

17. Adorno, *Aesthetic Theory*, 136.

18. Adorno, *Aesthetic Theory*, 122.

19. Adorno, *Aesthetic Theory*, 364.

Section V

EPILOGUE

Chapter 13

NORMATIVITY AND ITS LIMITS
Toward a Residual Ethics in Critical Theory

Jaimey Fisher

This volume of essays on the current state and future prospects of Critical Theory ends with two vigorous and fundamental critiques of Critical Theory's traditional positions. From their systems-theoretical perspectives, Harro Müller and Wolfram Malte Fues conclude the volume with a critique of what they see as Critical Theory's excessive normativity. That systems theorists should criticize Critical Theory for the creation of strong, positive norms proves of course nothing new: one of Luhmann's and other systems theorists' fundamental criticisms of Habermas has long been that he overvalues certain social systems and then grounds ultimately invalid moral norms in their privileged positions.[1] For many systems theorists, as well as for Müller and Fues in this volume, the extreme functional differentiation of systems in the modern world has subverted any privileging of one system or subsystem over any other, a position that undercuts norms generated in one sphere and intended to affect action in others.

Müller and Fues, however, turn their systems-theoretical critique not on Habermas—a long-time whipping boy for systems theorists—but on Adorno. Müller criticizes *Dialectic of Enlightenment*'s normativizing differentiation of the world into bad (identity thinkers and instrumentalists) and good (nonidentity thinkers). For Müller,

Adorno's later theory problematically privileges the aesthetic system—in a clear echo of the privileging of the religion system of yore—above other equally valid systems. Fues offers a brief critique of Habermas in detracting from theories with universal, positive norms, but focuses by name not so much on Habermas, the personification of Critical Theory's "second generation," but rather on Adorno, whose negative dialectics he sees at times as too subjective. The cornerstone of their critique still rests in the excessive normativity of Critical Theory, but now they set their sights on the dominant thinker of Critical Theory's "first generation": Adorno.

Müllers and Fues' positions constitute both a continuation—of systems-theoretical critiques based on Critical Theory's excessive normativity—and a shift—to a focus on Adorno over Habermas. In both senses, their positions are indicative of the essays in this volume, many of which problematize the second generation's strong normative positions while negotiating between the normative impulses of the first and second generations of Critical Theory. In this essay, I would like to discuss—in both a reading of and response to the pieces in this volume—the status of normativity as one of the lynchpins of the transitions between the first and the second generations. A surprising number of the essays in this volume focus on or at least highlight Habermas's universal, positive normativity, its stakes and consequences. From there, some essays suggest a recasting of Habermas's normative approach within a Habermasian framework, while others lobby for a more fundamental corrective of Habermas's approach, often via Adorno. Given the recurring theme of normativity in Critical Theory throughout this volume, I shall underscore both Habermas's general understanding of norms as well as what I term Habermas's process of normativity, that is, how he grounds—especially in language—and then deduces the positive norms he does prescribe. I shall suggest that many authors see Habermas's normativization of Critical Theory as limited—in fact, many of them want to reinstate what such transcendental grounding and deducing of norms excludes, that which becomes residually excessive to it.

As both Peter Dews and Christoph Menke point out in their essays, Habermas self-consciously undertook a revaluation of positive norms in Critical Theory. This revaluation became the cornerstone for the shift from the first generation of Critical Theory, represented above all by Adorno and Horkheimer, to its second generation, personified in Habermas. Hand in hand with Habermas's effort to overcome the normative deficit of Critical Theory was a revised, more optimistic relation to rationalism—the belief that rationality could positively serve to guide community consensus[2]—that Peter Uwe Hohendahl discusses in his history of rationality in the Frankfurt School. Habermas faulted, for instance, in an essay for Adorno on the occasion of his sixtieth birthday, Adorno's "loss of nerve" in not following through his own powerful critique of modern society, his backing off from positive norms that might guide political and social behavior in the contemporary world.[3] Habermas in fact criticized Adorno and Horkheimer in their "darkest, most pessimistic" passages of conceding the counter-Enlightenment position that civilization without repression is impossible.[4] Habermas thus deliberately conceived of his project as a response to the perceived deficit of norms in the first generation and set out to ground and deduce strong, positive norms for Critical Theory in what he was to call his "cognitivist ethics."

Though I do not want to retrace in detail how Habermas has attempted to accomplish his goal of grounding and deducing strong norms within Critical Theory, I do want to say a few words about the persistence of a certain understanding of normativity in his work. To this end, Hohendahl's essay on the development of the concept of rationality in the Frankfurt School serves well: he undertakes a careful recounting of at least three distinct phases of Habermas's work. There are three distinct phases in which Hohendahl emphasizes a consistently alternative relation to rationality—and in these same three distinct phases, I would underscore, as well, a consistently alternative understanding of grounding and then deducing (eventually strong) norms. Habermas's first major work, *The Structural Transformation of the Public Sphere*, displays, on the one hand, loyalty to the critical teachings of Adorno and Horkheimer—especially in its culture-industry-inflected critique of mass media—but, on the other hand, also demonstrates a more differentiated approach to rationality. I would underscore, however, that Habermas also begins to engage in an alterative understanding of normativity: he sketches the bourgeois public sphere in such a way as to provide a normative grounding for his critique of modern mass media. Such a move foreshadows his reconstructive method as well as, even at this early stage, a different understanding of normativity to be realized in his later linguistic grounding of reason and norms.

In *Knowledge and Human Interests*, Hohendahl points out that Habermas demonstrates two marked departures from Adorno and Horkheimer: not only does Habermas, as is widely observed, sustain something of a linguistic turn, but he also renegotiates and downgrades the role of historical critique that plays so prominently in Marx, Adorno, and Horkheimer. Using as well as departing from Gadamer, Habermas offers a deep grounding, in knowledge-constitutive interests, for human communication and social action. Such a move to a strong grounding of norms inevitably shifts the critical emphasis that Habermas's self-identified forebears—Marx, Adorno, and Horkheimer—located in historical critique. Habermas, in fact, consciously departs, or at least downgrades, their historical immanent critique in favor of his reconstructive project. [5] Hohendahl emphasizes how such a move allows Habermas to differentiate reason and partially rehabilitate instrumental reason, reason deployed, for instance, to control humans' environment. For my analysis here, one should observe, in this middle phase of Habermas, both the continuity and the development of a different understanding of normativity: Habermas continues to try to ground norms, but this time in an even more radically transcendental context than the quasi-historical grounding of *The Structural Transformation of the Public Sphere*, where one first senses his normative divergence from the first generation of Critical Theory.

By the time of *The Theory of Communication Action*, Habermas has clearly, as Hohendahl observes, preferred normative considerations over historical ones. Habermas demonstrates both facets of what I term his divergent process of normativity: first, in his normative grounding in "communicative action," revising the linguistic grounding of *Knowledge and Human Interests* but affirming, nonetheless, an inclination to strong, deep grounding of norms; and, second, in his reconstruction of the general conditions of communicative action via a transcendental deduction—one weaker than Kant's strong transcendental deduction in his critiques, but one nonetheless far from first-generation Critical Theory. His process of normativity—strong grounding of norms and then (however weak) transcendental deduction—has a number of consequences unimaginable for the first generation of Critical Theory. For instance, as Hohendahl underscores, Habermas substantially decouples rationality from instrumental reason—something, we shall see, impossible for Adorno, given his basic methodological tendencies and his understanding of normativity, which I shall sketch below. What one sees, then, throughout these three phases of Habermas's work is not only a new attempt to overcome what he perceived as a normative deficit of the first generation, but also his development of a divergent understanding of normativity.

Many of the essays in this volume take, as a point of departure, precisely this strong normative force that Habermas introduced and eventually developed as a central aspect of Critical Theory. What is remarkable in many of these essays is the level of discomfort and dissatisfaction with Habermas's attempted repair of the "normative deficit" in the first generation. For instance, in her essay on "cyberia" and the massively networked Internet as public sphere, Jodi Dean criticizes precisely what I term Habermas's process of normativity: she senses the tendency in *The Structural Transformation* and other work to idealize the bourgeois public sphere as normatively grounding. Though at times she overstates the norms implied in Habermas's grounding in the bourgeois public sphere, her overstatement itself is quite symptomatic of potential problems with Habermas's understanding of normativity: due to Habermas's very understanding of normativity, there is the slippage I indicated at the outset between Habermas's desire to ground norms, and what are then (mistakenly or not) often interpreted as excessively strong norms. His understanding of normativity occasionally gives the impression that these are strong, positive norms—even if Habermas himself tries to emphasize the weak status of some of them. The basis of her critique is similar to Fues and Müller: by strongly grounding them in a specific historical context, Habermas confuses historical with universal norms.

In his essay, Brian Jacobs also criticizes Habermas for mistakes in his normativizing zeal, this time in misreading Kant and then (more implied then developed in Jacob's argument) overly normativizing a reply to Kant. Jacobs suggests that dominant interpretations of Kant—be they those deployed in psychoanalytic, deconstructive approaches, or in Habermas's work—tend to attribute a strong normative grounding of subject autonomy to the allegedly paradigmatic thinker of the Enlightenment. Jacobs suggests that Kant posited subject autonomy primarily as a pragmatic, practical intervention rather than a transcendental given: Kant in fact undercuts subject autonomy with his view that events are caused by a huge array of largely unpredictable "natural causes." Like the psychoanalytic and deconstructive interpreters of the supposedly autonomous subject, Habermas takes Kant's faith in subject autonomy as a given and defines his own normative understanding of the "intersubjective" against it. Rather than recognizing and incorporating that Kant's subject autonomy was a strategic, practical intervention in morality—that is, a provisional grounding of normativity—Habermas strongly grounds his normative intersubjectivity in an overly idealized, reactive moment.

Christoph Menke likewise describes a shortcoming of Habermas's process of positing strong norms. His essay takes up, what he calls, a "modern antimony" in modern moral philosophy, between those who base their moral philosophy on external human "nature" (Kant and Habermas) and those who question and limit traditional morality by probing its external consequences (Schiller, Nietzsche, and Foucault). Menke subtly suggests that Habermas posits an external human "nature," presumably in the ideal speech situation in which the *Verständigungsthese*—the idea that language is originally and fundamentally intended to convey understanding—rules the day, and then grounds moral norms in this external moment. Indeed, Habermas is clear that the original use of language is in pursuit of understanding and that other uses of language are "parasitic."[6] Menke's essay drives at, as we shall see, sketching an alternative ethics—an alternative process of normativity—that does not ground morality in a transcendentally-posited external human nature.

In his essay, Max Pensky also probes the limits of Habermasian ethics, for him in the pitfalls of Habermas's depiction of cosmopolitanism versus particularism. I would underscore how Pensky's critique of Habermas once again takes aim at Habermas's processes of deducing strong norms. Pensky suggests that Habermas's version of cosmopolitanism—a strong universal rights with complementary cultural identity as the grounds for ethical substance, a model deliberately circumventing national identity—misgrounds a posited norm. In order to avoid privileging national identity, not an incomprehensible objective given Germany's history, Habermas casts cultural identity as a strongly normative grounds for ethical behavior. Pensky, however, means to show how this normative model contradicts Habermas's own concept of universalist rights.

Despite a consistent problematizing of Habermas's support of strong, positive norms throughout the volume, a number of authors suggest revisions to his program while retaining some of its basic premises—lobbying for a revaluation of his understanding of norms, they remain nonetheless within a Habermasian frame. Most supportive of Habermas's normative project is Peter Dews' essay, "A Question of Grounding: Reconstruction and Strict Reflexion in Habermas and Apel." Like other pieces in this volume, Dews foregrounds Habermas's introduction of stronger norms into Critical Theory and focuses on what I have been terming his process of normativity, that is, the means by which he sees Habermas grounding and then deducing the strong, positive norms he advocates. But Dews' approach to Habermas's understanding of normativity also includes an extension of the Habermasian normative framework.

Dews attends to Habermas's rarely discussed dissertation on Schelling and suggests that from that early date Habermas's work reveals a fundamental tension between his renormativizing Critical Theory and his "desublimating reason," that is, making empirically valid claims. Though he acknowledges the widespread critique leveled against Habermas for excessively strong norms, Dews goes in an entirely different direction in his investigation of Habermas's process of normativity: he elaborates the role of tension between norms and desublimated reason in Habermas's debates with his friend and colleague, Karl-Otto Apel. In contrast to many recent critiques of Habermas, Apel criticizes Habermas for the opposite, namely, for letting the desublimation of reason, or the contingent, empirical side of his "reconstructive sciences" dominate valid transcendental norms. Against what he sees as Habermas's lack of transcendental norms, Apel advocates "strict reflexion," which permits one to deduce the norms that one acknowledges when one enters into the *Kommunikationsgemeinschaft* (community of communication). For Dews, this debate between Apel and Habermas echoes the debate between Fichte and Schelling, in which Fichte argued like Apel for stronger transcendental norms, while Schelling favored more reconciliation between "Spirit" and "nature." Thus Dews, like many authors in the volume, problematizes Habermas's understanding of normativity, but he, unlike the others, suggests that Habermas may not even be normative—transcendentally grounding—enough. His essay, via Habermas's dissertation on Schelling, leaves open the possibility for revising Habermas's normativity in the direction of stronger, rather than weaker, positive norms.

This position is unique in the volume: even those other authors who, like Dews, stay within a basically Habermasian framework tend to weaken or downgrade Habermas's universal, positive norms with their analyses of his understanding of normativity. While she retains some basic aspects of Habermas's public sphere, and, by implication, some of the basic norms of his later communicative program, Jodi Dean lodges an ambitious critique of Habermas's and Benhabib's normativizing of what she terms the rational and friendly public spheres, respectively. For the brave new networked world of "cyberia," Dean suggests replacing the norms of the Habermasian rational public sphere with those of civil society, which promotes a basic openness to modes of communication and embodiment that Habermas's "idealizing" of the bourgeois public sphere does not.

Dean, however, sees cyberia as a type (or rather, many types) of public sphere, in which a premium is placed on the emancipatory potential of communication: even if she criticizes how Habermas (allegedly) deduces strong norms from an idealized bourgeois public sphere, communication remains the grounding framework within which she operates. She is not advocating radical political or economic change or an Adornian turn to emancipatory aesthetics; her answer is still to be found in intersubejctive, communicative interaction according to certain rules. Despite her critique of Habermas's deduction of norms, Dean also does admit that certain rules need to be taken into account, that certain norms will persist. Though it may be true, as she points out, that it is crucial that these norms are not state-enforced, Habermas did not exactly celebrate the state's intervention in the public sphere either. By the end of her piece, in fact, Dean admits that some of the sites (or some of the public spheres, as a more recent Habermas or Negt and Kluge might write) should continue to protect the equality of communicating parties, that some public spheres should prioritize inclusion. Thus, by her conclusion, Dean has alerted us to the dangers of Habermas's excessive grounding and deducing strong norms while retaining basic precepts of his approach, including some of his strong, positive norms themselves. Utlimately, although she criticizes what I term his process of normativity—his hypostatizing grounding of a certain historical moment in excessively strong, positive norms—she still maintains many of the norms themselves, albeit within a civil-society model.

Brian Jacobs and Max Pensky also retain some of Habermas's basic assumption in their critiques of his norms. As mentioned above, Jacobs suggests that in his normative zeal, Habermas misread the function of norms in Kant—that Kant posited, for instance, subject autonomy and freedom as pragmatic interventions rather than as a transcendent given. Jacobs does not, however, elaborate a consequential alternative to Habermas's misreading process of normativity; instead, he seems merely content to indicate Habermas's misinterpretation and to point out some of the normative contradictions in which it ends. In his critique of Habermas's cosmopolitanism—which celebrates universal rights and grounds ethical norms in cultural identity, while circumventing national identity—Pensky also retains basic premises of Habermas's model. For instance, he does not dispute or denigrate Habermas's aversion to emphatic national identity or his strong internationalist inclination. Instead, he points out the contradictions of "authentic" cultural identity and suggests a specific reformulation of it. While he retools Habermas's cornerstone, that of a grounding in "authentic" cultural identity, Penksy does not dispute Habermas's commitment to universal rights or his suspicion of the nation-state.

Though Pensky does remain loyal to the Habermasian project of cosmopolitanism, he also goes further than Dean or Jacobs in offering an elaborate, internally-consistent alternative to that which he criticizes in Habermas. This alternative indicates a revision, if not a fundamental rethinking, of Critical Theory: it revealingly takes the first generation of Critical Theory as a corrective to some of the shortcomings of the second. In such a corrective, Pensky suggests that one would do well to incorporate some of the forgotten or neglected insights of the first generation, particularly of Adorno, into Habermas's problematic understanding of norms. As I suggest above, however, this corrective aims at Habermas's process of normativity, the very processes of strong grounding and transcendental deducing of universal, positive norms. Pensky does not aim to change the content of moral or ethical norm—one still encounters others and still cultivates and acknowledges cultural identity. But the process of these norms has changed. To examine such a shift, it is enlightening to look at how Adorno, as a representative figure of the first generation, might have sketched an alternative process of norms.

In his normative approach, Habermas's first step is to develop a transcendental grounds for his deduction of universal norms. Communication, especially language, becomes the indispensable means for Habermas's articulation of universal norms. We have seen above how some of the essays that criticize Habermas's excessive normativity still remain within a Habermasian framework; other essays look elsewhere, especially to Adorno and some of the less prominent aspects of the first generation of Critical Theory. When one keeps in mind the important role of language in the process of Habermas's strong norms, Adorno offers a radically different view of language that also suggests a very different understanding of normative grounding, and a different process of normativity.

In his expansive history of the Frankfurt School, Rolf Wiggershaus recounts how, in 1941, Adorno and Hokheimer flirted with making language the grounds for universal reason. Their letters on the matter seem prophetic for Habermas's later project: Horkheimer, for instance, suggested that language might be able to sustain the universality ascribed to, but not fulfilled by reason, "Speech establishes a shared relation towards truth, and is therefore the innermost affirmation of another existence, indeed of all forms of existence, according to their capacities."[7] Adorno responded very enthusiastically, suggesting projects like "language and truth" or "reason and language," titles easily lent to later Habermasian undertakings.[8]

It is not clear why Horkheimer and Adorno abandoned this project, but these letters hint at a depiction of language that would entail and incorporate a very different grounding, one that cultivates, in the grounding itself, a sensitivity to both positive norms and their (negative) limits. In his initial letter suggesting the potential for grounding universal reason in language, Horkheimer goes on to contrast the communal reason implied in and through language to the language of the camp guard whose words are a "terrible illogicality, no matter what their content is." For Horkheimer, although there is a consideration of universal-rational potential of language, there is also the terrible illogicality of the camp guard that exceeds the universal-rational. In his response to Horkheimer's suggestion, Adorno, despite his exhorting tones, offers his "passionate support to the new trend in the philosophy of language, together, of course, with its dialectical antithesis."[9] For both authors—even as they flirt with such a universal normative grounding in language—there is already heteronomy to this move. The dialectical method of process carries through to what becomes in Habermas a universal grounding.

Their early optimism about the universal-rational grounding in language seems by the time of *Dialectic of Enlightenment* to have largely evaporated. In *Dialectic of Enlightenment*, Horkheimer and Adorno describe a language hopelessly debased by modern society bent on reifying and mobilizing all instrumental means at its disposal. As indicated above, however, their depiction of language, here and in Adorno's "Essay as Form," does not posit some prelapsarian, pure mimetic speech (something with which a young Benjamin flirted); instead, Adorno in particular sketches a thoroughly dialectical language as both image (mimetic, with potential and hints of emancipation) and sign (discourse, which lapses into the instrumental). Whereas Habermas's grounding in the ideal speech situation makes a strong normative declaration of the original intent of language, Adorno's language is always already fallen into the sign, the discursive, the instrumental—yet it also nonetheless retains the mimetic moment that points to the coercionless synthesis of the elusive utopia. As in the work of art and its language character, language signifies simultaneously the fall, as well as the promise of the utopian.

Adorno's critique of the language of Hegel and other Idealists anticipates the discomfort some of the authors in this volume feel with Habermas's strong normative grounding in language. Committed to this thoroughgoing dialectic of language, Adorno criticizes Hegel and other Idealists for their attempts at ascetically sheering of language of that mythical remainder, that historical remnant, the persisting excess of the pure (chimerical, for Adorno) sign. Such remainders and excesses should not be stripped from language—an impossibility anyway—but deployed in the service of truth, the historical remainders deployed in a sensitivity for the contradictions of language as both image and sign.[10] This would indeed be a very different grounding than that which Habermas offers in his process of normativity.

Two essays in the current volume, those by Geulen and by Hewitt, take Adorno in moments that many scholars consider problematically normative—that is, offering mandates aimed at guiding behavior—and then use this subtle concept of language to free up the normative impasse. Geulen questions Adorno's positing of shame as the only "genuine" affect—an affective norm—and then, reading Adorno against Adorno, problematizes what she terms his subsequent megamelancholia. But Geulen is able to see the potential for moving past in his version of language, which preserves one of the most important moments of shame. Like language, shame registers outdatedness, both historical "progress" and remnant registered as social contradiction, because the norms that cause shame are constantly out of date and incommensurate to the affect they produce. Geulen recasts shame onto a (weakly normative) ground of dialectical language. Thus Adorno's understanding of normativity would entail, as we shall see, a constant (not merely reconstructed) sensitivity to their inherent historical contradiction, all in the place of a transcendentally good, understanding-oriented language.

Hewitt begins with what is usually taken as Adorno's strongly elitist-normative condemnation of jitterbug and jazz and suggests his work on these areas, despite arrested appearances, affords both positive and negative moments suspended between the bodily-discursive and somatic-prediscursive. For Hewitt as for Geulen, the hesitation and suspension that can beget meaning is found, above all, in Adorno's writings on language. Like Geulen, Hewitt shifts what appears to be an overly normative moment in Adorno to the contradiction of—rather than strong grounding in—language. Though neither author fully explores the double character of language—as both image and sign—that one finds in *Dialectic of Enlightenment* and "Essay as Form," both of their essays indicate language's complexity, subtlety, and dialectical unity as a potential means out of what seem overly strong, positive norms. By shifting what seem to be excessive norms to the contradictory grounds of language, they defuse the surface impasse of strong norms. As an alternative to the above efforts to recast Habermasian norms within Habermas, I would like to suggest that this double character in language can assist in a reconceptualizing of the processes (how one should ground, deduce, and apply norms) of normativity itself—as some of this volumes essays imply but do not fully develop.

Adorno's radically different, more dialectical understanding of language indicates that he would yield a much different notion of grounding and then deducing norms than Habermas. Above, we have seen how Habermas's normative grounding in language diverges significantly from first-generation Critical Theory—now I would like to turn to the second half of his process of normativity, to the deduction of moral and ethical norms. For Adorno, a dialectical moment parallel to his conceptualization of language also applies to his analysis of the strong (deduced) norms of the modern moral philosophical tradition. I would like to suggest that Adorno's analysis of one of the key ethical norms for modern philosophy—freedom in the "Models" section of *Negative Dialectics*—suggests a different process of normativity than Habermas's and, in fact, points toward an ethics that includes and constantly incorporates the excluded heteronomous excesses, building on the residues and the negative of the universal, positive norm.[11] Such a residual, negative ethics can serve as an alternative corrective to some of the problems of Habermas's process of grounding and deducing strong, positive norms, a solution indicated but not fully elaborated in a number of essays in the volume.

Just as in language, where the image and the sign are completely intertwined and, in fact, entail each, the prescriptive and descriptive moments of what Adorno terms the emphatic concept become intertwined in an unsublatable dialectic. Instead of a reconstruction that occasionally privileges the prescriptive over the descriptive, as in Habermas's renormativizing of Critical Theory, Adorno sees the prescriptive and descriptive as always inextricably linked. There is an inherent heteronomy of the emphatic concept, a heteronomy that persists throughout history in different historical inflections. There is never an original or pure moment of the emphatic concept, never a unilaterally stable grounding—it is always already marked by this fundamental heteronomy. In his critique of Habermas via Kant, Jacobs emphasizes Habermas's misunderstanding of Kant's heteronomy, and his subsequent lack of building such heteronomy into strong, positive norms. Adorno can recoup such heteronomy and build into norms and ethics in ways Jacobs never fully elaborates: Adorno's focus on emphatic concepts' simultaneously descriptive and prescriptive moments contrasts starkly to the strong norms that mark Habermas's moral philosophy. Instead of a conceptual, identically-conceived measuring stick applied from a transcendental grounding (as systems theorists might zealously mock), Adorno shows how the concept itself contains the contradiction of what it promises, and the permanent failure to live up to that promise. For Adorno, there is simply no noncontradictory ethics.

This kind of heteronomy throughout history, this inherent and permanent contradiction that would also have to serve as the grounds for any norms, demands a new understanding of normativity. The ethical becomes as much a method—a deliberately self-reflective process of normativity—as much as a transcendent deduction of norms. Given this focus on the contradictory emphatic concept, and on a method to extract its contradictions, Adorno engages in the ethical moment an immanent critique instead of (and against) a transcendental critique based on universal normative grounding. In contrast, Habermas's combination of immanent critique with reconstruction yields what some of the volume's authors regard as excessively strong norms. Instead of deducing positive normative force from some posited grounding, immanent critique elucidates the prescriptive already inherent within the emphatic concepts as well as their failure to live up to what they prescribe and promise. Since these concepts have contradictory social relations built in as permanent remainders and residues, a critique of them inevitably creates a nontranscendental, negative normative force.

In order to explore how this very different understanding of normativity might work, I would like to turn to Adorno'a analysis of one of the strongest and most positive bourgeois norms, freedom. Freedom also conveniently relates to Jacob's critique of Habermas's process of normativity concerning subject autonomy—the wider umbrella under which freedom resides—as well as resonates against the critiques of Habermas practiced by Pensky and Menke. Freedom constitutes an important norm for Habermas, one that he deduces from the normative grounding in the ideal speech situation: any individual in the idealized communicative collective should be free to initiate any utterance as he or she wishes. [12] In his analysis in *Negative Dialectics*, however, Adorno undertakes a very different critique of the emphatic concept of freedom in Kant, thus striking at the core of the modern moral philosophy and the transcendental deduction of universal, positive Enlightenment norms.

It is often and widely observed that Adorno retained an amazing consistency of thought across a tremendous range of topics, and, in his treatment of freedom, one finds that his emphasis on heteronomy and historical contradiction determines his approach to a historically-central moral norm. Just as in *Minima Moralia*, when he suggests that so-called outdatedness is persisting historical contradiction in his Ibsen entry, Adorno underscores the historical contradiction inevitably produced by freedom's constantly lagging behind itself:

> Emphatically conceived, the judgment that a man is free refers to the concept of freedom; but this concept in turns is more than is predicated of the man, and by other definitions the man is more than the concept of his freedom ... The concept of freedom lags behind itself as soon as we apply it empirically. It is not what it says, then. But because it must always be also the concept of what it covers, it is to be confronted with what it covers. Such confrontation forces it to contradict itself.[13]

First and foremost, in line with the heteronomy and the constant failure of concepts to coincide with what they claim, there is the nonidentity of the concept and what it is supposed to measure, the nonidentity of the concept of freedom and the person. The person is both free and unfree, altogether much else besides the concept—there is the constant excess to the norm. This gap of nonidentity creates a constant lagging—and it comprises (though not exclusively), a constant outdatedness, a historical remainder recalling the character of language. This sort of historical lagging does not, however, posit any kind of origins—it is there from the beginning, always already: "The identity of the self and its alienation accompany each other from the very beginning; whence the bad romanticism of the concept of alienation in the first place."[14] As in his concept of language and Geulen's shame—each extracting the mythical-historical remainders—freedom constantly registers, as soon as it is thought, its own obsolescence, its historicized failure to live up to its own claims. And, as the passage's conclusion suggests, such a contradictory unity of reason guarantees the impossibility of any noncontradictory ethics of freedom.

What would constitute such a reworking of normativity, of the very processes by which norms are grounded, deduced, and applied? Adorno moves from the critique of the Idealist concept of freedom via heteronomy to elaborating what the expunged excess, the residue, of freedom might be:

> But freedom itself and unfreedom are so entangled that unfreedom is not just an impediment to freedom but a premise of its concept. This can no more be culled out as an absolute than any other single concept ... There is no available model of freedom save one: that consciousness, as it intervenes in the total social constitution, will through that constitution intervene in the complexion of the individual. This notion is not utterly chimerical, because consciousness is a ramification of the energy of the drives; it is part impulse itself, and also a moment of that which it intervenes in. If there were not that affinity which Kant so furiously denies, neither would there be the idea of freedom, for whose sake he denies the affinity.[15]

After reiterating the contradictory unity of reason and the inherent heteronomy of freedom, Adorno begins to sketch another approach to normativity, one built on "compulsion" and on the nonidentity of the consciousness and the individual. Compulsion hints at the character of this nonidentity: it is based, in a surprisingly Freudian turn, on consciousness status as a ramification of the energy of drive. The nonidentity of consciousness and the individual forged therein yields "impulses," that is, an excess. In his critique of strong Idealist norms, Adorno demands the incorporation of that nonidentity, of those concept-defying residues—the negative excess of the norm into the deduction of norm itself.

Contradicting critiques of Adorno as arrested and static—that reception at which Geulen and Hewitt take aim—Adorno demands a reconciliation between the purged realm of the concept in philosophical consciousness and this excessive impulse:

> The impulse, intramental and somatic in one, drives beyond (transcends) the conscious sphere to which it belongs just the same. With that impulse freedom now extends to the realm of experience; this animates the concept of freedom as a state that would no more be blind nature than it would be oppressed nature. Its phantasm—which reason will not allow to be withered by any proof of causal interdependence— is the phantasm of reconciling nature and the mind. This is not as alien to reason as it would seem under the aspect of reason's Kantian equation with the will; it does not drop from heaven. To philosophical reflection it appears as downright otherness because the will that has been reduced to pure practical reason is an abstraction. The addendum/supplementary charge [*das Hinzutretende*] is the name for that which was eliminated in this abstraction; without it, there would be no real will at all. It is a flash of light between the poles of something long past, something grown, all but unrecognizable, and that which some day might come to be.[16]

The first sentence executes quite precisely the dialectical process Adorno invites, the reconciliation of a polarity that does not actually exist. Such a reconciliation, of nature and mind, might be there (à la Jacobs) in Kant, but subsequent philosophical abstraction— via "deduction"—has purged and purified the concept of such heteronomy. Against such a tradition of transcendental deduction of strong norms, however, Adorno pleads for the reconciliation of the concept with its excess, with "*dem Hinzutretende*," and together the concept and its excess tend to experience, now intertwined with freedom. Adorno replaces transcendental deduction from a strong grounding with this process of constantly reconciling the excess to the "deduced" norm.

It may appear incredible that this process of reconciling freedom and unfreedom, of holding in an unsublatable dialectic the positive concept and its negative excess, is to found the basis for any kind of ethics, but by the end of the freedom section of the "Models" portion of *Negative Dialectics*, it is exactly this that Adorno advocates: a minor ethics that in its very processes reconciles residues of, and excesses to, the coercive emphatic concept. It is precisely an awareness and a reconciliation of this residue of the emphatic, coercive concept that should form a counterethics:

> Freedom and intelligible character are akin to identity and nonidentity, but we cannot clearly and distinctly enter them on one side or the other. The subjects are free, according to the Kantian model, in so far as they are aware of and identical to themselves; and then again, they are unfree in such identity in so far as they are subjected to, and will perpetuate, its compulsion. They are unfree as diffuse, nonidentical nature; and yet, as that nature they are free because their overpowering impulse—the subject's nonidentity with itself is nothing else—will also rid them of identity's coercive character...[17]

The idealized subject, like the idealized language of Habermas's linguistic grounding of norms, needs to exclude; its identity (in its various connotation) rests on defining itself against the unfree, the noncoincidental, the residual compulsion, the mythical and historical remainder. But it is precisely the intertwining reconciliation of this impulse, this residue, with the emphatic concept that can allow the allegedly purified subject to rid itself of the coercive, violent moment of identity.

It is on these minor Adornian ethics that two of the most optimistic essays in the present volume build. Both, implicitly or explicitly, take issue with Habermas's processes of normativity and use, implicitly or not, Adorno's minor ethics of residues to correct Habermas's universal, positive norms. Christoph Menke's essay, as suggested above, critiques Habermas's positing of an idealized human "nature" and grounding his morality in it. Menke favors instead a process of morality that enacts the Adornian reconciliation of the nonidentitcal and unity of the purged excess: as one applies moral categories and abstracts, as one must in making moral decisions, Menke advocates for an awareness of what is lost, of what is remainder, of what is residue. Menke's essay interestingly (and problematically) takes the content of the abstract moral norms—for him, egalitarianism—as almost a given and then points to a revision of the very processes of how norms are to be applied.

Like Menke, Pensky uses Adorno to correct what he sees as a normative excess in Habermas—Habermas's grounding of norms in "authentic" cultural identity. Pensky lobbies to incorporate into Habermas's cosmopolitanism an Adornian ethics of the negative excess of the norm: an ethics based on the constant acknowledgement of loss, on a sensitivity for the residue and excess, created and/or exacted, when one participates in modern cosmopolitanism and its procedures. Like Menke's dialectics of morality, Pensky revises Habermas via the processes of normativity (how one enacts the normative mandate of cosmopolitanism) rather than the content of cosmopolitanism (one still encounters others, one maintains Habermas's universalist rights). Pensky's supplement to Habermas recognizes that participating in modern democracies requires a loss of Habermas's grounding "authentic" cultural identity—always already heteronomous—just as, as Geulen underscores, Adorno's "progress" to the vocation of the intellectual required a loss of the father's language. Just like language or freedom, cultural identity (the strong norm of Habermas in his model for cosmopolitanism) is already ravaged by loss, and this lost but residual remainder, argues Pensky following Adorno, ought to be recognized and reconciled with Habermas's strong, positive norm. Both Geulen and Pensky, on both a particular and universal scale, advocate the reconciliation of these moments of loss while continuing to speak.

In the above, I have attempted to sketch Adorno's different understanding of normativity: it is a method of constantly reconciling that residual or excess to the norm, with the norm in an unsublatable dialectic, a process therefore somewhat different than Habermas's weak transcendental grounding and subsequent deduction of norms. This alternative approach to norms indicates an Adornian process that counts as well for two essays in the book not as explicitly concerned with normative grounding or moral/ethical norms.

Martin Jay contrasts Adorno's concept of experience to that of Benjamin and Heidegger along axes similar to those I sketched above in Adorno's understanding of normativity. While warning against conflating Benjamin's and Heidegger's concepts of experience, Jay does suggest certain similarities in their approaches, including a shared criticism of Hegel's ("overly subjective") concept of experience, and the desire to sketch some experience as prior to the subject/object split. Both end up positing a pure, presubjective, transhistorical experience in an effort to return to a more fundamental truth than disenchanted humanism allows. Jay suggests that Adorno, though he, in part, inherited his concept of experience from Benjamin, avoids such an idealized understanding of experience. As he did with the concept of freedom, Adorno remains sensitive to the heteronomy of experience, to its inherent and constitutive contradictions. There is no pure experience, just as there is no pure freedom; just as one cannot deduce universal norms from some transcendental grounds, one cannot recover or restore pure experience from some more whole past. As with his treatment of norms, Adorno depicts experience as always already postlapsarian, always already compromised. Like freedom, experience for Adorno always already contains the positive and the negative and, only by incorporating both, one unleashes the potential for the flash of light that someday might come.

Similarly, Lutz Koepnick's essay works with what have come to seem to be immutable concepts in Benjamin reception, concepts from Benjamin's essay "The Work of Art in the Age of Mechanical Reproduction," especially auratic and postauratic art. Koepnick recounts various scholars' vigorous critiques of Benjamin for depicting the fading of the aura and the advent of postauratic art undialectically and ahistorically. Ultimately, Koepnick winds his examination of Benjamin back to a position that is somewhat parallel to that which I have been sketching above: that one should be wary of universal concepts, even of the auratic and postauratic, and instead favor conceptualizations that are contingent, heteronomous, or contradictory. Citing Hal Foster's *Return of the Repressed* and the wrapping of the Reichstag as examples, Koepnick underlines the persistence of the aura in the midst of the supposedly postauratic postmodern, indicating the heteronomy of what all too often is interpreted as unilaterally postauratic. As Koepnick interprets Benjamin's essay in this direction, he is interpreting in a manner directly parallel to that laid out above: that concepts tend to the heteronomously mixing, to the contradictory reconciling of that which appears to have been shorn away.

Pensky's essay attempts to correct Habermas's understanding of normativity with Adorno's dialectic of progress and loss—while, as I suggest above, maintaining a fundamentally Habermasian framework of universalist cosmopolitanism. Therein Pensky's argument reflects the basic straddling of the first and second generations of Critical Theory that runs throughout this volume: though many of the essays problematize Habermas's universal, positive norms, some—like Dean's, Dews', and Jacobs'—retain Habermas's basic framework, while others—like Menke's, Pensky's, Geulen's, and Hewitt's—turn substantively to alternative models, often to Adorno, to free up the normative impasses in Critical Theory.

With this long excursion through the understanding of normativity in Habermas and Adorno, I have attempted to sketch more fully this renegotiation of normativity between the first and second generations of Critical Theory. With the basic terms of the renegotiation in mind—strong grounding, transcendental deduction unto strong norms, versus constant reconciliation of residual excesses into an unsublatable dialectic—one can return to the fundamental critiques with which this essay commenced, those critiques lodged in the systems-theoretical approaches of Harro Müller and Wolfram Malte Fues. At the outset, I suggested that both authors problematize Critical Theory's generalizing of norms grounded in one (sub)system for functionally differentiated systems—a transcendental deduction unto such norms is no longer, in our complex, functionally-differentiated society, valid.

More specifically, both authors criticize the subject position—or, as Müller terms it, the observer position—from which such norms are posited. This is of course an important element of the conflict between Habermas's and Adorno's understanding of ethical norms: not only the constitution of normative concept, but the position from which one does deduce the norm. That one cannot deduce norms from any single grounding (sub)system parallels and supports Luhmann's argument that no observer position—be it first-,second-, third-, etc.- observer position—is any more universally valid than any other. Though he does not use the term "observer position" explicitly, Fues similarly critiques the "subject of modernity" and its position of the "mediating middle": Fues sees in modern philosophy, and especially in Hegel, a privileging of an observing, mediating subject that is supposed to exercise reason, to ground and deduce transcendentally, and arrive at strong, rational norms.

Reading with Adorno's heteronomous understanding of normativity in mind, however, one can find hints in both authors that augmenting norms with Adorno's relentlessly negative approach can help correct what they problematize in Habermas's positive norms. Müller's argument highlights Adorno's rhetorical strategy of positing binary oppositions—for example between authentic art and inauthentic art—and then rewriting the positive pole to include the negative one, such that authentic art is always already, also, inauthentic art. This strategy, Müller suggests, both creates paradoxes that are more indicative of the operations of multiple systems, as well as allowing Adorno to move among first-, second-, third-order observer positions, critiquing both others and himself. The implication, though not elaborated in Müller, is that Adorno's manipulation of different-order observations demonstrates the contingency of those observer positions, rather than their transcendentalness. This also corresponds to what I sketched above as Adorno's process of normativity, the heteronomy of the concept, the inclusion of the excess and remnant, as in Pensky's and Menke's correction of Habermas's positive norms.

In a similar manner, Fues looks favorably upon Adorno's sensitivity to the contradictions and limits of the subject of modernity: emphasizing dialectics' skepticism about its own project, Adorno remains sensitive to the impossibility of fully realizing the subject's positive, rational project. There can be no absolute origin or conclusion, both authors argue, and Adorno's always already heteronomy of the subject and concept in many ways responds to their critique better than Habermas's epistemology. For Fues, as well as for Menke, Pensky, Geulen, Hewitt, and Jay, Adorno locates his own subjectivity within those contradictions that are unavoidable, that should be acknowledged and built into strongly positive, uniform, identical concepts and subject-positions.

While Fues leaves open the question of whether Critical Theory will allow its more subtle, contradiction-sensitive side to win out over its more recent excessive normativity, Müllers sees a strict limit to the heteronomous in Adorno. Müller's essay reveals a basic tension between the negative, paradox-creating rhetorical strategy Adorno deploys in *Aesthetic Theory* and his tendency to privilege art, ultimately, as a form of redemption. For Müller, redemption constitutes the final limit of Adorno's heteronomy: at no point does Müller see Adorno ironizing or parodying it; instead, it remains

everywhere in the background, a reminder of Adorno's overly normative position on art.

Müller's critique concludes by dwelling on this excessively strong,
positive norm in Adorno, despite some of Adorno's more produc-
tively contradictory/paradoxical tendencies. It seems to me, though,
that attention paid to the process of normativity, as we have done
herein, suggests another reading. Adorno's redemption is a tentative
position taken inside of a larger framework of negativity:

> The only philosophy which can be responsibly practised in face of
> despair is the attempt to contemplate all things as they would present
> themselves from the standpoint of redemption... Perspectives must be
> fashioned that displace and estrange the world, reveal it to be, with its
> rifts and crevices, as indigent and distorted as it will appear one day in
> the messianic light... It is the simplest of all things ... But it is also the
> utterly impossible thing, because it presupposes a standpoint removed,
> even though by a hair's breadth, from the scope of existence, whereas we
> all know that any possible knowledge must not only be first wrested
> from what it is, if it shall hold good, but is also marked, for this very rea-
> son, by the same distortion and indigence which it seeks to escape...
> beside the demand thus placed on thought, the question of the reality or
> unreality of redemption itself hardly matters.[18]

Adorno's depiction here—in the ultimate section of *Minima Moralia*,
his minor ethics—is hardly asserting a strong, positive belief in
redemption. One can once again observe Adorno's very different
understanding of normativity: while observing from the standpoint
that redemption constitutes something of a weak norm, it is also
always already held in intimate complementarity with its opposite,
with the rifts and crevices, the indigent and the distorted. There is no
unilateral, strong grounding of redemption, only the process of constantly reconciling it with its opposites, its excesses. Adorno's thor-
ough-going heteronomy here responds to the systems-theorists'
critiques of Critical Theory's observer position: the hope of redemption framed within an overarching negativity also acknowledges the
impossibility of an observer, or mediating subject, positioned above
others. And in contrast to Habermas's commmunicative approach,
the passage echoes Adorno's positive and negative conceptualization
of language when Horkheimer and he were considering making language the grounds for universal reason: the negative must be held
along with the positive, the residual, excessive remnant to the concept, word, or norm folded into and maintained along with the concept, word, and norm itself.

Notes

1. For a clear and helpful summary of the assault functional differentiation makes on politics like Habermas's, see Robert C. Holub, *Jürgen Habermas: Critic in the Public Sphere* (New York: Routledge, 1991) 124-28.
2. Cf. Allen Wood, "Habermas's Defense of Rationalism," *New German Critique* 35 (Spring/Summer 1985): 146. Wood makes clear the link of rationalism to strong norms: "The rationalist holds that there is always an objectively correct answer to normative questions ... Rationalism rejects all non-cognitivist, relativist, subjectivist or emotivist views which hold that there is no objectively correct answer to normative or evaluative questions... "
3. Jürgen Habermas, "Ein philosophierender Intellektueller," *Frankfurt Allgemeine Zeitung*, 11 September 1963, quoted in Rolf Wiggershaus, *The Frankfurt School: Its History, Theories, and Political Significance*, trans. Michael Robertson (1986; Boston: MIT Press, 1994), 581.
4. Wiggershaus, 581.
5. Habermas's reconstructive project intentionally departed precisely the immanently critical moment in Marx that Adorno preferred. In his essay, 'The Development of Normative Structures," Habermas writes that the immanent critique of Marx, and by implication the first generation of the Critical Theory, needs to be substantially supplemented by "reconstruction": "[Marx] could be content to take at its word, and to criticize immanently, the normative content of the ruling bourgeois theories of modern natural law and political economy... However, if (as becomes even more apparent in times of recession) the bourgeois ideals have gone into retirement, there are norms and values to which an immanent critique might appeal... A philosophical ethics not restricted to metaethical statements is possible today only if we can reconstruct general presuppositions of communication and procedures for justifying norms and values." Jürgen Habermas, "The Development of Normative Structures," in *Communication and the Evolution of Society*, trans. Thomas McCarthy (1976; Boston: Beacon Press, 1979), 96-97.
6. Habermas, *Theory of Communicative Action*, vol. 1 (Boston: Beacon Press, 1987), 288: "It can be shown that the use of language with an orientation to reaching understanding is the original mode of language use, upon which indirect understanding, giving something to understand or letting something be understood, and the instrumental use of language in general are parasitic."
7. Wiggershaus, 505.
8. Wiggershaus, 505.
9. Wiggershaus, 506.
10. Adorno's and Habermas's contrasting approaches to language determine as well their respective interest in the style of their own and others' theoretical writings. Habermas does not seem to entertain much interest in the language of his colleagues, either adversaries or supporters, whereas Adorno's style—inherently resistant to sheering its language of excess baggage—is crucial to the pursuit of truth itself.
11. My reading here is indebted to Fredric Jameson's chapter four in *Late Marxism* (New York: Verso, 1993). My interpretation, however, also tries to move beyond Jameson's focus on the heteronomy of the concept of freedom by indi-

cating Adorno's contradictory norms and the ethics of excesses that can be derived from it.

12. For the link between Habermas's linguistic grounding and freedom, see Herbert Schnädelbach, "The Transformation of Critical Theory," *Communicative Action: Essays on Jürgen Habermas's* The Theory of Communicative Action (1986; Cambridge: MIT Press, 1991) 19-20.

13. Theodor Adorno, *Negative Dialectics*, trans. E.B. Ashton (1966; New York: Continuum, 1973), 150-51.

14. Adorno, *Negative Dialectics*, 216-17.

15. Adorno, *Negative Dialectics*, 265.

16. Adorno, *Negative Dialectics*, 228-29.

17. Adorno, *Negative Dialectics*, 299.

18. Theodor Adorno, *Minima Moralia: Reflections from Damaged Life*, trans. E.F.N. Jephcott (New York: Verso, 1993), 247.

Bibliography

Adelson, Leslie A. *Making Bodies, Making History.* Lincoln: Nebraska University Press, 1993.

Adorno, Theodor W. "Wörter aus der Fremde." *Noten zur Literatur.* Vol. 2. Frankfurt am Main: Suhrkamp Verlag, 1961.

———. *Ohne Leitbild. Parva Aesthetica.* Frankfurt am Main: Suhrkamp Verlag, 1967.

———. *Negative Dialektik.* Frankfurt am Main: Suhrkamp Verlag, 1970.

———. *Negative Dialectics.* Translated by E.B. Ashton. New York: Continuum, 1973; Reprint, 1983.

———. *The Jargon of Authenticity.* Translated by Knut Tanowski and Frederic Will. Evanston, Illinois: Northwestern University Press, 1973.

———. *Minima Moralia: Reflections from Damaged Life.* Translated by E.F.N. Jephcott. London: New Left Books, 1974. 3d ed., 1985. New York: Verso, 1993, 1996.

———. "On the Fetish-Character in Music and the Regression of Listening." In *The Essential Frankfurt School Reader.* Edited by Andrew Arato and Eike Gebhardt. New York: Continuum, 1988.

———. "Transparencies on Film." *New German Critique* 24/25 (Fall/Winter 1981/82): 186-205.

———. "On Popular Music." In *On Record: Rock, Pop, and the Written Word.* Edited by Simon Frith and Andrew Goodwin. London: Routledge, 1990.

———. *Notes to Literature.* Edited by Rolf Tiedeman. Translated by Shierry Weber Nicholsen. Vols. 1 & 2. New York: Columbia University Press, 1992.

_____. *Hegel: Three Studies.* Translated by Shierry Weber
Nicholsen. Cambridge: MIT Press, 1993.

_____. "Theory of Pseudo-Culture." *Telos* 95 (Spring 1993): 15-38.

_____. *Aesthetic Theory.* Edited by Gretel Adorno and Rolf
Tiedemann. Translated by Robert Hullot-Kentor.
Minneapolis: University of Minnesota Press, 1997.

_____. "Progress." In *Critical Models.* Edited and translated by
Henry Pickford. New York: Columbia University Press, 1998.

_____ and Max Horkheimer. *The Dialectic of Enlightenment.*
Translated by John Cumming. New York: Continuum, 1987.

Agamben, Giorgio. *Infancy and History: Essays on the
Destruction of Experience.* Translated by Liz Heron. London:
Verso, 1993.

Anderson, Benedict. *Imagined Communities.* London: Verso,
1983.

Apel, Karl-Otto. *Transformation der Philosophie. Band 1:
Sprachanalytik, Semiotik, Hermeneutik.* Frankfurt am Main:
Suhrkamp Verlag, 1976.

_____. "The Problem of Philosophical Foundations in Light of a
Transcendental Pragmatics of Language" (revised). In *After
Philosophy: End or Transformation?* Edited by Kenneth
Baynes, James Bohman, and Thomas McCarthy. Cambridge,
Mass: MIT Press, 1987. Originally published in B.
Kanitschneider, ed., *Sprache und Erkenntnis.* Innsbruck:
Tama, 1976.

_____. "Normatively Grounding Critical Theory through
Recourse to the Life-world? A Transcendental-Pragmatic
Attempt to Think with Habermas against Habermas." In
*Philosophical Intervention in the Unfinished Project of
Enlightenment.* Edited byAxel Honneth, Thomas McCarthy,
Claus Offe, and Albrecht Wellmer. Cambridge: MIT Press,
1992.

_____. "Zurück zur Normalitat ..." In *Diskurs und
Verantwortung.* Frankfurt am Main: Suhrkamp, 1992.

Baudrillard, Jean. *Der symbolische Tausch und der Tod.*
München: Matthes und Seitz, 1982.

_____. *Die fatalen Strategien.* Munich: Matthew und Seitz, 1985.

Benhabib, Seyla. "Deliberative Rationality and Models of
Democratic Legitimacy." *Constellations* 1.1 (April 1994):
26-52.

_____. "The Pariah and Her Shadow: Hannah Arendt's Biography of Rahel Varnhagen." *Political Theory* 23.4 (February 1995): 17-24.

Benjamin, Andrew. "Time and Task: Benjamin and Heidegger Showing the Present." In *Walter Benjamin's Philosophy: Destruction and Experience*. Edited by Andrew Benjamin and Pete Osborne. London: Routledge, 1994.

Benjamin, Walter. "The Storyteller: Reflections on the Work of Nikolai Leskov." In *Illuminations: Essays and Reflections* (in German). Edited by Hannah Arendt. Translated by Harry Zohn. New York: Harcourt, Brace and World, 1968.

_____. *Gesammelte Schriften*. Edited by Rolf Tiedemann and Hermann Schweppenhauser. Vols. 1-4. Frankfurt am Main: Suhrkamp, 1972.

_____. *Reflections: essays, aphorisms, autobiographical writings*. Edited by Peter Demetz. Translated by Edmund Jephcott. New York: Harcourt Brace Jovanovich, 1978.

_____. "A Child's View of Color." In *Selected Writings*. Vol 1, 1913-1926. Edited by Marcus Bullock and Michael W. Jennings. Cambridge, Mass: Harvard University Press, 1996.

Berlich, Alfred. "Elenktik des Diskurses: Karl-Otto Apels Ansatz einer transzendentalpragmatischen Letztbegrundung." In *Kommunikation und Reflexion*. Edited by Wolfgang Kuhlmann and Dietrich Bohler. Frankfurt am Main: Suhrkamp Verlag. 1982.

Bernasconi, Robert. *The Question of Language in Heidegger's History of Being*. Atlantic Highlands, New Jersey: Humanities Press, 1986.

Bernstein, J.M. "Why Rescue Semblance? Metaphysical Experience and the Possibility of Ethics." In *The Semblance of Subjectivity: Essays on Adorno's Aesthetic Theory*. Edited by Tom Huhn and Lambert Zuidervaart. Cambridge, Mass: MIT Press, 1997.

Bohman, James and Matthias Lutz-Bachman, eds. *Perpetual Peace: Essays on Kant's Cosmopolitan Ideal*. Cambridge, Mass: MIT Press, 1997.

Brunkhorst, Hauke. *Theodor W. Adorno. Dialektik der Moderne*. Munich: Piper, 1990.

Buchstein, Hubertus. "Bytes that Bite: The Internet and Deliberative Democracy." *Constellations* 4.2 (October 1997): 248-63.

Buck-Morss, Susan. "Aesthetics and Anaesthetics: Walter Benjamin's Artwork Essay Reconsidered." *New Formations* 20 (Summer 1993): 123-43.

Bürger, Peter. *Prosa der Moderne*. Frankfurt am Main: Suhrkamp Verlag, 1988.

_____. *Das Denken des Herrn: Bataille zwischen Hegele und dem Surrealismus*. Frankfurt am Main: Suhrkamp Verlag, 1992.

Butler, Judith. "For Careful Reading." In *Feminist Contentions: A Philosophical Exchange*. Edited by Seyla Benhabib, Judith Butler, Drucilla Cornell, and Nancy Fraser. New York: Routledge, 1994.

Campe, Rüdiger and Manfred Schneider. Preface to *Geschichten der Physiognomik. Text. Bild. Wissen*. Edited by Rudiger Campe and Manfred Schneider. Freiburg: Rombach, 1996.

Carnois, Bernard. *The Coherence of Kant's Doctrine of Freedom*. Translated by David Booth. Chicago: University of Chicago Press, 1987.

Caygill, Howard. "Benjamin, Heidegger and the Destruction of Tradition." *Walter Benjamin's Philosophy: Destruction and Experience*. Edited by Andrew Benjamin and Pete Osborne. London: Routledge, 1994.

_____. *Walter Benjamin: The Colour of Experience*. London: Routledge, 1998.

Cohen, Jean and Andrew Arato. *Civil Society and Political Theory*. Cambridge, Mass: MIT Press, 1992.

Collins, Jim. *Uncommon Cultures: Popular Culture and Post-Modernism*. New York: Routledge, 1989.

Connolly, William. *The Ethos of Pluralization*. Minneapolis: University of Minnesota Press, 1995.

David-Menard, Monique. *Hysteria from Freud to Lacan: Body and Language in Psychoanalysis*. Translated by Catherine Porter. Ithaca, NY: Cornell University Press, 1989.

Dean, Jodi. "Civil Society: Beyond the Public Sphere." In *The Handbook of Critical Theory*. Edited by David Rasmussen. Oxford: Blackwell Publishers, 1996.

_____. "Virtually Citizens." *Constellations* 4.2 (October 1997): 264-82.

DeCaroli, Steven. "Matters of Taste, Matters of Fact: The Emergence and Integration of Aesthetics and History within the Philosophical Discourse of Eighteenth-Century Europe." Ph.D. diss., Binghamton University, n.d.

Derrida, Jaques. "Force of Law: The 'Mystical Foundation of Authority'." *Cardozo Law Review* 11.5-6 (July/August 1990): 919-1045.

Descartes, Rene. *Discourse on Method and Meditations.* Translated by Laurence J. Lafleur. New York: The Liberal Press, 1960.

Dewey, John. *Art as Experience.* New York: Minton, Balch & Company, 1934.

Dews, Peter. *The Limits of Disenchantment.* New York: Verso, 1995.

Duerr, Hans Peter. *Scham und Nacktheit.* Vols.1-3. Frankfurt am Main: Suhrkamp Verlag, 1985.

Dworkin, Ronald. *A Matter of Principle.* Cambridge, Mass: Harvard University Press, 1985.

Falasca-Zamponi, Simonetta. *Fascist Spectacle: The Aesthetics of Power in Mussolini's Italy.* Berkeley: University of California Press, 1997.

Fichte, Johann Gottlieb. *The Vocation of Man.* Indianapolis: Hackett, 1987.

_____. *Introduction to the Wissenschaftslehre and Other Writings.* Translated and edited by Daniel Breazeale. Indianapolis: Hackett, 1994.

Foster, Hal. *The Return of the Real: The Avant-Garde at the End of the Century.* Cambridge, Mass: MIT Press, 1996.

Forster, Eckhardt, ed. *Opus Postumum.* Cambridge: Cambridge University Press, 1993.

Fraser, Nancy. "Rethinking the Public Sphere: A Contribution to the Critique of Actually Existing Democracy." In *Habermas and the Public Sphere.* Edited by Craig Calhoun. Cambridge, Mass: MIT Press, 1992.

Freud, Sigmund. "Trauer und Melancholie." In *Studien-Ausgabe.* Vol. 3. Edited by Alexander Mitscherlich et al. Frankfurt am Main: S. Fischer Verlag, 1989.

Fukuyama, Francis. *Das Ende der Geschichte. Wo stehen wir?* Munich: Kindler, 1992.

Gadamer, Hans-Georg. *Truth and Method.* New York: Crossroad, 1986.

Gellner, Ernest. *Nationalism*. London: Weidenfeld & Nicolson, 1997.

Geuess, Raymond. *The Idea of a Critical Theory. Habermas and the Frankfurt School*. Cambridge: Cambridge University Press, 1981.

Giddens, Anthony. *The Consequences of Modernity*. Stanford: Stanford University Press, 1990.

Goethe, J.W. *Hamburger Ausgabe*. 3d ed., vol. 3. Edited by Erich Trunz. Hamburg: Christian Wegner Verlag, 1958.

Greenspan, Alan. "Market capitalism: The role of free markets." Address to Annual Convention of the American Society of Newspaper Editors, Washington D.C., 2 April 1998. In *Vital Speeches of the Day* 64:14 (1 May 1998): 418-421.

Gronke, Horst. "Apel versus Habermas: Zur Architektonik der Diskursethik." In *Transzendentalpragmatik*. Edited by Andreas Dorschel et al. Frankfurt am Main: Suhrkamp Verlag, 1993.

Gueroult, Martin. "Canon de la Raison pure et critique de la Raison pratique." In *Revue internationale de Philosophie* 8.30, 1954.

Gunning, Tom. "The Cinema of Attraction(s)." *Wide Angle* 8.3-4 (1986): 63-70.

_____. "An Aesthetic of Astonishment: Early Film and the (In)credulous Spectator." *Art & Text* 34 (1989): 31-45.

Habermas, Jürgen. "Das Absolute und die Geschichte: Von der Zwiespältigkeit in Schellings Denken." Ph.D. diss., University of Bonn, 1954: 71.

_____. "Die Scheinrevolution und ihre Kinder." In *Die Linke antwortet Jürgen Habermas*. Frankfurt am Main: Suhrkamp Verlag, 1968.

_____. *Knowledge and Human Interests*. Boston: Beacon, 1972.

_____. "Postscript." In *Knowledge and Human Interests*. Boston: Beacon, 1974.

_____. *Zur Rekonstruktion des historischen Materialismus*. Frankfurt am Main: Suhrkamp Verlag, 1976.

_____. *Communication and the Evolution of Society*. Translated by Thomas McCarthy. Boston: Beacon Press, 1979.

_____. "Consciousness-Raising or Redemptive Criticism: The Contemporaneity of Walter Benjamin." *New German Critique* 17 (1979): 30-59.

_____. *Theorie des kommunikativen Handelns.* Vol. 1. Frankfurt: Suhrkamp Verlag, 1981. (*Theory of Communicative Action.* Vol. 1. Boston: Beacon Press, 1987.)

_____. "Philosophy as Stand-In and Interpreter." In *After Philosophy: End or Tranformation?* Edited by Kenneth Baynes, James Bohman, and Thomas McCarthy. Cambridge, Mass: MIT Press, 1986.

_____. *Der philosophische Diskurs der Moderne.* Frankfurt am Main: Suhrkamp Verlag, 1985. (*The Philosophical Discourse of Modernity.* Cambridge, Mass: MIT Press, 1987.)

_____. "Entgegnung." In *Kommunikatives Handeln.* Edited by Axel Honneth and Hans Joas. Frankfurt am Main: Suhrkamp Verlag, 1988.

_____. *The Structural Transformation of the Public Sphere.* Translated by Thomas Burger. Cambridge, Mass: MIT Press, 1989.

_____. "Reconstruction and Interpretation in the Social Sciences." In *Moral Consciousness and Communicative Action.* Cambridge, Mass: MIT Press, 1990.

_____. "Erläuterungen zur Diskursethik." In *Erläuterungen zur Diskursethik.* Frankfurt am Main: Suhrkamp Verlag, 1991.

_____. "Further Reflections on the Public Sphere." In *Habermas and the Public Sphere.* Edited by Craig Calhoun. Cambridge, Mass: MIT Press, 1992.

_____. *Postmetaphysical Thinking.* Cambridge, Mass: MIT Press, 1992.

_____. "Remarks on Discourse Ethics." In *Justification and Application.* Cambridge: Polity Press, 1993.

_____. *Justification and Application: Remarks on Discourse Ethics.* Translated by Ciaran Cronin. Cambridge, Mass: MIT Press, 1993.

_____. "Ein philosophierender Intellektueller." *Frankfurter Allgemeine Zeitung.* 11 September 1963. Quoted in Rolf Wiggershaus, *The Frankfurt School: Its History, Theories, and Political Significance* (in German). Translated by Michael Robertson. Boston: MIT Press, 1994.

_____. "Three Models of Democracy." *Constellations* 1.1 (April 1994): 1-10.

_____. "What Theories Can Accomplish—and What They Can't." In *The Past as Future*. Translated by Max Pensky. Lincoln: Nebraska University Press, 1994.

_____. "Stuggles for Recognition in the Democratic Constitutional State." In *Multiculturalism: Examining the Politics of Recognition*. Edited by Amy Gutmann. Princeton: Princeton University Press, 1994.

_____. *Accommodating the Other*. Edited by Ciaran Cronin and Pablo De Greiff. Cambridge, Mass: MIT Press, 1998.

Hables, Chris, ed. *The Cyborg Handbook*. New York: Routledge, 1995.

Hamacher, Werner. *Pleroma*. Stanford: Stanford University Press, 1998.

Hansen, Miriam. "Early Silent Cinema: Whose Public Sphere?" *New German Critique* 29 (Spring/Summer 1983): 147-84.

_____. "Benjamin, Cinema and Experience: 'The Blue Flower in the Land of Technology'." *New German Critique* 40 (Winter 1987): 179-224.

Hanssen, Beatrice, *Walter Benjamin's Other History: Of Stones, Animals, Human Beings, and Angels*. Berkeley: University of California Press, 1998.

Harvey, David. *The Condition of Postmodernity: An Enquiry into the Origins of Cultural Change*. Oxford: Basil Blackwell, 1989.

Hegel, G.W.F. *Phänomenologie des Geistes; Wissenschaft der Logik; Vorlesungen über die Geschichte der Philosophie*. Vols. 1, 3, 5 and 20 of *Gesammelte Werke in zwanzig Bänden*. Edited by Eva Moldenhauer and Karl Markus Michel. Frankfurt am Main: Suhrkamp Verlag, 1970.

Heidegger, Martin. *Hegel's Concept of Experience*. New York: Harper and Row, 1970.

Held, David. "Cosmopolitan Democracy and the Global Order: A New Agenda." In *Perpetual Peace: Essays on Kant's Cosmopolitan Ideal*. Edited by James Bohman and Matthias Lutz-Bachmann. Cambridge, Mass: MIT Press, 1997.

Hohendahl, Peter Uwe. "The Public Sphere: Models and Boundaries." In *Habermas and the Public Sphere*. Edited by Craig Calhoun. Cambridge, Mass: MIT Press, 1992.

_____. *Prismatic Thought. Theodor W. Adorno*. Lincoln: University of Nebraska Press, 1995.

_____. *Building a National Literature: The Case of Germany, 1830-1870.* Translated by Renate Baron Franciscono. Ithaca, NY: Cornell University Press, 1989.

Holub, Robert C. *Jürgen Habermas: Critic in the Public Sphere.* New York: Routledge, 1991.

Honneth, Axel. *The Fragmented World of the Social. Essays in Social and Political Philosophy.* Edited by Charles W. Wright. Albany, NY: SUNY Press, 1995.

Horkheimer, Max and Theodor W. Adorno, *Dialectic of Enlightenment.* Translated by John Cumming. New York: Herder and Herder, 1972. New York: Continuum, 1996.

Huhn, Thomas and Lambert Zuidervaart, eds. *The Semblance of Subjectivity: Essays in Adorno's Aesthetic Theory.* Cambridge, Mass: MIT Press, 1997.

humdog. "pandora's vox: on community in cyberspace." In *High Noon on the Electronic Frontier.* Edited by Peter Ludlow. Cambridge, Mass: MIT Press, 1996.

Huyssen, Andreas. *Twilight Memories: Marking Time in a Culture of Amnesia.* New York: Routledge, 1995.

_____. "Monumental Seduction." In *New German Critique* 69 (Fall 1996): 181-200.

Jameson, Fredric. *Late Marxism. Adorno and the Persistence of the Dialectic.* London: Verso, 1990, 1993.

Jarvis, Simon. *Adorno. A Critical Introduction.* New York: Routledge, 1998.

Jauss, Hans Robert. *Aesthetic Experience and Literary Hermeneutics* (in German). Translated by Michael Shaw. Minneapolis: University of Minnesota Press, 1982.

Jay, Martin. *The Dialectical Imagination. A History of the Frankfurt School and the Institute of Social Research 1923-1950.* Boston: Beacon, 1973.

_____. "Adorno in America." In *New German Critique* 31 (Winter 1984): 157-82.

_____. *Adorno.* Cambridge, Mass: Harvard University Press, 1984.

_____. *Downcast Eyes: The Denigration of Vision in Twentieth-Century French Thought.* Berkeley: University of California Press, 1993.

_____. "Mimesis and Mimetology: Adorno and Lacoue-Labarthe." In *The Semblance of Subjectivity: Essays on*

Adorno's Aesthetic Theory. Edited by Tom Huhn and Lambert
   Zuidervaart. Cambridge, Mass: MIT Press, 1997.

_____. "Experience without a Subject: Walter Benjamin and the
   Novel." In *Cultural Semantics: Keywords of the Age*.
   Amherst, Mass: University of Massachusetts Press, 1998.

_____. "Is Experience Still in Crisis? Reflections on a Frankfurt
   School Lament." In *The Cambridge Companion to Adorno*.
   Cambridge, Mass: Cambridge University Press, forthcomoing
   spring 2001.

Kalkowski, Peter. *Adornos Erfahrung: zur Kritik der Kritischen
   Theorie*. Frankfurt am Main: Suhrkamp Verlag, 1988.

Kafka, Franz. *Der Prozess*. Hamburg: S. Fischer Verlag, 1960.

Kant, Immanuel. *Grundlegung zur Metaphysik der Sitten*. Edited
   by Karl Vorlaender. Leipzig: Felix Meiner, 1906.

_____. *Kritik der reinen Vernunft*. Edited by Raymund Schmidt.
   2d ed. Leipzig: Felix Meiner, 1930.

_____. "To Perpetual Peace: A Philosophical Sketch." In *Perpetual
   Peace and Other Essays* (in German). Translated by Ted
   Humphrey. Indianapolis: Hackett, 1983.

_____. "Was heißt: sich im Denken orientieren?" In *Werke,
   Sonderausgabe*. Edited by Wilhelm Weischedel. Darmstadt:
   Wissenschaftliche Buchgesellschaft, 1983 vol. 5.

_____. *Critique of Judgment*. Translated by Werner Pluhar.
   Indianapolis: Hackett, 1987.

Kappner, Hans-Hartmut. *Die Bildungstheorie Adornos als Theorie
   der Erfahrung von Kultur und Kunst*. Frankfurt am Main:
   Suhrkamp Verlag, 1984.

Kaufman, Gershen. *The Psychology of Shame. Theory and
   Treatment of Shame-Based Symptoms*. New York: Springer,
   1996.

Koepnick, Lutz P. "Rethinking the Spectacle: History, Visual
   Culture, and German Unification." In *Wendezeiten—
   Zeitenwenden: Positionsbestimmungen zur deutschsprachigen
   Literatur 1945-1995*. Edited by Robert Weninger and Brigitte
   Rossbacher. Tubingen: Stauffenburg Verlag, 1997.

_____. *Walter Benjamin and the Aesthetics of Power*. Lincoln:
   University of Nebraska Press, 1999.

Kracauer, Siegfried. "Cult of Distraction." In *The Mass
   Ornament: Weimar Essays*. Translated by Thomas Y. Levin.
   Cambridge, Mass: Harvard University Press, 1995.

Kymlicka, Will. *Multicultural Citizenship. A Liberal Theory of Minority Rights.* Oxford: Oxford University Press, 1995.

_____. "From Enlightenment Cosmopolitanism to Liberal Nationalism." n.p. 1997: 2.

Luhmann, Niklas. *Soziale Systeme: Grundriß einer allgemeinen Theorie.* Frankfurt am Main: Suhrkamp Verlag, 1984.

_____. "Ich nehme mal Karl Marx. Interview mit Walter van Rossum." In *Archimedes und wir. Interviews mit Niklas Luhmann.* Edited by Dirk Baecker and Georg Stanitzek. Berlin: Merve Verlag, 1987.

_____. *Die Gesellschaft der Gesellschaft.* 2 vols. Frankfurt am Main: Suhrkamp Verlag, 1997.

_____. *Paradigm Lost. Über die ethische Reflexion der Moral.* Frankfurt am Main: Suhrkamp Verlag, 1990.

Marcuse, Herbert. *One-Dimensional Man, Studies in the Ideology of Advanced Industrial Society.* Boston: Beacon, 1964.

_____. *Negations: Essays in Critical Theory.* Boston: Beacon, 1968.

_____. *Counterrevolution and Revolt.* Boston: Beacon, 1972.

McCarthy, Thomas. *The Critical Theory of Jürgen Habermas.* Cambridge, Mass: MIT Press, 1978.

_____. Introduction to *The Theory of Communicative Action.* By Jürgen Habermas. Vol. 1. Boston: Beacon, 1984.

Mead, George Herbert. *Mind, Self, and Society.* Chicago: University of Chicago Press, 1934.

Menke, Christoph. "Critical Theory and Tragic Knowledge." In *The Handbook of Critical Theory.* Edited by David Rasmussen. Oxford: Blackwell Publishers, 1996.

_____. *Tragödie im Sittlichen. Gerechtigkeit und Freiheit nach Hegel.* Frankfurt am Main: Suhrkamp Verlag, 1996.

_____. *The Sovereignty of Art: Aesthetic Negativity in Adorno and Derrida.* Cambridge, Mass: MIT Press, 1998.

Mirandola, Pico Della. *On the Dignity of Man.* Translated by Charles Glenn Wallis. Indianapolis: Library of Liberal American, 1965.

Müller, Harro. "Systemtheorie/Literaturwissenschaft." In *Neue Literaturtheorien. Eine Einführung.* 2d ed. Edited by Klaus-Michael Bogdal. Opladen: Westdeutscher Verlag, 1997.

_____. "Autonomie und Funktion." In *Literaturwissenschaft. Ein Grundkurs.* Edited by Helmut Brackert and Jörn Stückrath. Reinbek: Rowohlt, 1992.

Neckel, Sighard. *Status und Scham: Zur symbolischen Reproduktion sozialer Ungleichheit*. Frankfurt am Main: Campe Verlag, 1991.

Nicholsen, Shierry Weber. *Exact Imagination, Late Work: On Adorno's Aesthetics*. Cambridge, Mass: MIT Press, 1997.

Nussbaum, Martha. "Kant and Cosmopolitanism." In *Perpetual Peace: Essays on Kant's Cosmopolitan Ideal*. Edited by James Bohman and Matthias Lutz-Bachmann. Cambridge, Mass: MIT Press, 1997.

Pensky, Max. "Universalism and the Situated Critic." In *The Cambridge Companion to Habermas*. Edited by Stephen K. White. Cambridge, Mass: Cambridge University Press, 1995.

_____. "Habermas and the Antinomies of the Intellectual." In *Habermas: A Critical Reader*. Edited by Peter Dews. London: Basil Blackwell, 1999.

_____, ed. *The Actuality of Adorno. Critical Essays on Adorno and the Postmodern*. Albany: State University of New York, 1997.

Petro, Patrice. *Joyless Streets: Women and Melodramatic Representation in Weimar Germany*. Princeton, NJ: Princeton University Press, 1989.

Piers, Gerhart, and Milton B. Singer. *Shame and Guilt. A Psychoanalytic and a Cultural Study*. Springfield, Ill: Charles C. Thomas, 1953.

Plumpe, Gerhard. *Ästhetische Kommunikation der Moderne*. In Vol. 2 of *Von Nietzsche bis zur Gegenwart*. Opladen: Westdeutscher Verlag, 1993.

Ritter, J. et al. eds. "Scham." In *Historisches Wörterbuch philosophischer Grundbegriffe*. Vol. 8. Munich: Kosel Verlag, 1992.

Roberts, David. *Art and Enlightenment. Aesthetic Theory after Adorno*. Lincoln: University of Nebraska Press, 1991.

Rutschky, Michael. "Erinnerungen an die Gesellschaftskritik" *Merkur* 38.1 (January 1984): 28-38.

Rychner, Max. "Moral an Kleinigkeiten." In *Sphären der Bücherwelt. Aufsätze zur Literatur*. Zurich: Manesse Verlag, 1952.

Schelling, Friedrich. Letter to Johann Gottlieb Fechte. 3 October 1801. *Fichtes und Schellings philosophischer Briefwechsel*. Edited by I.H. Fichte and K Fr.A Schelling. Stuttgart and Augsburg: Cotta, 1856: 97.

Schiller, Friedrich. Letter to Jena Korner. 23 February 1793. *Schillers Briefe*. Vol. iii. Edited by Fritz Jonas. Stuttgart: Deutsche Verlagsanstalt, 1892-96: 285. Translated in F. Schiller, *On the Aesthetic Education of Man* (in German). Edited and translated by Elizabeth M. Wilkinson and L.A. Willoughby. Oxford: Clarendon Press, 1967: 300.

Schlüpmann, Heide. "Kinosucht." *Frauen und Film* 33 (October 1982): 45-52.

Schnädelbach, Herbert. "The Transformation of Critical Theory." *Communicative Action: Essays on Jürgen Habermas's* The Theory of Communicative Action. Cambridge, Mass: MIT Press, 1991.

Schulze, Gerhard. *Die Erlebnisgesellschaft: Kultursoziologie der Gegenwart*. Frankfurt am Main: Campus Verlag, 1992.

Schurz, R. *Ethik nach Adorno*. Frankfurt am Main: Stromfeld Roter Stern, 1985.

Sedgwick, Eve. "Shame and Performativity: Henry James' New York Edition Prefaces." In *Henry James's New York Edition. The Construction of Authorship*. Edited by David Whirter. Stanford, Stanford University Press, 1995.

Serres, Michel. *Der Parasit*. Frankfurt am Main: Suhrkamp Verlag, 1987.

Stafford, Barbara Maria. *Good Looking: Essay on the Virtue of Images*. Cambridge, Mass: MIT Press, 1996.

Steinberg, Michael P. "The Collector as Allegorist: Goods, Gods, and Objects of History." In *Walter Benjamin and the Demands of History*. Edited by Michael P. Steinberg. Ithaca, NY: Cornell University Press, 1996.

Stimilli, Davide. "Über Schamhaftigkeit. Zur historischen Semantik einiger physiogonomischer Begriffe." In *Geschichten der Physiognomik*. Edited by Rüdiger Campe and Manfred Schneider. Freiburg im Breisgau : Rombach, 1996.

Stone, Allucquere Rosanne. *The War of Desire and Technology at the Close of the Mechanical Age*. Cambridge, Mass: MIT Press, 1996.

Syberberg, Hans Jürgen. *Vom Unglück und Glück der Kunst in Deutschland nach dem letzten Kriege*. Munich: Matthes und Seitz, 1990.

Theunissen, Michael. "Negativität bei Adorno." In *Adorno-Konferenz*. Edited by Ludwig von Friedeburg and Jürgen Habermas. Frankfurt am Main: Suhrkamp Verlag, 1983.

Thomas, Douglas. "Hacking Culture." n.p., n.d.

Tompkins, Silvan S. *The Negative Affects*. Vol. 2 of *Affect Imagery Consciousness*. New York: Springer, 1963.

Thyen, Anke. *Negative Dialektik und Erfahrung: Zur Rationalität des Nichtidentischen bei Adorno*. Frankfurt am Main: Suhrkamp Verlag, 1989.

Tugendhat, Ernst. *Vorlesungen über Ethik*. Frankfurt am Main: Suhrkamp Verlag, 1996.

Wagner, Irmgard. "Arbeiten am Schamdiskurs. Literatur der Nachkriegszeit in psychoanalytischer Perspektive." In *Die dunkle Spur der Vergangenheit. Psychoanalytische Zugänge zum Geschichtsbewußtsein. Erinnerung, Geschichte, Identität*. 2d ed. Edited by Jörn Ruesen and Jürgen Straub. Frankfurt am Main: Suhrkamp Verlag, 1998.

Wellmer, Albrecht. *Zur Dialektik von Moderne und Postmoderne: Vernunftkritik nach Adorno*. Frankfurt am Main: Suhrkamp Verlag, 1985.

_____. *Persistence of Modernity: Essays on Aesthetics, Ethics, and Postmodernism* (in German). Translated by David Midgely. Cambridge, Mass: MIT Press, 1991.

_____. *Endgames. The Irreconcilable Nature of Modernity. Essays and Lectures*. Cambridge, Mass: MIT Press, 1998.

Whitebook, Joel. *Perversion and Utopia. A Study in Psychoanalysis and Critical Theory*. Cambridge, Mass: MIT Press, 1995.

Wiggerhaus, Rolf. *The Frankfurt School. History, Theories, and Political Significance*. Cambridge, Mass: MIT Press, 1986.

Williams, Bernhard. *Shame and Necessity*. Los Angeles: University of California Press, 1993.

Wolin, Richard. *Walter Benjamin: An Aesthetic of Redemption*. 2d ed. Berkeley: University of California Press, 1994.

Wood, Allen. "Habermas's Defense of Rationalism." *New German Critique* 35 (Spring/Summer 1985): 145-64.

INDEX